The Prophets

Volume Two
The Babylonian and Persian Period

KLAUS KOCH

The Prophets

VOLUME TWO
The Babylonian and Persian Periods

FORTRESS PRESS   PHILADELPHIA

Translated by Margaret Kohl from the German *Die Propheten* II:
Babylonisch-persische Zeit by Klaus Koch, copyright © 1978
Verlag W. Kohlhammer GmbH, Stuttgart, Berlin, Cologne and Mainz,
The Federal Republic of Germany, in the series Urban-Taschenbücher, no. 281

English Translation Copyright © 1982 by Margaret Kohl

Published in the United Kingdom by SCM Press, Ltd., London

First Fortress Press Edition 1984

Library of Congress Cataloging in Publication Data
(Revised for volume 2)

Koch, Klaus, 1926-
   The prophets

   Translation of: Die Profeten.
   Bibliography: v. 1, p.   ; v. 2, p.
   Contents: v. 1. The Assyrian period—v. 2. The
Babylonian and Persian periods.
   1. Prophets. I. Title.
BS1198.K6313   1983   224'.06   79-8894
ISBN 0-8006-1648-0 (pbk. : v. 1)
ISBN 0-8006-1756-8 (pbk. : v. 2)

Printed in the United States of America   1-1756

94   93   92   91   90   4   5   6   7   8   9   10

CONTENTS

I

Prophecy of Conversion in the Neo-Babylonian Period

1. Law in the Shadow of Prophecy: Deuteronomy

1.1 The law and the prophets

The prophets of the Assyrian period never appeal to any divine commandment as the basis of their arguments in their criticism of the social conditions of their day. They demand faithfulness to the community (*ṣᵉdāqā*), or they lament its absence. This faithfulness springs from a (mon)anthropology which sees the individual as a part of particular institutions which make life possible. But in the Babylonian and Persian eras, the prophets begin for the first time to concede a special ethical role to divine statutes. And this was a revolution. In order to understand it, we must first of all look at a non-prophetic book, Deuteronomy, together with its historical background. The beginning of the Babylonian period was marked by the cultic reforms of King Josiah (622/1 BC). In the short term these failed; but in the long run they had a tremendous impact. Josiah's reforms were based on a newly discovered book of Yahweh's Torah – in all probability Deuteronomy. So before we go on to discuss the critical prophets of the Babylonian period, I must first say something about the relationship between Yahwistic religion, law and prophecy.

For almost two thousand years it was a matter of course for Christians and Jews alike to assume that the religion of the Old Testament is radically distinguished from all other religions by its ties with a divinely conferred *tōrā*, the law revealed through Moses. Even in the early nineteenth century, the prophets were still viewed simply as the preachers of this age-old legal code. Their passionate involvement was put down to their readiness for total obedience to God's commandments – a readiness which they failed to find among their fellow countrymen. When the New Testament sums up the Old as 'the law and the prophets', this seems to be an accurate description of the relationship between the two; prophecy, with its many voices, comes later, to help interpret the law, which was fundamental in its importance.

It was the achievement of Julius Wellhausen (1844–1918) to discover that it was an anachronism to make the law the primal foundation of Old Testament religion, though this was what it had always been alleged to be. In the pre-exilic period there is no sign that divine laws were assigned any fundamental importance; and Moses certainly left no formulated legal code behind him. Nor can we find anything of the kind in the prophets: 'Their creed is not to be found in any book. It is barbarism, in dealing with such a phenomenon, to distort its physiognomy by introducing the law. It is a vain imagination to suppose that the prophets expounded and applied the law.'[1] The advent of the law can be dated; and its date, moreover, is relatively late. When, in 622/1, Josiah introduced Deuteronomy as the law of the state, this was the first time that a book emerged under the name of Moses, the legendary hero of old. But this was *the response of the priests* of Josiah's time *to the challenge of the prophets of reform*. Within a few decades, however, the new law was certainly to change the Israelite religion fundamentally; and, in Wellhausen's view, it made the prophecy that had evoked it superfluous: 'There was now in existence an authority as objective as could be; and this was the death of prophecy.'[2]

Wellhausen was still able to neglect the part played by legal codes in ancient oriental civilizations. But since his time, more and more books of law and cultic edicts have come to light from the countries surrounding Israel – Babylonian (such as the famous Hammurabi Code), Assyrian, Hittite, Sumerian – all of them considerably earlier than the Josiah period, earlier indeed than Moses. Its form and content indicates that one considerable section of Old Testament legal tenets, the casuistic genre, 'If (anyone commits this or that offence), then (he is to be punished as follows)', is derived from Babylonian cuneiform law.[3] Is influence of this kind supposed to have made itself felt for the first time under Josiah, of all people, who was particularly hostile towards foreign interference? It would seem more plausible to suppose that Babylonian legal practice and language had already been passed on to the Israelites through the Canaanites, after the Israelite settlement of Palestine. At the same time, casuistic law is only one strand. A second kind of legal enactment seems to have been in use in Israel before it became a nation: the apodictic sacral law. This is most evident in series of prohibitions, such as 'You shall not kill, steal, commit adultery.' Apodictic prohibitions are to be found elsewhere in the ancient East as well, but to gather them together into series is a genuinely Israelite achievement, and is usually associated with the conclusion of a covenant at sacred places (Ex. 20–24; 34; Deut. 5; Ps. 50). Alt[4] worked out the differences between the two types of law and showed that the apodictic series are more closely connected with the Yahweh cult. But no position of central importance can be detected even for these in pre-exilic religion.

None the less, Alt's exposition caused the pendulum to swing in the other direction, inducing some scholars to presuppose that the divine law enjoyed decisive religious significance in the pre-exilic period, as if Wellhausen had never been, and making them try to trace back the prophets' social criticism to legal traditions (for Amos, see Vol. I, Section 4). But to establish the bare existence of communal (casuistic) and sacral or cultic (apodictic) legal norms is one thing; to assign them central importance for man's relationship to God and for prophecy is quite another. Pre-exilic Israel was anything but a religion of the law. It is true that from the beginning faithfulness to supportive social institutions, such as clan and people (*ṣᵉdāqā*), counted as the highest ethical goal, and as the factor eliciting every possible correlation between good deeds and salvation, making an undisturbed relationship to God possible. But often though *ṣᵉdāqā* is mentioned, it is never – never, that is, before the emergence of Deuteronomy – explained by any reference to commandment or law. The historical sequence is therefore: *first the prophets, then the law*, not the reverse.

1.2 A law of unique character

Historical research views Deuteronomy as the book which was found in 622/1 BC during repairs to the temple on Zion (II Kings 22f.). Josiah of Judah (who was in process of freeing himself from the political and cultic suzerainty of Assyria) was deeply impressed by the Torah writing that had been discovered; and through covenant and oath he elevated it into a generally binding norm for living, making its observance part of the attempts at political emancipation which were already under way. The book's authority was repealed after Josiah's early death, but it none the less became the religious guideline for the section of the people who remained in their Palestinian homeland after the fall of Judah. Occasionally doubt is cast on the relationship between Josiah's law and Deuteronomy, on the grounds that the latter is too utopian ever to have been elevated into the official law of the state by a king thinking in terms of practical politics. But this line of thinking evidently fails to realize both the programmatic character of ancient oriental legal codexes and the utopian features of Josiah's policy. It is at least quite in accordance with the end of the Assyrian period that the national independence of Israel should present no problem for the law. If it were either a post-exilic or an exilic document, one would expect the liberation of Israel from the power of foreign nations to be touched on at least as a problem.

Deuteronomy makes a high claim. In its earlier form it closed with an address in the singular, to the total self of the cultic community:

> See, I have set before you this day life and good, death and evil,
> In that I have commanded you this day to love Yahweh your God;
>   by walking in his ways and by keeping his commandments, his
>   statutes and his ordinances.
> Then you shall live and multiply; and Yahweh your God will bless
>   you in the land which you are entering to take possession of it.
> I set before you life and death, blessing and curse.
> Therefore choose life! (30.15f., 19).

Life in the land depends on following the book. And yet this book by no means offers a thoroughly worked-out code of law. The legal enactments which, generally speaking, go back to older casuistic or apodictic series of laws, are largely embedded in admonitions, references to past events, and other arguments couched in an admonitory, compulsive style of personal address for which no analogy can be found in ancient oriental law. The book is therefore often classed as a *legal sermon*. To this is added a highly individual, emotional language for which we have no earlier parallel in Hebrew, and which uses impressive, easily remembered phrases, such as 'love Yahweh your God', and many fixed sequences of words, such as 'commandments, statutes and ordinances.' It was often imitated from exilic times on, even being introduced into historical works and prophetic writings. Was it this kind of language that made the concept of law an essential element in Israelite religion? And what is the relationship of this concept to the activity of the critical prophets who preceded it?

1.3 The revolution in Israel's constitution

In every section the Deuteronomists pick up traditional legal tenets and historical traditions; but they interpret them so radically that disparate material is fused into an impressively unified picture of the constitution of a future twelve-tribe people of Israel. The institutions that had been passed down were certainly preserved, but altered in such a way that in the whole of the ancient world there is hardly a single writing – not even Plato's *Republic* – which can equal Deuteronomy in its solemn, revolutionary passion. The cult is Deuteronomy's first concern, because this was the real focus of the people's life; but the economic, administrative and communal sectors are covered as well.

1.3.1 The centralization of the cult and the secularization of everyday life. After a historical paraenetic preface, the laws begin with the demand for a unification of the place of worship (12.13f.):

> Take heed that you do not let your burnt offering rise at every place that seems good to you. But at the cultic place which Yahweh will choose in one of your tribes, there you shall let your burnt offerings rise.

It is difficult for the modern reader to realize what this demand meant for an ancient oriental cultic religion, which is what Israel was at that time. In the ancient world, it seemed a matter of course that a place of worship should only be set up at the indication of a numinous power. Its establishment, that is to say, was not dependent on considerations of reason or human expediency. But since divine powers made themselves felt everywhere, every self-contained settlement in Israel possessed a cultic hill, or a piece of elevated ground, with altar, *maṣṣēbā* (orthostat) and *'ašērā* (wooden post) as its minimum equipment; and the same had been true, even earlier, among the Canaanites. In contrast, the Deuteronomists now demand the restriction of cultic ceremonies to a single sanctuary, which Yahweh has solemnly set aside from the whole country, probably through the mouth of a prophet. There the Levitic priesthood from all Israel will gather together; and there every Israelite has to make a pilgrimage three times a year, in order to surrender himself to ecstatic joy. The law demands the destruction of all other local sanctuaries, including *maṣṣēbā* and *'ašērā* (16.21f; 12.2 – a later interpolation). All this meant an iconoclasm without parallel. Even this one appointed site was no longer to be seen as an earthly place surrounded and filled by Yahweh's holiness, which is what Isaiah still saw Jerusalem as being. It was only to be viewed as a place where Yahweh had 'deposited' his *šēm*, his cultic name (12.21 and frequently elsewhere). He is therefore present there only in his manifestation through word and language. His real existence is invisible, in heaven.

This centralization of the cult went hand in hand with a secularization of ordinary life. The slaughtering of animals for human use – till then always a sacrificial act – was now released from the sphere of what was clean or unclean, and was made a matter of free choice (12.15). The tenth part of fields and herds was still to be a cultic levy, to be surrendered at the chosen place; but every third year it was retained by the village or township and distributed to the needy. It therefore lost its cultic standing (14.22–29). Regulations of this kind are a step towards what might be called secularization. A change in Israel's religion begins to make itself felt – a transition to a 'deutero-religion', where the worship of God is detached from ties with any local place (compare, later, Zoroaster, Buddha, or Greek natural philosophy). This certainly did not mean that everyday life became an entirely profane affair. On the contrary, the individual had to observe the difference between clean and unclean in matters of food, birth and death even more carefully than before. And of course lament, prayer, *tōrā* instructions, blessing and curse were not only possible everywhere – they were actually necessary. But the principle – erroneous in the eyes of the Deuteronomic authors – that divinity made itself actively felt everywhere, and could everywhere be worshipped, was now abandoned.

Anyone who is accustomed to reduce history to mere struggles for power will suspect here the influence of priestly circles which, wishing to establish their sole authority, will have staged the discovery of the Book of the Torah as a pious fraud. But this does not fit in with the restriction of the religious status of even the one remaining cultic place or with the fact that the priests' income was diminished rather than increased. Other scholars have explained the Deuteronomic cultic law as the revival of an ancient Yahwistic institution which had meanwhile been lost. According to this view, before Israel became a state, there was only one central sanctuary, shared by the amphictyonic tribal league; it was this that Deuteronomy now aimed to revive.[5] However, nowadays, the hypothesis of an early central sanctuary has been abandoned almost everywhere. The most probable explanation is still the earlier one: that Deuteronomy was taking the social criticism of the eighth-century prophets into account. In his criticism of the baalized Yahweh religion, for example, Hosea had prophesied the impending destruction of the many sanctuaries (Hos. 8.11–13; 10.1–3, 8). To some extent the Assyrian invaders had already brought about the fulfilment of this divine word. Where the sanctuaries had survived, the Deuteronomists now order their removal, once and for all. Amos' biting condemnation, even of sanctuaries as highly regarded as Bethel and Gilgal (4.4f.; 5.4–6), may also have had its subsequent effect.

1.3.2 Improvement in the situation of the needy. Many of Deuteronomy's regulations are humanitarian in their purpose:

> You shall not pervert the *mišpāṭ* of the sojourner in your care (and) the fatherless, or take a widow's garment in pledge.
> Remember that you were a slave in Egypt and Yahweh your God redeemed you from there. Therefore I command you to fulfil this saying (24.17f.).

In accordance with this principle, Deuteronomy enjoins that impover-
ished fellow countrymen should be lent money. The levying of interest
is forbidden (23.19), though this regulation was hard to implement
among people dependent on borrowing and loans; for under
Palestinian conditions, good harvests continually alternated with bad
ones, and a loan was often the only way of warding off hunger, if the
harvest failed. Pledges are considerably restricted; a creditor is not
allowed to take in pledge either a hand-mill or a garment which a
poor person needs to cover him at night (24.6, 13). A day labourer
has a right to daily payment (24.14). At harvest time, a corner where
the poor can glean must be left standing in every field, olive grove
and vineyard (24.19ff.). Some regulations seem positively to call in
question the whole social structure – for example, when a slave who
has fled from his master is guaranteed freedom as soon as he has
reached the bounds of another township (23.15f.); or when the ancient
provisions of the sabbath or sabbatical year are made to cover debts
as well: it had originally been religious usage to leave the fields fallow
every seventh year, but now all financial obligations have, under the
law, to terminate at the beginning of the seventh year (15.1ff.). Other
articles of the law protect women from male tyranny (22.13–29;
24.1–4). The justification for all these rules of behaviour is the
liberation of the people's ancestors from slavery in Egypt. Called and
destined to be a holy people, succeeding generations can only imitate
the acts of their God and help the people in their midst who have lost
their rights, as God helped them in the past (24.22 and frequently
elsewhere).

Clan distinctions were softened or set aside in the cultic sector as
well as in the legal one. The ancient regulation that only the free adult
male could play a part in the cult was now restricted to the Feast of
the Passover. In all the other festivals children, slaves, Levites
possessing no land, widows and orphans, even the denizens of alien
tribes, were allowed and even commanded to take part (12.7; 16.11,
14). This too meant the 'liberalization' of traditional notions of sanctity
and purity. According to the concentric monanthropology of the
eighth-century prophets, legal status and the right to participate in
legal acts, in the cult and in defence was still bound up with the
possession of *naheiā*. This now ceased to be the prerequisite for
participation in the cult. Although Deuteronomy sees possession of
the promised land as the precondition of all blessing, the individual's
religious status is no longer tied to the possession of land; this means
that the soil is now demythologized. From this time on, all are equal
before God, not merely fundamentally and in principle, but in actual
cultic practice as well.

It was probably the passionate intervention above all of Amos and Isaiah, on behalf of people who had few legal rights, which triggered off this constitution for a future Israel – a constitution in which social distinctions are at least levelled out more than ever before, even if they do not disappear completely (compare e.g. 24.17f. with Amos 2.7).

1.3.3 Authority and the separation of powers. The aim of the lawgiver was to weld Israel together into a single, unified will. It was for this purpose that even the cult was centralized; yet on the political level centralization was, if anything, resisted. In the light of ancient oriental conditions, it would seem obvious to view *the king* as the head of the people. It is true that in Deuteronomy a sovereign head is envisaged for the future holy people, but the king's sphere of competence is so drastically restricted (17.14ff.) that what remains is no more than a caricature of an ancient oriental ruler. He is forbidden to surround himself with a multitude of chargers or wives; so he is denied what was for Solomon the prime cause for pride (though for Isaiah it was a ground for criticism; cf. Isa. 2.7ff.; 31.1–3). Whereas hitherto, as 'the anointed one', the king had been a sacral personage, with authority over temple and cult, now the cult is entrusted entirely to the priests. A copy of Deuteronomy is pressed into the king's hand and he is enjoined to read it daily, so that he does not think more highly of himself than he does of any of his brethren. Nothing whatsoever is said about actual royal rights. If we remember to what degree the court and the monarchy were the source of transgression for the prophets of the Assyrian period, it is easy to understand the law as a reaction. None the less, the provisions of the law are so brief that Josiah found it possible to reconcile them with his ambitious political goals – which the Deuteronomists could not have envisaged.

Priests belonging to the tribe of Levi stood at the head of the social structure, next to the king; and in cultic matters they were independent of him. Here too a restriction was made, and the priests were denied the right to own their own land. Their only 'inherited land', their *naḥᵃlā*, was Yahweh (this was not yet the case in I Kings 2.26 or Amos 7.17). More attention is paid to the *nābī'*, whom Yahweh raised up charismatically 'from your brothers' in every generation. The *nābī'* alone was capable of receiving divine words directly and of passing them on. Consequently he had to be obeyed implicitly, unlike priest or king. The prophet, having no regular income and being dependent on himself, was a critical court of appeal. He had merely verbal authority, but he was closer to God than anyone else in the nation. Admittedly he was subject to the 'professional risk' that if his prediction proved false he would be unmasked as a lying prophet and condemned to death (18.15–22).

Not only were the chief offices in the state now differentiated by a kind of separation of powers. The local levels of community life were changed too. In place of the autonomous 'democracy' of free men in the gateway of the local community, Deuteronomy envisages *judges and officials* for every township. These have to see to it that the rights of the weak are no longer set aside (16.18–20). On the other hand, whatever spills over into the cultic sector, is the task of the *elders*, who were a representative body. In difficult cases the priests and the top judges at the central sanctuary could be called upon; these sought for a decision through the divine judgment. Here too we may ask whether the interference with traditional institutions was not connected with the prophetic criticism of intolerable conditions 'in the gates' (e.g. Amos 5.10).

1.4 Ethical principles and anthropology

1.4.1 By proclaiming carefully formulated edicts (which were ascribed to Yahweh) as the highest norms by which action was to be judged, the Deuteronomists changed the morality which had hitherto been considered valid, with its conception of *ṣᵉdāqā*. For Amos and Isaiah, the institutions which had grown up meanwhile – family, people, cultic community – were still the supreme values. Every Israelite knew instinctively in any given case what *ṣᵉdāqā* required of him. It is true that in Deuteronomy the earliest stratum still uses *ṣᵉdāqā* in the traditional sense for the preservation of a poor person's *mišpāṭ*; that is to say, it was the guarantee of his existence – a guarantee that was in accord with faithfulness to the community (24.3; 16.20). But the later revision (which is shown by the plural form of address) already terms the edicts themselves *ṣaddīq* – which means they were actually determinative of what faithfulness to the community meant (4.8). This already prepares the ground for what was later to become a conviction: that the divine commandments, not a spontaneous feeling of solidarity, are the guide to all that is meant by a saving faithfulness to the community. For the Deuteronomists, 'natural' ties with the community are losing their religious dignity. For example, in the pre-Deuteronomic story in Genesis 38, the widow Tamar counted as *ṣaddīq* because she set aside custom and morality out of faithfulness to the kindred of her dead husband, and in order posthumously to give him a male descendant. Now Deuteronomy 13.6[7]ff. makes it everybody's duty to inform against even the closest member of his family, and to deliver him up for execution, if he is guilty of enticing others to false religious practices. Faithfulness to kindred or clan and faithfulness to

the divine covenant therefore begin to divide. This was undoubtedly
the sign of a profound social crisis which was intensified even further
by the events of the exilic period.

1.4.2 It is not only where people are concerned that, for Deuteronomy,
the ancient ṣᵉdāqā is no longer sufficient: it does not suffice towards
Yahweh either. But it is *love* that mainly determines the new relationship, not edicts or regulations. Presumably the book originally opened
with the words (6.5f.): 'You shall love Yahweh your God with all your
heart, and with all your soul, and with all your might' (and the
corresponding end, 30.15ff., was similar; see above). Earlier, love of
God as a way of behaviour had been unknown in Israel. It is an idea
that only emerges for the first time in Hosea (Hos. 3; cf. Jer. 2.2). The
word 'love' may go back to the political context, where it was used for
the vassal's covenant-like relation to his overlord; so it may not have
as strong an emotional connotation in Hebrew as in English. None
the less, it now brings out the fact that a personal element was of
decisive importance in the relationship to God. From this time on,
Yahweh was more than an indispensable link within a total community
embracing Israel as a whole. So whereas the relationship to other
people was objectified through laws, the relation to God, conversely,
was personalized.

1.4.3 'Today' Israel is once more to become 'the holy people' as it had
been before, in the time of Moses; and it was thereby to become the
highest (ʿelyōn) for the peoples of the earth (26.19; 14.2). Israel's
relationship to the other nations was therefore to be guided by a
concentric monanthropology. (The corresponding concentric circles
within Israel itself had come to an end through the separation of
powers.) But Yahweh was understood as being mankind's real centre,
while for his holy people he became ʾᵉlōhīm – the irresistible numinous
impulse and force (26.17).
   If Israel was 'holy', this meant that an active power was transferred
to the people as a whole which had hitherto only surrounded priests
and the cultic place. The religion of the Israelites became the representative or vicarious worship for all mankind. In order that this purpose
might be fulfilled, the people were to be fused together into an
economic, cultic and spiritual unity, and the underlying and sustaining
institutions of society changed in the way I have indicated.
   This strongly programmatic objective was coupled with a rejection
of contrary tendencies that could sometimes be fanatical. 'So you shall
purge the evil from your midst' is the categorical demand with regard
to any dissidents among Israel's own people (21.21 and frequently

elsewhere). The peoples living in the land given to Israel are to be rooted out completely (20.16). Happily, edicts of this kind never guided Israel's actual historical settlement of the country; but they continually had a fatal aftermath in the later history of Christendom and Judaism.

1.4.4 Practical utopia as response to the prophetic challenge. The Deuteronomic provisions remind us at every step of the utterances of the critical prophets; yet they are very different from these in character. The untenable conditions in Israel provided the occasion for prophetic predictions of disaster; while the prophetic yearnings were moved by hope for a purified, reunited Israel (and a holy one: Isa. 4.3; 6.13, a later interpolation). The Book of the Law is largely in accord with this criticism and this expectation of salvation. But every eschatological feature has been erased. Whatever glory the future may bring, life under Moses and Joshua was already successful and harmonious! There is no pointer whatsoever towards any marvellous transformation of human beings and the earth. Surprisingly enough, Israel's liberation from foreign domination is evidently not a problem on which a word need be wasted. Consequently a metahistory is superfluous as well (cf. Vol. I, Section 4.9.5).

A theoretical framework of this kind can hardly be prophetic in origin. Moses is the fictitious author of the law, and the figure who legitimates it. He is appealed to, as a *nābī'*, a prophet; but the language is not characteristically prophetic at all. Yahweh is talked about in the third person, and this suggests that the Deuteronomists are deliberately assigning themselves a secondary position compared with contemporary prophets, who proclaim what they have to say speaking in the first person for Yahweh himself. The priests and legal administrators who are at work here have grasped that the intention of critical prophecy went far beyond moral chidings, and that prophecy was impelled by an ideal concept of the true constitution of the Israelite people of God. What was an implicit hope for the prophets now becomes a practical utopia. We must not be put off by the fact that in Deuteronomy much that the prophets announced as Yahweh's work becomes the task of man. Israel never thought in the category of a divine work that excluded the work of human beings. All the movements of history are explained by the warp and weft of monotheism and 'monanthropism'. So it is quite understandable that – as the example of the prophetess Huldah shows (II Kings 22) – the prophets and nabis by no means rejected the law as Deuteronomy outlined it.

1.5 The nabi's answer to the introduction of the law: Huldah

The Book of the Torah, so unexpectedly discovered in the temple, caused Josiah to proclaim the first constitutional monarchy in history and to submit his authority voluntarily to a divinely legitimated constitutional document. In addition it made him destroy the cultic places, with *maṣṣebā* and *'ašērōt*, and 'clean up' the sole remaining sanctuary in Jerusalem by destroying all the objects that had any astral connections. The link with the Deuteronomic demands is obvious. At the same time, in the ancient world the introduction of a law book never meant that from that time on every legal enactment was going to be followed exactly. (The civil service mind had not as yet developed!) Only the law of centralization was strictly applied, because that was in line with the emancipation of Israel's foreign policy. The one chosen place was, as a matter of course, taken to mean Jerusalem (which does not mean that this was necessarily the intention of Deuteronomy in its original form).

Before Josiah put the measures into force, he sent the chief priest and other dignatories to Huldah the *nᵉbī'ā* (feminine form of *nābī'*), to enquire of Yahweh about the discovery in the temple and the consequences that were supposed to follow from it. Evidently there was not only a chief priest (*hak-kōhēn*) in Jerusalem, who held office in addition to the other priests; there was also a chief *nābī'* (*han-nābī'*). The office could be held by a woman too (cf. Isa 8.3). Her answer will originally have contained a demand for the conclusion of a covenant and for the destruction of the cultic places outside Jerusalem. What has been preserved is an additional prophecy to the king who has sent the message (II Kings 22.19f.):

A   It is thus, that you have made your spirit elastic, have bowed
         yourself before Yahweh,
      by *hearing* what I said [. . .] that a curse was in preparation.
      You have rent your clothes, and wept before me.
B   So I also have *heard* you, murmurs Yahweh.
      Therefore, behold, I will gather you to your fathers,
      you shall be gathered to your grave in peace.

The prophecy was not destined to be fulfilled literally. Josiah did not die peacefully. He fell in battle at Megiddo twelve years later, fighting against the Egyptian Pharaoh. This put an end to his work of reform. But the saying shows, all the more for that, how much the leading nabis adopted the aims of Deuteronomy as their own. The contemporary prophet Jeremiah may have taken up the same attitude (see below). Seen in the light of the prophets' social criticism, Josiah's bold experiment represents a decisive victory for prophetic monanthropology and its constitutional ideal. But, as we see from Zephaniah and Joel, the end of the Assyrian period brought renewed premonitions of disaster, which sensed the advent of another terrible foreign power, following the downfall of Assyria. From this perspective, Deuteronomy's attempt at restitution was premature, and its optimism about an imminent turn for the better in Israel's history was unjustified. Events were to prove the pessimistic voices right.

2. Jeremiah ben Hilkiah

2.1 The revival of critical prophecy in the Neo-Babylonian period

In 627/6 a prophet again emerges to whom we owe a great prophetic book: Jeremiah. We can follow his activity for forty-five years, longer than for any other of the prophets. Once more a critical prophet appears on the stage at the moment when the wheels of world politics begin to turn. About the same year in which Jeremiah began to prophesy for the first time, the Chaldaean prince Nabopolassar conquered Babylon and set up an independent kingdom there, robbing the Assyrian state, which had been unshaken for decades, of its economic and religious capital. It was an omen that would certainly have been duly registered by all Assyria's satellites, not least by Judah. Was this the dawning fulfilment of the divinely authorized prophecies of Nahum and others about the bloody city of Assyria? But then it could only be a short step to the eschatological salvation which the prophets had also proclaimed! Long-suppressed hopes sprang up. Borne up by these, the young high-hearted king, Josiah, devised plans in Jerusalem to shake off the hated foreign power. The moment of Jeremiah's prophetic entry on to the stage coincided with a mighty wave of expectation in his country. Had not Isaiah already prophesied the downfall of the Assyrian power, linking this with the vision of a messianically reunited Israel? The fall was now immediately impending!

When in 612 Nabopolassar, in alliance with the Medes, completely conquered Nineveh and gave the Assyrian colossus its death-blow, the mass of the Israelite people had no doubt that this was the beginning of what Yahweh's prophets had predicted for a hundred years, and that it could only be a few years at most before the Deuteronomic utopia came true – or even a messianic kingdom. Josiah's foolhardy policy is only comprehensible against a background of this kind. And, through their prophecies of salvation, a multitude of nabis encouraged the people in their hopes.

But the exuberant enthusiasm is countered by the renewed voice of critical prophecy. Beginning with Zephaniah, it finds its continuation in Jeremiah, Habakkuk and Ezekiel. These men were certainly convinced that the Assyrian power was going to fall. But they saw a new despot looming up behind her who was going to fall upon Israel and Judah in a way that was to be a thousand times worse. Judged metahistorically, the social and religious behaviour of the people had not improved in the least. So the *dābār* that had threatened them ever since Amos was now hovering over the country and having its effect on history. It was a time bomb whose ticking was terrifying clear to the prophets' ears. When, after 605, Nabopolassar's son Nebuchadnezzar began to subjugate the southern part of the former Assyrian empire and Judah with it, the direction from which the new menacing disaster would ultimately come became clear.

The downfall of people, state and religion is therefore a theme that was taken up again by Jeremiah (and Ezekiel) at a time when according to public opinion the worst was over and the danger of annihilation had apparently been finally overcome. None the less, the new unfavourable predictions of the future differ from those uttered by the prophets of the Assyrian period.

(a) Whereas Amos and his fellow combatants had prophesied unconditional disaster, there are now increasing indications of an alternative which is still open to the prophet's listeners. Their repentance or conversion is presented as a possible way of changing the course of history. This justifies us in now talking about prophecy of conversion.

(b) We find an almost tragic feature in the suffering that is the mark of both present and future; the people who are affected are to be lamented as well as indicted. Compassion is evident. The prophets discover that they too are rooted in the situation, and they confide to the written scroll their private temptations and their consolations – Jeremiah especially, but Ezekiel too (and perhaps Deutero-Isaiah? Isa 50.4ff.).

(c) The resurgence of a reunited Israel following the catastrophe is not merely proclaimed in general terms; it is given quite precise form, personally, strategically and anthropologically. An attempt is made to give specific shape to the turning point which is to bring about salvation. When the collapse came about in 587/6, the disaster was considered to be finished and done with. In the late Ezekiel and in Deutero-Isaiah the main stress lies on the prophecy of salvation.

(d) The domination of the known inhabited world by a great non-Israelite power (the Babylonians and later the Persians) is not viewed by the prophets merely as an emergency measure which Yahweh resorts to because he needs a rod for his anger (as Isa. 10.5 puts it). This domination has an essential function in maintaining the order necessary for man and beast in the framework of the divine *creation*. The nationalistic particularism of pre-exilic religion is now modified at an essential point.

Taking Jeremiah as an example, we must now look more closely at this prophecy, which has undergone such important changes compared with the eighth century.

2.2 The special characteristics of the book of Jeremiah. The four periods of his prophecy

2.2.1 More of Jeremiah's prophetic sayings have been handed down to us than those of any other prophet. But the text is not a homogenous whole. Three literary strata can be distinguished:

A. Brief poetic sayings uttered in the first person, in the name of Jeremiah himself, and strung together in series. These dominate chs. 1–25 (30f.). There is generally no problem about tracing these back to the prophet himself, and probably also to the original scroll which ch. 36 tells us that Jeremiah wrote (see below). Whether the basic material of the oracles about the nations (chs. 46–51) belongs here too is a matter of dispute.

B. Third-person reports about Jeremiah's fate or the *dābār* he proclaimed: (19.1–20.6;) 26–29; 37–44. The final section is evidently a coherent account by an eye-witness, and it is often attributed to Baruch, Jeremiah's scribe and friend. We cannot be certain whether the same author is behind the other stories in chs. 26–29, which refer to other periods of the prophet's life and have a different orientation. (The narrative in chs. 33; 34 probably belong to C.)

C. Long first-person speeches in prose, with third-person headings. Now interspersed in A, they all mark transitions to new themes in the book's structure (1.4–10; 7; 11; 18; 21; 25; 32; 34; [35]). The vocabulary differs from the Jeremianic vocabulary in A and B. In spite of this, the kernels of certain fragments (the temple speech in ch. 7, for example) undoubtedly go back in essentials to Jeremiah's own poetic utterances, and we have to assume that the same is true of the rest, pending proof of the contrary. The possibility of repentance and future salvation for Israel is now much more emphatically stressed than in Jeremiah's own sayings. (In the older prophetic books, too, expansions are evident, but these are different in style: there brief sayings are generally interpolated in a style and genre imitative of the prophet himself; this is true of the Book of Isaiah, for example.) Jeremiah C is designed for public delivery or reading. It is understandable that scholars should use the word 'sermon' (and some people actually scent the preliminary form of a synagogue sermon, even though the earliest evidence for anything of the kind is only to be found 500 years later, in a completely different kind of society). These speeches are evidently translations into simpler language used for paraenetic purposes. Were they perhaps employed at assemblies for lamentation in exilic Palestine, when there was no longer any ordered cult or any holy places? Will it perhaps be permissible to move their *Sitz im Leben* – their situation in life – close to the little book which is called in modern Bibles (though not in the original text) the Lamentations of Jeremiah? This book will hardly be the work of the prophet himself, but it probably belongs to this period.

In what follows I shall be confining myself mainly to A and B, though I shall draw on C from time to time, in an original poetic version which I have hypothetically reconstructed.

2.2.2 If we consider the existing text chronologically, we can restrict Jeremiah's activity to *four periods*. In each of them Jeremiah appears on the stage as the firm opponent of the ruling circles in temple and court. He intervened in day-to-day politics more than any other of the prophets known to us; and this meant that the climate surrounding him continually worsened.

The four periods were as follows:

(i) Under Josiah, 626–622; criticism of the cult before the Deuteronomic reform (anti-Baal polemic), chs. 1–6*; and the 'Little Book of Consolation for Ephraim' (i.e., North Israel), chs. 30f. (no third-person narratives).

(ii) The first four years of Jehoiakim's reign, 609–605: religious and political opposition, chs. 1–26+; 35f.; with oracles about the foreign nations, chs. 46ff. ('I' sayings and third-person accounts.)

(iii) From the fourth year of Zedekiah's reign down to the fall of Jerusalem, 593–587/6: pro-Babylonian pronouncements and sayings promising salvation, chs. 27–29; 32–34; 37–39 (third-person accounts).

(iv) After 586: the unsuccessful attempt to move the remnant of the population in Palestine and Egypt to repentance, chs. 40–44 (only (B) accounts).

This means that there is a gap of about twelve years in each case between periods (i) and (ii) and between periods (iii) and (iv). The first silence begins with Josiah's reform. Did Jeremiah welcome the new Deuteronomic law so fervently that he saw it as the possible sign of conversion, and so took up a waiting attitude which lasted for years? Or is it merely by chance that nothing dating from these years has come down to us? The silence from 605 onwards is more easily

explicable. The king's order of arrest forced Jeremiah into the underground until the first capture of Jerusalem by the Babylonians, with
the subsequent deportation of his powerful opponent.

2.2.3 Jeremiah was the son of a priest belonging to Anathoth, a place
three miles north of Jerusalem. Unfortunately we do not know whether
his father was employed at the village's cultic high place or at the
temple in Jerusalem. Perhaps he died early, since Jeremiah never
mentions him. Since Jeremiah himself did not become a priest, he was
able to own land (ch. 32) and hence was independent enough
financially to be able to afford his own scribe, from 609 onwards.
Although Jeremiah was more at odds with the nabis of his time than
any of his predecessors, he may nevertheless himself have been an
institutional nabi, even though he was a critical prophet at the same
time. He is called a nabi in some of the stories about him. In ch. 14
he appears as intercessor in a repentance liturgy, which we ought
probably to see as an official observance taking place at the temple.
In 19.2 he is able to summon priests and elders (these being the
religious representatives of the people as a whole) to a 'curse' ceremony. His call to fight against the troops seen in a vision – a call
uttered more than once – is also reminiscent of the function of the
nabis in the pre-exilic wars. After the fall of Jerusalem, at least, for
the remnant of the population he counts as Yahweh's sole existing
nabi. Yet he himself is conscious that he is most certainly an outsider,
compared with any ordinary nabi.

2.3 The wickedness of idolatry and the enemy from the north: the early period, I

2.3.1 The cauldron vision. Jeremiah 1.13–16 reports a vision which
according to the context belongs to the beginning of Jeremiah's
proclamation and which, as chs. 2 to 6 show, manifestly influenced
his thinking for years.

A   The word of Yahweh came to me . . . 'What do you see?'
     I answered: 'A boiling (water) pot, whose front side is facing
     away from *the north*.'
     Then Yahweh said to me, 'Out of *the north* breaks forth *evil*
     upon all the inhabitants of the land (of the earth?).
B   For see, I am calling
     all [. . .] kingdoms of *the north*.
     They shall [. . .] each of them set up his throne
     at the entrance of the gates of Jerusalem [. . .].
A   Because of all their *evil* in forsaking me
     and in burning incense to other divinities.

The visionary account (a vision with a dialogue between God and man, followed by an interpretation) was a textual pattern or genre which had already been used by Amos (7f.) and Isaiah (6); and the form had already received its mould even before it came into their hands. Visionary experience is therefore transmitted to the audience through the medium of an already existing framework. Only the content of the visionary picture itself seems to be spontaneous and individual, not the way in which it is seen. As in other cases (e.g. Amos 9.3f.), the prose account is followed by a poetic prophecy. Because of the visionary introduction, the indication of situation (A) and the prediction of a divine intervention and its realization through intermediaries (B) change places. (On the genre cf. Vol I, section 3.3.)

The bubbling water pot, which Jeremiah may actually have had in front of him, suddenly becomes transparent, showing a seething mass of nations from the far north. Seen from Jerusalem, and according to the geography of the time, the Assyrians came from the north. But though they had enslaved Judah for over a hundred years, it is not the Assyrians that are being thought of here. Jeremiah sees a far more dangerous, anonymous, sinister power, which is going to come rolling up, over the heads of the Assyrians. The collapse of what has hitherto been the great power of the time by no means signifies the dawn of freedom and salvation for Palestine, as Jeremiah's countrymen suppose.

Jeremiah paints the onrush of the sinister opponent in poem after poem full of a wild poetic beauty (e.g. 5.15–17; 6.22–28). The spoiler of the nations and 'a great destruction' is moving up cruelly and inexorably (4.6; 6.1) in the form of an ancient and established nation (5.15), leaving behind it a charred desolation (*šammā*, 4.7; 10.22).

'His horses swifter than eagles!
Woe to us, for we are annihilated!' (4.13).

Isaiah had already used overflowing water as a metahistorical expression for a company of nations sweeping up for a final attack; though at that time he was still thinking of the Assyrians (8.7f.; 17.12–14). Probably, like Jeremiah, he was going back to a myth about the conflict of the nations which was a familiar part of the language of the Jerusalem cult. The sea of chaos surrounding the earth and beneath it had been mastered and tamed by Yahweh in primordial times; it now finds its outflow in the sea of nations which is beating from all sides against Zion, the mount of God, but which is thrown back by Yahweh at the last minute (Ps. 46).[6] The prophets are afraid that what the cult celebrated as a past event will come upon the people in the future. But why should disaster now come from the *north*, of all places? Various interpretations have been put forward. Earlier commentators point to a Scythian attack on Syria-Palestine which took place between 630 and 620 BC, according to the Greek historian Herodotus (I, 103–106). But according to ancient oriental records this is improbable. Other scholars point to 'the sea peoples' who had flooded into Syria-Palestine from the Aegean 500 years earlier, threatening even Egypt. In spite of the defeat of these invaders by Ramses III, the attack is supposed to have remained traumatically in the remembrance of the peoples affected. But during the period of the monarchy the inhabitants of Jerusalem experienced the north in a diametrically opposite way. It was felt to be the region of saving power, because it was the site of the mythical mountain of God, Zaphon, where Yahweh with his attendant spirits held court and determined the fate of the earth (Ps. 48.2; Isa. 14.13f.). It is Jeremiah who makes a new polarity evident for the first time (like Joel 2.20; Ezek. 38.6, 15; 39.2). The universal corner-stone – the mountain of God – now turns into a reservoir of supernatural disaster. Implicit in this may be the fact that in Babylonian times there was an increased slackening of the ties between the understanding of God and cultic or worldly realities in Israel. But even if the divine centre now splits off from its position in the north of the globe, sinister beings are still left behind there; and these could now be thought of as bringing about disaster, just as earlier they could be thought of in saving terms. Desacralization therefore leads to demonization.

Another equally important reason for a reorientation was provided by the shifts of population at that time, when Indo-Germanic horsemen from the north several times brought unrest to the Middle East.[7] The north, which for the Israelites stretched from Asia Minor to northern Persia, with huge unknown stretches of land behind the Caucasus and the Caspian Sea, had always, from time immemorial, been a political storm centre. Here, as elsewhere, the critical prophets show themselves to be close observers of world events. The level of practical politics within the metahistory is never overlooked. Like all prophetic visions, the cauldron vision does not aim to open up knowledge of higher worlds; it is designed to grant the prophet involved a vision into the depths of reality. It is a profundity of insight that allows something to be seen, in a kind of x-ray, which is not discernible to the normal human eye, but which none the less has definite existence. The account lays bare historical facts and circumstances which listeners can then – in a process of subsequent insight – accept as logical and meaningful.

2.3.2 Palpable evil, with actual spatial existence. Why does Jeremiah take so pessimistic a view? In addition to 'the north', the text uses a second

key word 'evil', *rā'ā*. Evil displays itself on the one hand through the
onrush of an enemy who is superior in military power. On the other
hand the Judaeans are practising evil. Have the two things anything
to do with one another? Or is it merely by chance that the same term
is used at the beginning and end of the passage? It is not only our
evaluation of the visionary account which will be governed by the
answer; our judgment about the whole of Jeremiah's early period
depends on it too.

In the prophetic genres, key words generally form the pivot in the
logical progression from the 'now' to the 'impending'. Why should
this be any different here? The word *rā'ā* is used ninety times in
the book and becomes the common denominator, both for human
transgression that has already taken place and for a catastrophe that
is going to break in from outside. (Derivations of the root *r"* appear
in Jeremiah more frequently than in any other prophet.) For the
prophet, *rā'ā* is not an abstract power. It is an aura, with effects on
the world, an aura encircling the particular agent, who brings about
his own destiny. Numerous passages show how closely action and
destiny are linked for Jeremiah and his school, and how the correlation
between the two is concentrated in this concept.

> Your ways and your doings
> have brought this upon you.
> This is your doom, and it is bitter;
> it has struck (back) to your very heart (4.18).

Anyone who follows other divinities (*'lōhīm*) is inflicting evil on himself (7.6; 25.6); he is creating an aura of evil deeds round himself which
will one day come to maturity and break over the perpetrators like
boiling water (Jer. 1) – when 'the time of their *rā'ā* comes' (2.27f.).
Yahweh's power explicitly helps to make wickedness, as an act that
has been committed, soon turn into wickedness as destiny. Wickedness
that is invisible to the human eye is perceived by the eye of Yahweh
(18.10). It is 'its (the nation's) own *rā'ā* which I have spoken against
it (as prophecy)' (18.8). Yahweh will one day bring the fruit of the
people's own intention upon them, as *rā'ā* (6.19). God develops future
rā'ā through his *dābār*. If the men and women affected repent, this *rā'ā*
will have no effect on them (18.11). But even a God can no longer
purify present-day Judah from its evil (6.29). So what the cauldron
vision shows as threatening from the north is the final result of an evil
which the Judaeans have themselves brought about (so also 4.15–18;
6.1–8). Jeremiah seems here to adopt the view that all the evil
committed collectively by his people has withdrawn into the north for
a while, but that it will be transformed by Yahweh at the appropriate

time into hostile military energy and will be used again against the perpetrators. For this purpose Yahweh introduces his own negative energies, metahistorical active powers, such as the wind of his spirit (*rū^aḥ*, 4.11–13), his word which works like fire (*dābār* 5.14), but above all the force of his anger. The white heat of his angry breath (*ḥ^arōn 'ap*, 4.7f.) makes the enemy from the north irresistible; Yahweh's wrath fills even the prophet to bursting point (6.11). Seen from the personal aspect of the divine will, this means that Yahweh 'visits' (*pqd*) those who are not prepared to understand his way (*derek*), which is the foundation of history (5.1–9.29; 6.6, 15); indeed it means that the God who in past ages led Israel to victory in her holy wars is now – in a paradoxical reversal of all salvation history – issuing the trumpet blast that summons to the holy war against his people (6.4–6).

In this way the cauldron vision already suggests how much Jeremiah's sayings turn on the cohesion between action and destiny. It is true that the prophecies of disaster uttered by men like Amos or Isaiah were cruelly realized through the agency of Assyria; but the behaviour of the people has not changed; it is as corrupt as ever. So the nation is running into an even worse abyss. This conclusion is inescapable, both for Jeremiah and for his God.

2.3.3 Burning incense to Baal.

Like the prophets of the eighth century (though in merely general phraseology) Jeremiah can attack acts of social violence (6.7) and the shedding of innocent blood in Jerusalem (2.34); he can even go as far as the sarcastic assertion that there is not a single person in the city who is prepared to do the right, *mišpāṭ* (5.1 [28f.]). But the centre of gravity of his criticism of contemporary life is to be found elsewhere. The cauldron vision already makes this clear.

Here, in a phrase which is uniquely his own, Jeremiah points to the power of Judaean wickedness to trigger off events: 'It is your wickedness that you have forsaken me and burn incense to other divinities (*^xlōhīm*)' (19.3f.; 44.3f, 7f.). As a polemical watchword, the phrase apparently became so well known that the Deuteronomist chroniclers (who ignore Jeremiah's existence completely) put it into the mouth of the prophetess Huldah (II Kings 22.16f.).

The phrase 'to burn incense', *qiṭṭēr*, is used for a ritual offering of vegetable food which – apparently with the addition of incense or other powder – rose as an aromatic smoke to the deity. The cultic use of incense is mentioned for the first time by Jeremiah (6.20) and counts as idolatrous even in post-exilic times (Isa. 66.3). *Qiṭṭēr* was also considered illegitimate (except in Amos 4.5). Hosea (4.13; 11.2) mentions it among the baalized rites practised at the cultic sites on the hilltops; Jeremiah links it with worship of the heavenly host, or of its master *(ba'al)* or its queen (19.13; 32.39; 44.17–19, 25), Baal being for him *the* provocative word.

The influence of Hosea is unmistakable, and stronger than that of any other of Jeremiah's predecessors. Like Hosea, Jeremiah means a Baal whom his countrymen equate with Yahweh. He picks up Hosea's phraseology. 'Harlotry' counts as the chief occupation of his contemporaries (3.1–3, 6f., 9, and frequently elsewhere). The young Jeremiah uses even more drastically brutal expressions, painting his countrymen as female camels in heat (2.23–25) and rutting stallions, 'each neighing for his neighbour's wife' (5.8). For European ideas he is sometimes positively obscene: 'Look up to the heights! Where have you not been fucked?' (3.2). Like Hosea, Jeremiah assumes that there is a marriage bond between Yahweh and the people, though God is now married to two sisters, Israel and Judah. (Polygamy was in no way shocking for Israel in pre-Christian times. Even God could be thought of as having several wives.) Just as in the days of Hosea, the people under attack indignantly reject the accusation of worshipping any god other than the god of their ancestors (2.23). So Jeremiah seems to be treading entirely in the footprints of his north-Israel model. Most scholars therefore assume that what is in question is the same idolatrous cult – that is to say, baalized fertility rites which are only nominally connected with Yahweh.

And yet can we be certain that someone who talks about Baal in the southern kingdom round about 620 is talking about the same figure meant by a North Israelite a good hundred years earlier? In southern Palestine the worship of Baal had never become really widespread in pre-Israelite times. So the Judaeans had actually no reason for taking over Canaanite Baal practices in the same naive way as their North Israelite contemporaries. Moreover Jeremiah never suggests that the Baal he attacks is responsible for fertility, and that corn, wine, oil and flax, for example, can be expected of him (as Hosea does; cf. 2.8f.). Has 'harlotry', which Hosea meant quite literally, now become an image for any assiduous activity that is reprehensible in itself? We have to remember that for Semites Baal is not a proper name. It means 'lord, master', and signifies one who is purposefully active by way of other powers (field, domestic animal, wife) (cf. Vol. I, section 5.3). A 'functional god' of this kind is able to change his sphere of competence more rapidly than a deity characterized by specific names. It is noticeable that Jeremiah links the service of Baal which he condemns principally with the contemporary nabis, and indeed with all of them; they prophesy 'in Baal' and hence in *šeqer*, in deceit. The priests are their associates, not so much in their cultic ceremonies as in their *tōrā*, the instructions about what is clean and unclean which they have to pass on to the laity (2.8; 5.31; 6.14). This suggests that Baal was an authority who was approached primarily for the sake of oracles, which were expected to provide information about the future of the social group and the way it ought to act.

What is behind this?

Apart from a North Israelite intermezzo (II Kings 11.18) we are first told about the cult of Baal in Jerusalem fifty years before Jeremiah, during the reign of Manasseh (from 687). He is said to have set up an altar to Baal in a temple at Jerusalem, and to have worshipped Baal's wife Asherah and the whole heavenly host (II Kings 21.3–7). Manasseh was a faithful adherent of the Assyrian emperor. Accordingly we may assume that he was taking up the practice of his grandfather Ahaz, who was also pro-Assyrian and who, when he met the emperor in Damascus, took the measurements of an altar there and set up a copy of it on Zion, moving the ancient Yahweh altar to the side (II Kings 16.10–18). Of course Davidic kings like Ahaz and Mannasseh still viewed Yahweh as the highest of the gods, even if not the only one. But, in an attempt at syncretism, they identified him with an Assyrian-Damascene Baal whose rites they introduced into worship, making them part of Israel's cult. As far as we know, the Assyrians laid no special stress on fertility rites and sexual cults. What had become increasingly important for Assyrian religion was the astral form in which the great gods manifested themselves, and the insight into the world order and the future which was to be won from them by way of astrology. In the Syrian-Aramaic area this astralized religion, which gradually penetrated from the East, was assigned to a new god, Baal-Shamem – the lord or master of heaven – as head of the pantheon. This was a religion with which the Assyrian emperors could associate themselves.[8] It will have been this heavenly Baal whom the Judaean kings fused with Yahweh and whom Jeremiah had in mind. Hence the reference to the lord of heaven (cf. Zeph. 1.4f.). A functional god for the mastering of particular conditions or sectors of life (mountain, field, wife) turns into the master *per se* – i.e. a supreme god.

If we look at Jeremiah's utterances against this hypothetical background, his polemic becomes comprehensible. For him as for his opponents, burning incense counts as the central sacrificial act, because it is through this that the human offering rises to the master of heaven who rules above. In order to avoid any false conclusions, the prophet deliberately stresses that it is Yahweh who is the guardian of the rainy season, in contrast to the heavenly powers who allegedly determine destiny (5.24).

Yet Jeremiah's monotheism does not presuppose any exclusive

almighty power on Yahweh's part. It leaves room for numinous forces acting in a contrary direction. Baal certainly signifies a nullity, but it is an obliterating nothingness *(hebel)* which works on his worshippers and destroys them. Perhaps we might go a step further. There is a saying belonging to a later phase of the prophet's life to the effect that the idolatrous wickedness created by the people themselves will in the end carry off the perpetrators to the north, so that they may serve the other divinities there (16.10–13). This suggests that Jeremiah imagines that the seat of Baal is to be found in the north, where he is near the Assyrians and other northern peoples. There mighty mountains tower up into heaven. Anyone who devotes himself to the worship of Baal thereby evokes as it were magnetic forces from the north, or is attracted by them. If we make this assumption, the complex of ideas that sustains the cauldron vision and makes it comprehensible would be a completely whole and self-contained one.

Anyone who interprets a text historically has to do justice to a prophet's opponents as well. The Christian observer feels outraged when the God of the Old Testament is identified with a supreme heathen god; the clear rejection which Jeremiah enunciates seems to him a matter of course. On the other hand he is surprised by the deadly conclusions which the prophet draws from something which we are accustomed to assign to liberty of belief. Downfall and destruction only because people practise the rite of burning incense? In ancient Israel things looked different, to both sides. Israel shared its Hebrew and Canaanite language with neighbours who knew nothing of Yahweh; and in describing their God Israel was forced to use the word for divinity (*ᵉlōhīm*) that was applied as term of praise by these peoples too. In this way a 'syncretistic' bridge grew up all by itself. Consequently, in the pre-Hellenic era Israel saw its God at work in the divinities of other nations as well. Even as late as the Persian period, the Israelites had no scruples about identifying their own heavenly God with the Iranian god of the heavens, Ahura Mazda. On the other hand people were allergic to a cultically worshipped Baal for the very reason that a numinous being of this kind was *not* merely a nullity, but represented a perilous field of force. The heavenly Baal who was now enjoying such esteem in Jerusalem, however, had probably very little to do with the ancient fertility god of the same name. Consequently Manasseh's behaviour, which was sanctioned by all the priests, was not necessarily seen from the very outset as an offence against the first commandment of Yahweh worship. On the other hand we can understand why Jeremiah held a different view. But why was he so inexorable in his assertion that such idolatry would inevitably be punished by the death of the guilty person? This finds a

closer justification in the later disputes (see section 2.7 below) than it
does here, in the early period.

*2.4 History as a purposeful course of events, and the apostasy and repentance
of the nation: the early period, II*

2.4.1 Divine and human derek *as the backbone of history.* The burden of
Jeremiah's charge against his opponents, with their fashionable astral
cult, is their disregard of the history experienced by Israel as the
foundation of its present and future life. For him, the heavenly Baal
is a new version of the Baal figure who had already seduced the people
in earlier days, and who from time immemorial had led his worshippers
astray, away from the true path of history. For contrary to what his
name claims, Baal is no true master, but a power impotent in history
– one who has neither moulded what is past nor can bring forth what
is still in the future. He can at most breathe forth annihilating oracles;
he is not capable of a positive *dābār*. The first utterance in the book
which is couched in the genre of prophecy – the saying about
the change of gods (2.5–11) – stresses that the turning away to
nothingness had been the fateful turn of national history. It was a turn
that followed directly on the conclusion of divinely effected salvation,
and it was still making itself felt in the grievances of the present day:

> Thus has Yahweh spoken:
>
> A What wrong did your fathers find in me,
>   that they went far from me?
> They followed an annihilating breath
>   and became nothing . . .
> Instead of saying: where is Yahweh to be found?
>   the one who brought us up out of the land of Egypt,
>   leading us in the desert,
>   in the land of the steppes and the abyss [. . .],
>   in the land that no man passes through
>   and where no man dwells.
> I let you come into the land [. . .]
>   to eat of its fruits and good things.
> Hardly had you come in, you defiled my land,
>   made my heritage an abomination.
> The priests did not ask: where is Yahweh to be found?
> Those who pass on the Torah did not know me,
>   the shepherds rose up against me.
> The nabis prophesied by the Baal,
>   followed after *the powerless one.*

B Therefore:
   I will still contend with you,
      murmur of Yahweh's,
   with your children's children will I contend.
C For
      cross to the island of the Kittim [. . .]
      send to Kedar and inform yourself carefully!
   [. . .] Has ever a nation changed its divinities?
   And these are not divinities!
   But my people have changed their glory
      for *the powerless one!*

The saying is permeated through and through by a fundamental antithesis. On the one hand is the powerless one (*lō' yō'īl*) who is also called Baal, the nullifying breath (*hebel*), the abomination (*tō'ēbā*), to whom leading groups among the people are devoted. On the other hand stands Yahweh, who is originally and in reality Israel's divinity (*'elōhīm*) – indeed, who constitutes Israel's power and her splendour and her effective strength, her *kābōd*, her glory – whose cause only Jeremiah now supports. Yahweh does not rule somewhere or other in the beyond. On the contrary, he is the driving force of positive history, which is depicted as a purposeful course of events. Bringing the people up out of Egypt and into the cultivated lands was Yahweh's achievement. This brief historical sketch ends with the settlement of the promised land. Jeremiah is presupposing the viewpoint of a self-contained epoch of salvation history – a viewpoint which we otherwise find in the Old Testament in cultic contexts.[9] From the zenith and terminal point of salvation history, in which the subject is God, Jeremiah leaps over to the present and its subject, man.

To call to mind the power invested in its leadership ought to be the task of the ruling classes. The priestly question 'where is Yahweh?' will hardly have been intended as an invitation to theoretical speculation; it is a pointer to observances which celebrated the salvation history of earliest times as the foundation sustaining present opportunities for living. (Was this perhaps recalled through dramatic and symbolic performances, rather like the mediaeval mystery plays?) It was from reflection on this history, its presuppositions and its course, that the appropriate instructions about holy and unholy behaviour grew up (the *tōrā*), as well as the reliable prediction of the future made by the nabis. What a nabi proclaims as future event thus has to prove and legitimate itself against the background of past history, and the course it took. But in Jeremiah's opinion this is being inexcusably neglected.

What Jeremiah attacks as wickedness, in view of the present

situation, has a long previous history. For some mysterious reason the zenith of salvation history, the gift of the land and its good things, also became the beginning of a history of disaster: 'Hardly had you come in, you defiled my land.' Like Hosea and Isaiah before him, Jeremiah does not see the history of the people as a unilinear and homogeneous continuum. He is aware of a primordial period of salvation history which had risen to a final climax, only then to break over into a period of growing disaster. The tradition that Israel deflected to Baal cults as soon as it settled in the promised land is an old one (Num. 25); it receives historical support to the extent that, in making the transition to agriculture, the early Israelites felt the need for vegetation rites, for which Baal worship offered suitable models. But here and elsewhere the process, which actually took centuries, is explained as apostasy belonging to a particular point in time.

Yahweh's *way in history* ended in a healthful constitution for living and for society (*mišpāṭ*), which human beings have to discern and to preserve. But it is precisely this that ruling circles in Israel are rejecting and wantonly destroying, in the belief that it keeps them in leading strings. The consequence is inescapable chaos (5.5f.):

A   They should understand that they are on Yahweh's way (*derek*),
     the *mišpāṭ* of their God.
   But they have together broken the yoke
     and burst the bonds.
B   Therefore a lion from the forest shall slay them,
     the desert wolf shall harry them . . .
C   For many are their rebellions (*pešaʿ*),
     mighty their acts of apostasy (*mᵉšūbā*).

With *derek yhwh* we meet for the first time a phrase which plays a particular part in Jeremiah. What is apparently meant is the strand of national history woven by God and co-fashioned by men and women which opens up positive opportunities for living, and which was discernible above all in the salvation history of primordial times. At that period, in the epoch lasting from the exodus from Egypt until the settlement of Canaan, Yahweh was more actively and unambiguously involved in earthly happenings than he is in 'the present time', which is qualitatively of less value. But every generation can establish a link with that first era.

Walk in the ways [of the beginnings] (*rōš*),
   ask for the paths of primordial days,
what the *derek* of the good is!
   So walk therein! (6.16).

This period is known in Hebrew as 'fore-time' – the prehistoric age (*rōš, rīšōn*, 17.12; *qedem*, 30.20) or primordial time (*'ōlām*). It may in certain circumstances be extended backwards to creation and – by Isaiah, for example – forwards to the time of David. It was an era in which God, as the ground of all positive reality, brought into being the orders for living designed for his chosen people. Every later age is capable of 'bending back' to this era; the time that is of such constitutive importance can at all times be actualized, brought forward into the present. (In a similar way, New Testament writings later see the history of salvation from the beginning of Israel down to Jesus' resurrection as an epoch, a segment, which is actualized or made contemporary in the worship and, especially, the sacraments of the church.)

It is noticeable that Jeremiah never talks about a *derek* of Yahweh's at the present day. But in the turn to eschatological salvation, Yahweh's guiding providence will once again move clearly into the foreground. Then he will let the liberated Israelites arrive at 'a straight path' on which it will be impossible to go astray (31.9, 21). Through the gift of a new reason, a 'unified *derek*' for the whole people will come into being; and the nation will then be bound to God in unceasing reverence and fear (32.39–a later interpolation?). (Even the neighbouring peoples who are now so ill-disposed towards Israel will in days to come learn 'the [way] of my people' in order 'to swear by my name' and to become part of the people of God; 12.16 – a later interpolation.)

Yahweh's *derek* is also manifested to Israel so that she may walk in it and find her salvation. This, at least, is what seems to be meant by 18.15:

> They (? the false gods) made them (the Israelites) stumble in their
> ways,
>   the paths of primordial times.
> So that they walk in paths belonging to a way
>   that has not been cleared.

The ways have been fore-given from earliest times, which means that they have been laid down as salvation history; and they lead to a favourable future. But they are not being used. The people 'pervert their way', which comes from Yahweh (3.21), in order to construct, in a kind of *hybris*, a way of their own, which is in fact no way at all. Through what he does, every human being makes a *derek* for himself, *derek* meaning both the way that leads through life and the conduct of life itself. But if a person designs his *derek* as a path into nothingness, without any connection with the fundamental way of God, he will stumble and fall. No one can achieve a history all by himself. It is 'not

in man (to form) his way' (10.23). Israel is opening up her own paths
to the great powers of Egypt and Assyria, and is coming to grief in the
process (2.17f.). At the present time Jeremiah's contemporaries are
building their history with vice. It is no wonder that Yahweh is
teaching these wickednesses (*rā'ōt*) to take over this abortive *derek*
altogether (2.33; 3.21; 4.18)!

2.4.2 *šūb*. The people is not unconditionally bound to follow the
way undeviatingly, whether this is the way of God or its own. Under
certain conditions it is able to turn back. For this, Jeremiah used the
word *šūb* (it occurs over 100 times in the book). We already find this
word among the eighth-century prophets, where it probably refers to
cultic rites of repentance, which included a confession of sins; though
for Amos or Isaiah these rites represented opportunities once open
that had been wasted (cf. Vol. I, section 4.4). Jeremiah, on the other
hand, loves in his argument to vary the word's root and its derivations
in a brilliantly inventive way (*šōbēb, šōbāb, mᵉšūbā*). He uses *šūb* to
designate both the turning *away* from *derek*, from the following of
Yahweh (*mēʾaḥᵃrē*, 3.19), and the turn *back* to him (*'el*), the conversion.
(In the second sense the expression, in its Greek translation, *metanoia*,
becomes the central concept of Jesus' preaching; but there it means
the inner repentance of the heart. Jeremiah still associates it with
demonstrable actions.)

Jeremiah makes clear to his North Israelite countrymen the double
potentiality of 'the turn' in two passages: the vision of the two women,
with the sayings appended to it (3.6–4.4), and 'the little book of
consolation for Ephraim' (chs. 30f.). We have to remember that for a
hundred years North Israel had disappeared from the face of the map
– had been totally erased. The upper classes, who had been deported
by the Assyrians to Mesopotamia, had disappeared completely there.
The peasants who had remained behind were dominated by a new,
foreign 'aristocracy', which had been channelled into the country. It
is in this particular situation, where – in practical political terms –
everything is at an end, that Israel's God intervenes and throws
open a new future for the nation. The key to the metahistorical
understanding of this is provided by the word *šūb*. For the modern
observer, a practical political explanation seems more obvious. What
Jeremiah prophesies seems to be connected with the military operations of Josiah of Judah who, confronted by the decline of the Assyrian
empire, hastened to conquer former North Israelite lands and to
unite them again with Judah. Unfortunately it is not clear whether
Jeremiah's predictions preceded the royal measures or accompanied
them. In either case it seems improbable that Jeremiah appeared on
the stage merely as court ideologist. For that his attitude towards the

royal house was far too critical all his life. He traces back what he says
to secret experiences of his own; and we have no reason to mistrust
his subjective sincerity.

According to Jeremiah's account, North Israel had made itself the
very personification of apostasy through its Baal rites (which Hosea
had fought against). For the sake of foreigners it had spoilt the
harmony of its own *derek*, making it pernicious. Acts like this mean
rebellion (*pš'*, 3.13) against the all-embracing God, a dissolution of
the covenant, adultery. They compel Yahweh to divorce his wife
Israel. And this is what has happened. But secretly God remains
faithful to the covenant (*ḥāsīd*, 3.12; cf. 31.3, 20). Contrary to human
law (which excludes the remarriage of a divorced woman) he grants
the new beginning by means of a *dābār*. Jeremiah has to call to the
north, 'Turn back, faithless Israel' (3.12), and, 'Turn back, faithless
sons, I will heal your faithlessness' (3.22). The prophecy is probably
thought of as having so mighty an effect that it reaches not only the
remaining population (which was still existing in the mountains of
central Palestine) but even the descendants of the men and women
who had been carried off to the faraway country in the north. At all
events, the actual presence of the people he is addressing is unnecessary
when the prophet becomes the mouthpiece of his God. He further
proclaims that Yahweh had heard a secret cry from the enslaved:
'Turn me, so that I may be turned (*šūb*, hiphil + qal), for thou
[Yahweh] art still my God.' The one to whom they call responds with
a prophecy of salvation:

B Behold
    I will turn again the turn of the tents of Jacob,
        on his dwellings will I have compassion.
    The city shall be built above its rubble,
        and a palace shall throne over its true constitution (*mišpāṭ*).
    Out of them shall come a feast of thanksgiving
        and the voices of merrymakers . . .
    Its sons shall rise up as in the fore-time,
        so that its congregation shall be established before me.
    And I will visit it on its oppressors;
        the bearers of its power shall be (more powerful) than them.
    Its ruler will come forth from its midst,
        I will grant him audience, so that he shall approach me.
    For who else would dare in reason
        to approach me? murmurs Yahweh (30.18–21).

With the divine announcement of a total reversal or turn of events
(*šūb šᵉbūt*) for the shattered North Israelites, Jeremiah is probably

picking up a cultic phrase which was used at the New Year festival,
to celebrate the beginning of the rainy season, as a sacramentally
effected turn in the fortunes of fellow participants in the cult (Ps. 85.1).
Removed from this context in the recurring sequence of the years, it
now signalizes the change from the disaster of earlier times to healthful
conditions 'as in the fore-time' (cf. Hos. 14.2, 5). The view of Israel's
history as a line whose direction changes diametrically in two places
becomes clearly evident here (see also Vol. I, 7.6.3). So what is being
emphasized is a historical turning point which one would be inclined
to call eschatological, if only future salvation were not described in
Jeremiah in such sober and everyday terms that hardly anything at
all can be perceived of any wondrous 'excess' – any going beyond
everything that has hitherto existed. The cities will be rebuilt, a
monarchical constitution will come into being with its own North
Israelite head of state. He is not described as king (was this title
reserved for the Davidic rulers in Jerusalem?) but he none the less has
the right of direct contact with the deity, such as is not enjoyed by
other mortals.

How reserved all this sounds, compared with the triumphal strains
of the messianic expectations of salvation in the Book of Isaiah! The
divine reversal, as an edict conferring a new state of affairs, comes
first. But it is characteristic of Jeremiah that this should draw a
conversion of the people in its wake. This is first of all true in the literal
sense: the people who have been deported will return to their homeland
and will receive a meaningful *derek* in which they can walk (30.10;
31.8, 16–18, 21). But there is a cultic application too: the people will
come confessing their sins and will make a pilgrimage to Zion (3.22ff.;
31.6). Ultimately, a rethinking and inner insight is an essential factor
– recognition of one's own sinfulness and one's deviations from the
true path (3.13; 31.19). This, then, is the future of the North Israelites.

For his own people, the Judaeans, Jeremiah as yet knows nothing
about an hour of repentance. And this does not change later in his
life, either. By turning to the Baal of heaven and leaning on the
inwardly brittle powers of Egypt and Assyria the Judaeans have
denied the liberation of the exodus, which raised Israel to the status
of responsibly acting son, and have fallen back into slavery (2.14–20).
Compared with North Israel, Judah has heightened apostasy into a
deliberate breach of faith (*bgd* 3.7f.); she has actually declined *šūb*, or
has only ostensibly implemented it (3.10; 5.3; 8.4f.). So the present
generation has shut the door on every alternative to the destiny
threatening them. (It is only personally, for his own self, that Jeremiah
knows that he is called to repentance, 15.19). This explains why the
theme taken up in the early period recedes completely into the

background from ch. 7 onwards. It is only the interpreters involved in the C stratum of the book who – in the exilic period, after the catastrophe had already taken place – prolong Jeremiah's own line of argument and call incessantly to the Judaeans to return from their evil way (*had-derek hārā'ā*), now that the *dābār* proclaiming disaster has been fulfilled (18.11; 25.5; 26.3; 35.15; 36.3, 7).

Through Jeremiah, therefore, the possibility of human repentance takes on an importance which it is still completely lacking in the prophecy of the Assyrian period. Yet this by no means implies that the prophet sees his prophetic word as something hypothetical, only valid should his listeners fail to repent. The link between misdeed and misfortune must be forged and completed first of all. Only then can repentance have its effect. Yet the stress on *šūb* means that human decision and insight play a very different part for Jeremiah from the part they play in the predictions of salvation made by Isaiah or Hosea. Perhaps this explains why Jeremiah can put forward so sober a picture of Israel in the era of salvation, and why the mythological images of his predecessors find no echo in him.

2.5 Persecution and underground existence under Jehoiakim

2.5.1 The anti-temple diatribe. For twelve years Judah had sworn by Deuteronomy, and had centralized the cult in Jerusalem. For twelve years the high-hearted Josiah had won back political independence for his country step by step. It is for these very years that we lack any sayings of Jeremiah's. Why, it is useless to speculate.

Perhaps during this period the prophet expressed enthusiastic agreement with Josiah's policy (because the reform was in accord with his insistence on the elimination of Baal rites), but was later ashamed of what he had said. Or perhaps he deliberately awaited developments in silence, because the national exuberance made him vaguely uneasy. Or perhaps there was simply no occasion for him to write down that he said; since it was only in exceptional cases that prophetic utterances were committed to writing.

In Jeremiah C there are two pronouncements in which Jeremiah seems to refer to Deuteronomy in approving terms. 9.13–16 talks affirmatively about Yahweh's Torah, which Israel has forsaken. 11.2–8 quotes a sentence from Deut. 27.26 in modified form: 'Cursed be the man who does not heed the words of the covenant.' This is no doubt a reference to Josiah's renewal of the covenant by way of this Book of the Law. But if the two sayings derive from Jeremiah at all, they date from a later period, when Deuteronomy no longer enjoyed official recognition.

Jeremiah's prophecy becomes indisputably in evidence once more when, after the defeat and death of Josiah, the victorious Pharaoh Necho installed Josiah's son Jehoiakim in Judah as an Egyptian vassal. Without the religious enthusiasm and the utopian dreams of his father, instead aiming ruthlessly at the assertion of power and at a life of luxury, Jehoiakim's exploitative policy evoked Jeremiah's unequivocal protest. For some months social criticism now comes to the fore, linked with a criticism of the temple which is of incomparable ferocity. The prophet already raises a dirge over the rulers although they are still alive, beginning with an uncanny *hoy*, which was usually sung at the grave, and which we can only reproduce in much feebler form through our 'woe'.

> Woe to him who builds his house without faithfulness to the
>   community (*ṣedeq*),
>   his upper rooms without a foundation of justice (*mišpāṭ*).
> He makes his fellow countrymen work for nothing,
>   he does not give them wages;
> who says: 'I will build myself a spacious house
>   and airy galleries.'
> He cuts out [windows]
>   panelled with cedar . . .
> Are you a king that you may compete in cedar?
> Your father (= Josiah), did he not eat and drink,
>   but create justice and faithfulness to the community (*mišpāṭ* and
>   *ṣᵉdāqā*)?
> He helped the poor and needy to their rights,
>   then it was good.
> Is this not to know me?
>   murmurs Yahweh.
> But your eyes and your reason (*lēb*)
>   know nothing but your own gain,
> the shedding of innocent blood,
>   exploitation and oppression! (22.13–17).

As in the earlier prophets, the connection between action and destiny is in the foreground, and *ṣedeq* and *mišpāṭ* count as the sustaining pillars of a sound society. As in Amos, the greedy striving for gain (*bṣʿ*, Amos 9.1) achieves the reverse effect, creating a sphere of disaster which necessarily attracts downfall and destruction. The saying must date from the early years of Jehoiakim. Nothing is said as yet about the idolatry with which Jeremiah reproaches him elsewhere. Consequently, there is as yet nothing here either about the father's zeal in introducing the divine law. Jehoiakim still seems to be observing Deuteronomy. Nevertheless, his social policy evokes a decisive protest.

But the whole people is on the same false track. Political collapse
has washed away all solidarity and has instead fostered a bigoted
piety. After all, the Egyptians had passed Jerusalem by and had not
laid a finger on the temple! So the priests and nabis agreed that this
was the finger of God himself, a revelation from the highest power
that Zion and Zion alone was God's own dwelling on earth and would
for ever remain inviolable. If Josiah had remained under Jerusalem's
sphere of influence, no injury would have happened to him! Deuteronomic notions about the cultic places which Yahweh had chosen for
his name, Isaianic prophecies about the unassailability of Zion (cf.
Vol. I, section 7.7) and older traditions of the Jerusalem cult about
the sea of nations which dashes itself against the walls of the temple
– all these elements add up to a perilous, magical over-estimation of
the cultic places. It was against this that, in the very first year of
Jehoiakim's reign, Jeremiah protested energetically in an anti-temple
diatribe delivered at the temple itself – did he perhaps belong there,
as nabi? – (ch. 7, stratum C; 26, stratum B).

A   Do not trust
           in words of deception (*šeqēr*):
           Yahweh's temple! Yahweh's temple!
           Yahweh's temple are these (buildings) . . .'
           (How is it then) with stealing, murder and adultery?
           and swearing falsely?
     You come and stand [. . .] in *this house* [. . .]
           and say 'we are delivered!' . . .
     Has then *this house* become a den of thieves?
           over which my name is proclaimed? . . .
     Go now to my place in Shiloh,
           [. . .] see what I have done to it!
B   But now [. . .]:
     I will do to *this house*
           in which you trust
           as I have done to Shiloh.
     And I will cast you away from my face
           as I have cast away all your brethren,
           the whole seed of Ephraim (7.4ff.).

With his conviction that before the building of Solomon's temple there
was only one legitimate sanctuary, in Shiloh, Jeremiah is under the
spell of the Deuteronomic idea of the divinely-willed centralization of
the cult in a single place at any given period. But when he predicts
destruction for the second cultic centre, in Jerusalem, which the
supporters of Deuteronomy saw as final, he is not deviating from the

actual wording of the document of reform, though he is no doubt departing from its spirit. In Jeremiah's opinion violent robbers can no longer enjoy the fellowship with God that confers salvation. The devout worshipping community is nothing but a band of robbers seeking for a way of escape at some secure place! Festive holiday clothes are the covering for people who are really garbed in theft, murder and other crimes. Jeremiah follows the argumentation of the prophets belonging to the Assyrian period (Amos 5.4–6; Micah 9–12, for example): God denies that the cult has any sacramental effect; the hypocritical participants in the cult are doomed, and God is giving over the cultic place itself to destruction. Jeremiah's listeners, who are gathered in the forecourt, are naturally completely convinced of the contrary. But that is trust in *šeqer* – a phrase which from this time on Jeremiah uses to designate ideological self-deception (13.25; 28.15; 29.31). *Šeqer* means far more than a clouding of the consciousness. It includes an aggressive way of behaving which damages the person himself and others. It is the opposite of faithfulness and *mišpāṭ* (5.1–3).

His listeners' reaction shows how deeply Jeremiah has hurt them. Mad with rage, the crowd falls on the speaker to lynch him: 'You must die!' This time the prophet escapes with his life only because of the courageous intervention of some of the king's ministers, who have got wind of the tumult in time, and because some of the elders point out that Micah had already proclaimed a similar message a hundred years earlier without being punished for it.

Does the anti-temple diatribe mean the death-blow for all cultic religion? For it is not a perverted Yahweh cult that is attacked (v. 9a, the exception, is a later interpolation); it is a liturgy that has been purified and reformed in accordance with the newly discovered law of Moses. Protestant commentators in particular view the speech as a milestone on the way to an ethical monotheism that no longer requires any holy places, but which worships its God in spirit and in truth, and practises religion through neighbourly love. Righteousness, not sacrifice: this is what God expects. Rites and ceremonies draw away the attention from the one thing needful. 'The cult itself is the nation's sin,' writes Volz about this passage.[10] Is this an accurate judgment?

There is no doubt that Jeremiah underlines the ethical character of a true bond with Yahweh, differing from most influential supporters of his people's religion in the importance which he attaches to it. The critical prophets do undoubtedly raise the moral character of Israel's religion to a higher level. From this time on the stringency of prophetic judgment was to be the companion of Israel's understanding of God and was to transform it profoundly. And yet, in spite of this, the interpreter must be careful not to attribute modern ideas to Hebrew texts. Yahweh's name really is proclaimed over *this house;* and the house is just as sacred for Jeremiah as it was for Deuteronomy, requiring a cult as a matter of course. Nor is the divine face an empty phrase for Jeremiah either. It represents a personal and local mode of the bestowed presence of a supreme power, which was impossible outside the sphere of the cult. Israel's 'auras' of wicked deeds would not take so catastrophic a course and would not so quickly issue in destruction had they not touched the unique sphere of the real divine presence on earth, in his sanctuary. So Jeremiah too is unaware of any perpetual link between man and Yahweh outside the worshipping community; nor does he recognize any true knowledge of God without cultic mediation.

2.5.2 Lasting persecution. Soon after the incident at the temple, the authoritative force of Deuteronomy must have been set aside. At all events, almost every chapter in Jeremiah dating from the Jehoiakim period stresses that the fundamental evil is that incense is (again) being burnt to Baal and the heavenly host, or that the house of Yahweh is being desecrated, even children being burnt as sacrifices (7.30–8.3; 11.15; 12.7; 13.10, etc.). Pre-Deuteronomic cultic practices dating from the Manasseh period have crept in again. Consequently Jeremiah sees these as the root of the evil (13.4). He certainly still occasionally engages in social criticism (9.3–6); but this has become secondary. It only underlines the compulsive nature of the impending downfall. Jeremiah's plain speaking in his discourses leaves nothing to be desired. Whereas in the early period he did not directly attack the monarchy, now things are different. He upbraids the queen mother, for example, who has a special position at the court, prophesying that her majesty will be exposed for what it is:

> Lift up [your] eyes and see
>   how they come from the north.
> Where is the flock that was given to you,
>   the cattle of your glory?
> What will you say when he visits it
>   over you [as head]?
> You yourself have accustomed (the foreign powers)
>   to familiar dealings with you . . .
> Because of the greatness of your guilt your garment shall be lifted
>   up,
>   your 'thighs' will be ravished (13.20–22).

He crosses swords with other leading groups as well. If Israel is destroyed through illusionary self-deception (*šeqer*), then this is thanks to the priests and nabis, who take their guidance from Baal in their oracles, instead of from Yahweh's way (5.30f.; 6.13f.; 23.17).

From this time on Jeremiah has to reckon with attempts on his life. The other people living in his village, Anathoth, discuss in whispers behind his back how he can be got rid of; he cannot even rely on his own family (11.19; 12.6). When he goes so far as to announce for the first time that the whole of Jerusalem with its people will soon go up in flames, action is taken. He is beaten and shut up in the stocks overnight by Pashhur, the priest who is responsible at the temple for nabis who have taken leave of their senses. Jeremiah certainly pays him back with a prophecy of disaster, which declares the priest from this time on to be 'Terror on every side', assuring him that he will be imprisoned in Babylon and will die there (20.1–6). But that does not make his own fate easier. He knows that he is harried by every dog, and is an outcast from society. (Religious history knows many martyrs. But few of them had to endure ostracism and persecution for so many years as Jeremiah.)

In 605 relations with the king reached boiling point. In the same year Nebuchadnezzar of Babylon defeated the Egyptian Pharaoh Necho at Carchemish on the Euphrates, and threw Egypt out of Asia. It was not long before Nebuchadnezzar had subjected the whole of Syria and Palestine. Jeremiah had seen the battle beforehand in a vision and, with a wild summons to the holy war in the name of his God, had supported the Babylonian army (46.1–12). Nebuchadnezzar was the enemy from the north whom Jeremiah had proclaimed for twenty years. At last he had appeared, emerging from the real political scene as an identifiable metahistorical figure.

Shortly before Judah's subjection to Babylonian hegemony, or soon afterwards, a general day of repentence (*ṣōm*) was officially proclaimed at the temple in Jerusalem. On this occasion his inner voice demanded of Jeremiah that he write down on a scroll all the words about the fate of his people with which he had been inspired. These culminate in the sure prediction that Nebuchadnezzar is going to attack Judah, destroy the land and carry off the people. For Yahweh is now going to bring about all the wickedness (*rā'ā*) which he has long since promised to inflict (36.29, 31).

Baruch, Jeremiah's friend and scribe, writes everything down on the scroll at his dictation. Since the prophet himself is forbidden to speak in the temple, Baruch reads the whole text aloud there. The ministers present are so agitated by it that they immediately report to the cabinet. Baruch is called to appear before them and has to read the scroll aloud once more. The ministers decide to lay the prophecy,

with its menacing threats, before the king himself. But since they know
how quick-tempered he is, they first of all tell Baruch and Jeremiah
to go underground. The narrator then tells dramatically how Jehoiakim has the text read to him as he sits in front of the fire in his palace.
Taking a knife, he cuts out with his own hand every three or four
columns as he hears them, throwing them into the fire. 'Yet neither
the king, nor any of his servants who heard all these words, was afraid,
nor did they rend their garments.' Jehoiakim's intention was probably
not simply to express his contempt of the nonsensical prophet; he also
wanted to destroy the magic character of the written word by burning
it. He finally orders the prophet and his scribe to be thrown into prison
immediately. But the two men remain in hiding. Yahweh commands
his prophet: 'Take another scroll and write on it all the former words
that were in the first scroll.' Jeremiah obeys, adding to his new edition
many other similar sayings. There is no doubt that this provided the
basic material for the book of Jeremiah as we have it.

The procedure is typical of the genesis of a prophetic book. The
prophets were not men of letters, and consequently their books are
not systematic accounts; they are collections of utterances. Yet putting
them into writing involved detailed revision, with the inclusion of
prose glosses and link passages. This makes it impossible in many
cases to reconstruct the original wording of the prophecies with any
final certainty.

Jehoiakim acted astutely enough, submitting himself to Nebuchadnezzar in good time and avoiding a war. This seemed definitely to
give the lie to Jeremiah's sombre visions, for Jehoiakim himself
was installed as Babylonian vassal. The prophet remained in the
underground for six or seven years. But he continued to be certain
that the disaster from the north was still impending. And events were
to prove him right.

2.6 The night of despair

2.6.1 The Confessions. Interspersed in chs. 11 to 20, which date from the
Jehoiakim period, are five poems of extraordinary lyrical beauty. In
them the prophet complains bitterly about his own fate and makes a
personal appeal to his God (11.8–12.6; 15.10–20; 17.14–18; 18.18–23;
20.7–18). These poems follow the pattern of the individual psalm of
lament, a genre which was in common use in the temple. And like the
psalms, these laments of Jeremiah's are sometimes answered with a
divine oracle of assurance that the prayer has been heard.[11] They are
sometimes introduced by a self-pitying monologue ('woe is me',
15.10), and sometimes conclude with a curse on the prophet's own
life (20.14ff.). As an expression of personal reflection, these poems go

beyond anything known to us in Israel and the ancient world. For the first time in the literature of the world, the voice of an individual is heard (some years before the Greek Sappho), the voice, moreover, of an individual tormented by boundless suffering. These poems can best be compared with Augustine's *Confessions*, and this has given them the name by which they are known to scholars. (They were earlier known as Jeremiads.)

(i) A saying accusing the Judaeans of bringing evil (*rā'ā*) on themselves is followed by the eruption of a prophetic cry (11.18–20):

> Yahweh made it known to me, and I knew,
>> then I [looked upon] their deeds.
> But I, like a trusting sheep, was dragged to the slaughter,
>> and I did not know it.
> But over me they made plans:
>> 'Let us destroy the tree in its [sap]!
> We will wipe him out of the land of the living
>> so that his name will be remembered no more.'
> Yahweh Sabaoth!
> Thou dost set up *ṣedeq*,
>> triest the inner heart and the mind (*lēb*).
> Let me see thy vengeance upon them
>> for I commit to thee my cause!

The God who is invoked enters entirely into the feelings of the petitioner and utters a sombre prophecy of diasaster over his opponents:

> Therefore, so has Yahweh spoken:
> A concerning the man of Anathoth
>> who seek your life:
>> 'You should not prophesy in Yahweh's name!
>> Then you will not *die* by our hand.'
> B Therefore, so has Yahweh Sabaoth spoken:
>> Behold I will visit it upon them!
>> The young men will *die* by the sword.
>> Their sons and daughters shall *die* of hunger,
>>> no remnant of them shall be left.
> C For I will bring evil on the men of Anathoth
>> in the year of their visitation.

The village community is shamed to the depths that one of themselves should undermine the very foundations of the nation by what he said, and should make himself the most hated man in the country. So they threaten to murder him. Yahweh puts himself on the side of his prophet to the extent of condemning the whole of Anathoth to die,

although up to that point the death of the prophet had been no more
than planned.

(ii) The poems that follow are more sombre still. The suffering
which Jeremiah feels constrained to express increases. God shows less
and less understanding; instead he confronts Jeremiah with the
prospect of even more bitter experiences. In a second poem (12.1–6),
linked directly to the first, the prophet goes into the fundamentals of
the situation. He complains that the path (*derek*) of the wicked who act
contrary to the community prospers, even though they only pay lip-
service to religion. He wishes them his own fate and a day of holy war:

> Separate them out like sheep for the slaughter!
> Sanctify them for the day of killing!

This time he dares to enter into an explicit dispute with Yahweh. The
divine response is certainly not lacking, but it is not a comforting
answer. According to our ideas it sounds positively sarcastic. Jeremiah
is forced to hear: 'You have till now raced against men on foot and
they have made you weary. How will you in the future race against
horses?' His own family is going to turn against him, so 'trust them
not!'. Even the most intimate circle of the human community is going
to expel him. He has to fight against everybody.

(iii) Growing isolation because of his prophetic calling is the subject
of two other poems as well (15.10–11 [–14?], 15ff.). These switch over
into a wild attack on the all-powerful God:

> If words of thine were found, I devoured them,
>   thy words became bliss to me . . .
> I never sat down in a cheerful group
>   to be merry there . . .
> (Vanquished) by thy hand, I sat alone
>   for imprecations occupied me.
> Why was my pain unending? . . .
> Thou hast indeed become to me as a deceitful brook,
>   as waters on which there is no reliance (vv. 16–18).

The 'responding' oracle tells the petitioner that he has been heard,
but rejects him, though showing comprehension of his infinite pain:

> If you return (*šūb*), I will turn you,
>   that you may again turn to me . . .
> They shall turn (*šūb*) to you,
>   but do not turn to them!
> I have made you for this people
>   into a bronze wall that cannot be captured.

To present an iron front outwardly, whatever the turbulence within him, can have been only a very limited consolation for Jeremiah.

(iv) In the third and fourth passages the petitioner is chafed by the failure of the correlation between action and destiny to function where his opponents are concerned. They never stop scoffing at him: 'What has happened to Yahweh's *dābār*? Let it come!', probably playing on the much-heralded attack by the enemy from the north, which Jeremiah had been proclaiming for the last twenty years. Jeremiah had made it perfectly clear that he personally was certainly not longing for the disastrous day. But since they are persecuting him treacherously, he now changes his mind: '*Bring* upon them the day of evil!' (17.14–18). They 'complete' evil for the prophet although he has done nothing but good, indeed has striven by his intercession to turn away the divine anger. Now his patience is at an end:

> Deliver up their sons to famine,
>> pour them out before the sword!
> Forgive their iniquity no more,
>> their sins before thee – do not wipe them out! (18.19ff.).

In reply to unrestrained cries like this the voice of Yahweh is no longer heard. God can be silent even towards a prophet.

(v) The fifth and final pair of poems attacks the inexorable God at the beginning (20.7–9):

> Thou hast deceived me, Yahweh, and I have let myself be deceived.
>> Thou wert stronger than I and hast prevailed over me . . .
> For me has Yahweh's word (*dābār*) become
>> shame and derision all day long.
> But if I thought: I will no longer think of it,
>> no longer speak in his name –
> Then it was in my heart as it were a burning fire
>> shut up in my bones.
> I was not able to keep it to myself
>> and could not.

What Yahweh has done to him is being imitated by his human opponents; they too want to tempt and overpower him (20.10). It is almost as if God himself is the author of the evil. But afterwards the prophet admonishes himself with the traditional theme of the psalms: a certainty of being heard.

> Yahweh is with me as mighty warrior,
>> therefore my persecutors are bound to stumble.

But the mood immediately changes again. One curse follows

another. The Old Testament, which is certainly not sparing of curses, can hardly show anything comparable:

> Cursed be the day
>   on which I was born! . . .
> Cursed be the man
>   who brought the glad news to my father:
> 'Born to you is a son and heir, rejoice greatly over him!'
> Let [the day] be like the cities
>   which God overthrew (i.e. Sodom and Gomorrah),
>   because it did not kill me in the womb,
>   so that my mother would have been my grave . . .
> . . . Why did I come forth from the womb?
> So as to see toil and trouble so much
>   that my days will end in shame?

Jeremiah cuts himself off even from his nearest relatives. He invokes misery and downfall on the innocent messenger who had once brought his father the happy news of his birth. Jeremiah is as much at odds with all other human beings as – in the hour of his despairing cry – he is with his God.

2.6.2 The conflict between the person and the office. Anyone who tries to imagine what Jeremiah's life was like will not be surprised at the note of torment in these poems. In the face of a biography as full of tension as this, who could fail to understand his wish to lead an ordinary, normal life at long last – to marry, to be at rest, and to laugh like other people? Perhaps we are put off by his cry for revenge (11.20; 15.15; 20.12). This does not fit in with our ideas of how a religious person should behave. We must remember, however, that in a society where there is no established legal system recognized by the state and no police force, revenge, carried out by the kindred of the injured person, is the only effective way of protecting human life from arbitrary attack. It was one of Israel's ancient traditions that Yahweh himself would retaliate on behalf of people who could no longer rely on their kindred. And it is just this that Jeremiah hopes for.

What also seems surprising to us is the 'magical' conception of the divine word which, as *dābār*, has a compulsive force that moulds history, and an explosive power – so much so that if the person who is inspired by it and who has to utter it keeps silent, the word tears him apart. There is no longer any question of obedience or disobedience. Amos (Amos 3.8) and Isaiah (Isa. 8.11) were already aware of this uncanny compulsion under which they were forced to stand and speak. Were they living in a state of trance? Did psychological abnormalities force the prophets to cry out words of this deeply sombre kind? Perhaps a certain deviation from the norm really is among the preconditions that make a prophet what he is, endowing him with particular parapsychological capabilities. But we have to remember that the prophetic interpretation of the *dābār* in no way differed from the understanding of the word passed down to us in the Hebrew language. It is also noticeable that the constraint to second sight and the compulsion to hear an inner voice is balanced by a liberty in dealings with other people which seems unusual, and which shows no sign of any inner coercion at all. When they are disputing with their opponents, these prophets argue with icy clarity, in a language that is both rationally comprehensible and artistically moulded. Jeremiah is continually overwhelmed and mastered by Yahweh. His opponents will never succeed in mastering him.

We are also disconcerted by the way in which massive reproaches are levied against God and are positively hurled in his face. Although the exaggeration here is also typical of Jeremiah elsewhere. Old Testament prayers are never kept within the bounds of the well-tamed language in which a Christian nowadays suppresses his hate or any other impious feelings when he prays. The Israelite, in contrast, seems rather to assume that his complaint will only be effective if he expresses his feelings spontaneously and if he pours out his whole heart. Western prayers sound much more inhibited and formal.

In spite of these obvious roots in an ancient civilization, in the Confessions Jeremiah makes a strikingly modern impression. He shows a conscious awareness of the dichotomy between person and office which we otherwise only find in modern times. It is no wonder that Jeremiah, more than any of the other prophets, should have roused an imaginative sympathy that has provided the inspiration for a number of imaginative works (down to Franz Werfel). The man from Anathoth knows that he has been forced into a role which in no way corresponds to his own personal leanings. Shy and sensitive as he is, the intrigues carried on behind his back chafe him more than the physical deprivations and external sufferings which were to be their result. True, he does not conceal that at the beginning he had pleasure in discovering and proclaiming Yahweh's message. But that time is past, and now despair is his daily bread. The intimate dialogue with the invisible background of all reality has estranged him from all visible, human society. He clings desperately, in a mixture of hate and love, to the last tie left to him. What happens to him can hardly be reconciled with the belief that auras of action create destiny, even though he himself has always had to make this the basis of his arguments in talking to the people. So sensitive a thinker as Jeremiah cannot make himself over so completely to the collective, or see himself so entirely in the light of the collective results of action, as the transmitted material, including some of his own prophecies, suggests. It was this that brought him into conflict with his own God.

A present fashion which goes under the name of the criticism of religion is accustomed to consider religious texts with the latent assumption that they are simply designed to serve the interests of either economic or political power. But who can explain Jeremiah's protest in the light of the interests of any particular social group? For it deviates from the convictions of his people, his class, and indeed his traditional religion.

2.6.3 Biographical classification. The interpretation of the Confessions I have put forward is not undisputed. In seeing them as the voice of a man crushed between his religious role and his personal inclinations, are we perhaps viewing the texts too much through the eyes of our own time? Graf Reventlow was a pioneer in turning the customary interpretation upside down. He believes that here (as well as in certain songs of lament in the Psalter) an individual is speaking in the name of the corporate personality of the cultic community. According to this interpretation, Jeremiah comes forward at cultic ceremonies as the spokesman of persecuted and humiliated Israel. But even apart from his references to the people of Anathoth, the way in which Jeremiah is overwhelmed by the pressure of the divine *dābār*, and also his increasing loneliness, are elements so individually coloured that it is hard to postulate a collective context. So we must continue to assume that towards the end of the seventh century BC in Judah there really was a profound crisis in the social structure, and that a seemingly modern, individual awareness came into being whose pre-eminent witness was Jeremiah.

The Confessions mark a transitional stage in the prophet's life. We possess no individual laments dating from later periods, although Jeremiah remained active for many years, and was still persecuted. The nadir of his inward depression seems only to have been reached during the reign of Jehoiakim. Jeremiah pulled himself together again afterwards, although life hardly became any easier for him. Personally he remained without hope. He still had hope for his nation, although he knew that his people's ambitions were as alien to his ideas as ever. From this time on, Jeremiah practised a submission to God which finds no parallel in the Old Testament. (For a contrast, we need only look at Job.) Was it sufficient from now on for him to be a branch on Israel's stem, content to know that this tree would one day put forth new leaves?

He himself must have included the Confessions in the collection of his sayings; for it is inconceivable that any later hand would have put such blasphemous utterances into the prophet's mouth. Probably the poems are deliberately dovetailed into the particular context. (For example, the first complex is followed by a lament of God himself, whose heart bleeds as he sees the land of his own patrimonial inheritance surrendered, 12.7–12). Did Jeremiah fit the Confessions into his writings when he went underground in 604 and wrote down the first scroll there (ch. 36)? And did he accordingly see the writing as a documentation made for God, and at the same time as a symbolic act which, by giving the *dābār* substance in writing, 'attached' its power more firmly to the actual wording than could be the case if – uttered orally – it was blown away by the wind? Elsewhere in the book, too, references to Jeremiah's own prophetic position are woven into the texture (6.27–30; 10.23–25?).

If we are to comprehend the self-pity of the Confessions, we have to remember that the other parts of the book again and again show pity for others as well – and pity most of all for the fate of the nation. Although the downfall of Judah has become inescapable, because of the correlation between action and destiny, and although its fortunes have been sealed through the *dābār*, its fate still wrings the prophet's very bowels as he proclaims it (4.19–22). In his torment he ejaculates the prayer: 'How long shall this endure?' He confesses 'because of the shattering of my people I myself shall be shattered' (8.18–9.1) and despairingly implores that the impending divine anger may be poured out upon the heathen in Judah's stead (10.25) – though knowing the moment he speaks how senseless such a petition is.

But it is not only the prophet who is wrung by compassion. The God of Israel himself suffers profoundly too:

Woe is me over the hurt that has broken me,
over the heritage of my own people
. . . my tent is laid waste! (10.9–22; cf. 12.7ff.).

Nothing shows more clearly than texts of this kind that pre-exilic religion knows nothing of any theoretically almighty divine power. Instead, it is penetrated through and through by a sense of this God's unconditional faithfulness to the community and his solidarity with the group of men and women to whom he is bound. At the same time the metahistorical character of the spheres or auras of sin and disaster becomes evident. Although he is more than willing to help, Yahweh is unable to avert the downfall once wickedness has become an entity of its own, or a power within the world itself. There is a tide in the events of history which even a God may not stay.

2.7 The power of the stars, or divinely conferred natural laws? The Jehoiakim period

2.7.1 Foreign religious practices in the temple and human sacrifice in ge-hinnom.
Why is Jeremiah so zealous, proclaiming for decades one thing and
one thing only: the country is moving towards destruction; there is no
longer any hope for Judah? Why does he take the incessant persecu-
tions on himself? In the case of so reflective a mind, the persistent
proclamation of disaster can only be understood if Jeremiah was able
to justify it adequately to himself and other people. Why is the
catastrophe so inexorable? This question was of course asked by
Jeremiah's own listeners. 16.10 to 13 gives the answer (from stratum
C, stylized?):

> When you tell this people all these words,
>   and they then ask you:
> Why has Yahweh pronounced over us
>   all this great disaster? . . .
> What is the burden of our guilt (*'āwōn*) and the sin (*ḥaṭṭā't*)
>   we have committed?
> Then you must say to them:
> A   The reason is: your fathers forsook me . . .
>   followed *other divinities,*
>   *served* them and worshipped them,
>   but me they forsook . . .
>   You are behaving more evilly (*rā'ā*) than your fathers . . .
>   Behold, you follow, each of you
>   the stubborness of his evil will (*lēb*) . . .
> B   Therefore I will hurl you
>   out of this land into a land
>   which you do not know . . .
>   There you will *serve other divinities*
>   day and night.

The saying is not lacking in logic. Jeremiah's contemporaries have
forsaken their own God, who had once procured the land for them,
and have given themselves up to foreign deities. It is no wonder that
their own God should now expel them from their own country into
the country whose supernatural powers they are craving so much.
Evidence is therefore provided to back up the prophecies of disaster.
And almost every chapter belonging to the Jehoiakim phase refers,
like this passage, to a depraved cult as the root of the evil.

And yet, is it not fanatical and inhumane to condemn a whole
country to downfall because of a false religious practice, to damn a
whole people simply because they use the wrong 'hymn book'? It is

reasoning of this kind that has prompted today's widespread opinion that the 'Old Testament' God is nothing but a relentless, other-worldly judge, who insists on the strict observance of quite arbitrary laws – a God who has little in common with the God we find in Jesus' teaching, who is the quintessence of love. But the idea of God as judge plays no part whatsoever for Jeremiah, any more than it did for the prophets who preceded him. The cult he opposes so bitterly seems to him corrupting, not only because of its theory but also, and much more, because of its practice; for it actually requires human sacrifice.

A   They produce something evil (*hā-rā'*) in my sight,
        murmur of Yahweh's.
     They set up monsters in [my] temple.
     They have built a *place of fire* as a cultic place
        [. . .] in the *valley* of Ben-Hinnom.
     To burn their own sons there,
        and their daughters in the fire (7.30f.).

The cultic objects are horrible because they require children as burnt sacrifices. The cult of idols which Jeremiah condemns does not only undermine the sense of general solidarity; it does not merely allow the rise of a false and hectic zeal which no longer takes any account of the shared humanity of man with man. It even leads to the murder of innocent children. That makes it unforgiveable.

B   Therefore . . . – murmur of Yahweh's –
     it shall not henceforth be called *place of fire*
        or the *valley* of Ben-Hinnom (= of whimpering?)
     but the valley [of the slaughtered].
     They will be buried on the *place of fire* (7.32).

The notion of Gehenna as hell was later to be derived from the name of the Hinnom valley (*gē-hinnōm*). There, in a dramatic and symbolic act, Jeremiah ceremonially smashes a pitcher before Judah's religious representatives, in order to predict, and 'magically' to provoke, the future smashing of Jerusalem. The city as a whole will become a place of fire on which the inhabitants will burn as their children had once done.

(The kings of Judah) have filled
    this place with the blood of innocents.
They have built the high cultic places of Baal,
    to burn their sons in the fire.
Which I never commanded, never said,
    which never came into my mind! (19.4f.).

Again the main reproach is that innocent people are being killed, and allegedly for the most elevated religious reasons!

2.7.2 Was the origin of the idolatry Canaanite or Assyrian? What bloody cult was it that was spreading in Jerusalem at the end of the seventh century? When the prophets attack corrupt rites, biblical scholars have always been accustomed to think of indigenous customs dating from the pre-Israelite period, which popular Israelite piety took over from the Canaanites, and which from time to time found an entry into the official religion. Where child sacrifice in Ge-hinnom is concerned, the suspicion is supported by the fact that among the Phoenicians (who came from the Canaanite area) first-born sons were also sacrificed in particularly critical situations. In II Kings 23.10; Jer. 32.35 the Ge-hinnom rites are associated with a power that is given the name *mōlek*. This gave rise to the tale of a Semitic god Moloch, who could only be appeased by the flesh of little children. (The subject has attracted painters, important and unimportant, down to our own century.) But historically speaking no such God ever existed; *mōlek* means either a kind of sacrifice which releases a human life from the destiny of death; or it is merely the epithet 'king' applied to a specific deity. Jeremiah shows no signs of the modern tendency to make the Canaanites the scapegoat whenever the Israelite religion becomes corrupt. On the contrary, he blames the king, the priests and the nabis – anyone but the ordinary people – for the introduction of the rites. In addition he presupposes that the people responsible are justifying the rites by an appeal to Yahweh's commandments. This is the only way we can interpret the emphatic defence made by Jeremiah's God: 'Which I never commanded, never said, which never came into my mind' (7.31; 19.5; Ezek. 20.25f. differs). There is no doubt that Jehoiakim and his clique also equated with Yahweh the god whom Jeremiah rejects as Baal, seeing in him a particular extension of Israel's God, as once did the people in the Northern Kingdom, whose Baal worship Hosea attacked. But Jeremiah's speeches point to quite different features in the case of the 'master' Baal, the god who has now reached Jerusalem.

Ever since his vision of the enemy from the north, Jeremiah had intimated that this time Baal and the divinities associated with him were a foreign import. Consequently he has to prophesy that the guilty will be deported to countries where they really can serve other gods, since these gods are at home there. (See the symbolic act in ch. 13, with the belt that is sunk in the Euphrates.) The details we are given about the detested cultic practices and theories point to the religion of Assyria, the paramount political power of the day. Two common features make the relationship strikingly evident:

(i) The 'abominations' set up in the temple are connected with the place of fire in the Hinnom valley where children are burnt (7.30f.; 19.2–6 [II Kings 23.4–11]). We hear about cultic rites in this valley, or about the presence of foreign cultic objects in the temple at Jerusalem, only from the time of Ahaz (Isa. 30.33) and Manasseh, both of them kings who were well disposed towards the Assyrians.

(ii) The Baal who was worshipped at both places is flanked by the queen of heaven (7.18 [44.17f. = Asherah, II Kings 22.5f.]), the sun, the moon and the host of heaven (8.1f.; 19.13). Incence is also burnt to these divinities on the roofs of the houses (19.13; 32.39).

The closeness to neo-Assyrian customs is astonishing. There too we find parents who put their sons and daughters 'through fire' at a cultic place (*hamru*) outside the city. Recipients of the sacrifice are the weather god Adad-Melki (who can also own an additional temple inside the city) and his wife Beletseri = Ashratu. Among the Aramaeans (and in this period Assyria was increasingly infiltrated by Aramaeans) Adad was elevated to the rank of supreme god. He was closely associated (or was even identical) with Assur, the first of all Assyrian gods, or with the Aramaean Baal of heaven (*b'l šmn*). As oracle god, Adad acted in close association with the sun.

Among the Assyrians this 'burning' appears in fact to have been a mere act of consecration, perhaps the surrender to cultic prostitution.[12] But on the evidence of prophetic polemic, it would seem that in Israel the matter was taken literally.

Up to now little consideration has been given to the background of Jeremiah's polemic against idolatry. Taking up some suggestions of Eissfeldt's,[13] I would venture to maintain that here we come face to face with traces of a revolution which we find in the history of almost all the great religions of the ancient world – a revolution which was beginning at this period and whose extent has hardly been investigated at all up to now. At that time an astralization of the idea of God began to gain general acceptance. According to this view, the great gods reveal themselves pre-eminently in the constellations assigned to them. Incidentally, we are still influenced by this revolution today when we identify the planets (like the days of the week) with the deities as whose manifestations they were discovered and in connection with whom they were celebrated at that time. In Mesopotamia, observation of the stars over a period of centuries had led to the discovery of mathematical regularities in the astral heaven. From time immemorial, the relation of the constellations to the gods of mythology had been a matter of course in this part of the world. So it necessarily

followed that the interplay of the gods who rule the world was subject
to eternal laws, which the wise and those versed in the stars could
discern.

This had eminently practical results. The inductive and instru-
mental manticism predominant in Mesopotamia (cf. Vol. I, section
2.1) found a demonstrable basis in these theories. For the influence of
the stars on the earth and the life of human beings was plain. Without
the sun there would neither be any life on earth nor any alternation
between day and night. Yet the sun's effect varies in the cycle of the
year, evidently according to its position in the zodiac. So the signs of
the zodiac, together with the sun, clearly affect earthly destiny. Aries,
and Taurus, Libra, Aquarius and the rest, are archetypal images and
the primal stages of all corresponding phenomena on earth. Their
course is calculable; so how much more calculable is the pattern
of their correspondences in earthly life! And surely what can be
established about a particular heavenly body must apply to all of
them? In this way there came into being 'the edifice of a *cosmic* religion,
based upon science, which brought human activity and human
relations with the astral divinities into the general harmony of
organized nature'.[14] Monotheistic tendencies can be combined with
this approach. If the gods invariably follow laws which can be
formulated in mathematical terms, is it not probable that these laws
spring from a democratic declaration of will on the part of the assembly
of the gods themselves? (This was perhaps the Babylonian solution.)
Or is the more obvious answer not a 'heavenly master' who creates
the laws and guides the course of the stars (the solution probably
chosen by the Syrians and Assyrians, as well as in Jerusalem)?

Enlightened Europeans tend to turn up their noses at astrology
nowadays (even though millions of people are still its devotees, as the
horoscope pages in the magazines show). But present-day astrology
is only a degenerate offspring of an imposingly designed world picture
which fascinated not only the Israel of Jeremiah but also, two centuries
later, the greatest Greek philosophers, Plato included. This astral
world picture was the product of an impressive Enlightenment, based
on the results of the first scientific research in human history, and not
on figments of the imagination. For the ancient world, the results of
astrology seemed as evident as the laws of the classic natural sciences
do to us today. The public of the time was presented with the possibility
of a scientific 'futurology' which certainly had a religious basis but
which could easily be detached from the special features of the
Assyrian-Babylonian cult and could be linked with almost any other
religion. The supporting proof was not only the assent of the mind;
there was also the evidence of success and power. As countless letters

from the court astrologers show, in all their campaigns and acts of state the great Assyrian conquerors clung with unparalleled scrupulosity to the predictions of those who were versed in the stars – and they were victorious! Why should Judah forgo the integration of so successful a divine power into her own religious system? Why not incorporate the heavenly Baal, with his host, in their own native Yahweh? Historically it is more or less certain that the Assyrian kings by no means forced their vassals to take over their own cultic forms. So what happened in Jerusalem was voluntary, and was emphatically furthered under Manasseh (II Kings 21); it was Manasseh whom Jeremiah accordingly viewed as the originator of the evil.

Afterwards, Josiah's reforms once more abolished the objects associated with the foreign cult, and its viewpoint (cf. Section 1.5 above). But Jeremiah's polemic during the later Jehoiakim period presupposes that the same evil practices were spreading once again. According to what we read, soon after the period of Jeremiah's speech in the temple Jehoiakim abrogated the Deuteronomic law, openly or tacitly, and turned back to the religious policy of his grandfather.

But why did so enlightened an astral religion require the sacrifice of children? Here I can do no more than hazard a guess. The burning of children, or making the victims pass over 'in the fire' is stressed (II Kings 21.6; 23.10; Ezek. 20.31). Now fire – pure fire – seems to be the element of the heavenly bodies. They sparkle like translucent bowls whose contents are alight. Did this lead to the supposition that through fire a special bond could be forged with what was heavenly? And were the sons and daughters in the Hinnom valley therefore perhaps sent as messengers from those making the sacrifice to 'the heavenly master'? We are at least bound to presume that there was some convincing theory behind those horrible burnings. Why otherwise should a king sacrifice his firstborn? (For then as now, science and inhumanity were not mutually exclusive.)

2.7.3 The antithesis: the laws of nature promulgated by Yahweh. Jeremiah is not rising up against the cultic practices of some primitive civilization. He is protesting against the intellectual world of his age – the international 'march of mind'. Of course the burnings of children play a decisive role. Because action and destiny are connected, these burnings lead inexorably to the consequence that the whole of Jerusalem must burn. But there are other reflections as well. Anyone who absorbs astral references and connections into his cult is abandoning Yahweh, and disavowing and dissociating himself from Israel's history of salvation (and disaster), which was impelled and driven onwards by the divine *dābār* and by intuitive manticism (cf. Jer. 2.6ff.).

Yahweh is much too dynamic a God, far too personal a power, to be
shut away in the glass case of any astral mechanism. Moreover an
unalterable motion of the stars, controlled by the master of heaven,
has something terrifying about it, and is bound to inspire people with
fear. There is no reason for this:

> Learn not [the] way (*derek*) of the nations,
>   do not tremble before signs of the heavens!
> [. . .] The nations tremble at them,
>   [. . .] the laws of the nations are naught (*hebel*)!
> Be not afraid of them,
>   for they do no evil,
>   and just as little do they do good (10.2f., 5b).

Does the prophet guess something of the fatal results of a mechanistic
world picture, where the individual becomes a cog in the maching,
and the idea of human liberty mere madness? Jeremiah was probably
the first who rose up against a deterministic concept of nature in the
name of the biblical God, thereby entering upon a battle whose effects
were felt down to the dispute between religion and science in the
nineteenth century, and which is still not finished and done with, even
today.

In order to martial arguments against his influential opponents,
Jeremiah seems compelled – more than Hosea earlier – to put forward
his own interpretation of the cohesions of nature, and to fit this into
what he says about God. In doing so he probably draws on the
traditional wisdom of his people. Of course he cannot deny that the
heavenly bodies influence earthly events. But when he is considering
the interrelation of the cosmic powers he has recourse to the conception
of law – this being the very first time in the Bible that we come across
this concept. Earlier, the sea, which was felt to be so uncanny (Prov.
8.29), had given people the notion of a law-like determination which
was etched into particular things (*ḥōq*) and was never infringed. But
the determination was restricted to that specific case. Picking up this
idea, Jeremiah, talking about the sea, even speaks of an *eternal*
determination of law; and then goes on:

> He gives showers of rain, and spring rains
>   and autumn rains each in their season.
> The weeks of the laws (*ḥuqqōt*) of harvest
>   he will keep for us.
> But the weight of your guilt ('*āwōn*) weighs these down,
>   your sins have kept the good from you (5.22–25).

Here the rhythm of the rainy seasons and the harvest is seen as a law which corresponds to the bounds limiting the ocean. These natural laws are necessary – helpful both to human beings and to the earth. But Jeremiah's monanthropology does not (as yet) presuppose that such laws have unrestricted validity. Where a collective guilt-disaster correlation has been created by men and women, laws can only act to a limited degree: the periods of the rains and the harvest will be diminished (cf. 3.2f.; 14.1–7). But in another passage God presents himself as the one who has graven the determinations of law (*ḥōqēq*) into the sun, the moon and the stars, as he has into the sea, in order to guarantee the rhythmical cycle of the times and seasons; these laws of nature and others like them find their parallel in divine behaviour towards the total framework of Israel's history, which is, correspondingly, also in accordance with law. In the case of the movement of the heavenly bodies, the infrangibility is stressed so much (31.35–37; 33.25f.) that human behaviour can evidently have no influence on it. In saying this, however, Jeremiah is initiating a development which concedes inherent laws to the realm of nature. The prophetic monanthropology which had been expounded without any reservation before Jeremiah's time declared that, apart from the one God, man was the sole autonomous cause of things in the sphere of reality as a whole. This was narrowed down, and applied only within the lower sphere of the cosmos. Nevertheless, the upper regions were not thought to be ruled by independent powers, to whom worship might perhaps be due; they were governed by enntities that were subject to the law of Yahweh even more strictly than men and women on earth. Natural laws and the rhythms of time are closely connected with one another. It is probably part of his defence against astral speculations about time, that for Jeremiah the time which God foresees and observes plays a greater part than it does among other prophets. Jeremiah looks ahead to the *year* of the visitation of evil-doers (three times), to the *time* of their wickedness, which will then b consummated in the corresponding destiny (four times), or to the *time* of their visitation (eight times). Whereas ancient Israel had hitherto assigned to an arbitrary divine power of discretion the final implementation and ending of an action-destiny correlation, this assumption now seems to have been abandoned. Even though Yahweh is not incorporated in the motion of the stars and is more strictly separated from their course than any heavenly Baal, yet it is he above all who observes the bounds and measures of time.

Perhaps it is tendencies like this which explain why the old traditional name for God, *Yahweh Ṣᵉbāʾōt*, is suddenly taken up again and again. Wherever the prophet rebukes the people for their worship of the host *(ṣābāʾ)* of heaven, he at the same time stresses that Yahweh himself represents the heavenly hosts ($s^eba'\bar{o}t$) (8.2f.; 19.11–13). Is this name for God therefore intended to stress the dependence of the starry powers on this dynamic divine centre?

2.7.4 The degeneration of reason. In Jeremiah, therefore, we do not only find a self-contained view of history; a corresponding view of nature emerges at the same time. That explains why he insists on the reasonable nature of his proclamation. There is nothing irrational about Jeremiah's God. Anyone who rejects Jeremiah's words is not unbelieving; he is unreasonable. He does not understand how to use his eyes and ears in a proper and useful way (5.21). Jeremiah's fellow-countrymen do not hear the voice of Yahweh, even though it opens up a positive future for them. Instead they follow unrealistic fantasies which have taken root in their minds as 'hardness of heart' ($s^er\bar{i}r\bar{u}t\ l\bar{e}b$, eight times). Jeremiah picks up ideas about an incurable spiritual blindness which we already found in Isaiah (Isa. 6.8f.), although for Jeremiah the blindness is not caused by God himself. If people let their reason degenerate, that is their own affair. Their $l\bar{e}b$ (i.e., their heart, but as the source of reason) is incurably sick. It is incapable of producing good auras of action any longer. Sin has been etched with an iron pen into the very centre from which their actions spring (17.1):

> Can a negro change his skin,
>   or a panther its spots?
> So you cannot (any more) do good,
>   since you have taught (yourselves) to do evil (13.23).

The people are living in an illusory world. They are trusting to a delusion and are listening to prophets who proclaim this delusion, and who swear and act in *šeqer*. It is nothing but self-deception to say 'Yahweh' and to mean a God who is bound inexorably into the astral system. So who is going to prevent the collapse of the nation?

2.8 Zedekiah and the Egyptian period

2.8.1 Opposition to the optimistic nabis. While Jeremiah was still underground, the history of his country developed dramatically. After Nebuchadnezzar had been defeated in Egypt in 600, the arrogant Jejoiakim of Judah risked rebellion. Babylonian troops moved up to crush it. Jehoiakim himself died, and his inexperienced son Jehoiachin failed to defend the city. On 6 March 597 Jerusalem fell; and some thousands of the upper classes, priests, craftsmen and soldiers were deported to Babylon, together with the king. In Jehoiachin's place Nebuchadnezzar installed Zedekiah as vassal; but Zedekiah was merely tolerated by a large section of the population; he was not approved of. For the exiles, and for many people in Jerusalem, Hehoiachin was still Israel's only chosen representative.

But Jeremiah, who had emerged from hiding, supported Zedekiah as the divinely willed king. He saw Jehoiachin as Yahweh's signet ring, which God had slipped off his finger and thrown away for ever (22.24ff.). For devout Judaeans, the conquest of the holy city was a religious shock without parallel. For over 400 years Jerusalem had stood out against every foreign power, and in so doing had provided history with the irrefutable proof of Yahweh's promise that the dynasty of David would endure for ever, and that Zion was God's earthly dwelling, which he would protect unconditionally (Ps. 46). And now this same Yahweh had surrendered his city! for Jeremiah, on the other hand, the fall of Jerusalem could well have been a reason for triumph. Had not the invasion from the north, herealded for so many years, now really taken place at last? The people had been deported, just as he had proclaimed (10.18; 13.19; 15.2; 16.13; 20.5f.). All the same, the city had not been burnt down, as he had predicted, and it had been conquered without much bloodshed. Moreover the temple remained standing, and its ceremonies continued, even though it had been robbed of some precious vessels indispensable for the cult. (Jeremiah soon felt forced to ask whether the real onslaught of the enemy from the north *had* already taken place, or whether it was not still to come.) Priests and prophets belonging to the temple admitted that the pitiable military defeat could only be explained as the result of a false religious outlook which Yahweh evidently abhorred. The fashionable combination between the service of Yahweh and rites offered to the heavenly Baal was now, in all probability, abandoned, and Deuteronomy was once again given pride of place. Only this can explain why from this time on Jeremiah ceased to attack idolatry, the service of Baal and the burning of children. After Zedekiah's accession, these things no longer existed in Jerusalem.

But after a brief period of depression, the renewed reform which, in my own view, took place under Zedekiah, once again evoked exuberant optimism; for according to Deuteronomy, foreign rule could present no problem for people who were obedient to the *tōrā*; and Israel's ideal constitution would come about all by itself. So although the nabis now prophesied 'in' the Deuteronomic Yahweh, and no longer 'in Baal', they could not do enough to proclaim the impending turn to the nation's destiny and a new *šālōm*. The victory of the Babylonians was merely to be seen as a temporary punishment.

Jeremiah, borne out though he is by the fundamental force of history, sees himself confronted by a new overwhelming opposition.

This time his opponents are prophets whom he cannot reproach with
being inspired by false gods. Like him, they appeal to Yahweh; and
with their assertion that God will never cast off his people, they are
much more in harmony with religious tradition than the intransigent
Jeremiah. Because of this, Jeremiah even occasionally loses confidence
in himself, as we can see from his Confessions.

At the very beginning of Zedekiah's reign, Jeremiah feels compelled
to perform a demonstrative symbolic act. When diplomats from the
neighbouring countries appear at the Jerusalem court, in order to talk
over the changed situation, Jeremiah meets them with an ox's yoke
on his shoulders. This was intended as a visible sign of the finality
with which God had installed Nebuchadnezzar as emperor over the
whole earth (ch. 27). All hope for individual national independence
is going to prove illusory. Whenever the prophet appears in public
during the next four years he binds the yoke on himself. And the
society of his time – which permitted itself a unique critical authority
in the shape of prophets of this kind – lets him have his way, without
interference. Until one day, in the temple, the chief priest Hananiah
comes to meet him, tears the yoke off his shoulders and breaks it, after
he has proclaimed:

> Thus says Yahweh Sabaoth, the God of Israel . . .
> The [. . .] vessels of Yahweh's house
>   which Nebuchadnezzar took away . . .
> And Jehoiachin . . . king of Judah
>   and all those deported from Judah . . .
> within two years
>   I will bring them back, (28.2–4).

Jeremiah is taken aback. Up to now he has respected Hananiah as an
equal; moreover he is full of ardent sympathy for the fate of his nation.
So he merely replies:

> Amen! May Yahweh do so;
>   may Yahweh make your [word] come true!

And he goes away. It is only some time later that Yahweh inspires
him with the conviction that Hananiah was wrong. So he turns back
and proclaims to his associate:

> A   Listen, Hananiah,
>   Yahweh has not *sent* you!
>   But you have let this people trust
>   in a lie.

B Thus says Yahweh:
   Behold I will send you from the earth,
      this very year you shall die.

The narrator remarks laconically that Hananiah died in the seventh
month. (Was this psychological warfare, or was it some parapsychological power on Jeremiah's part?) The strugle between Yahweh prophet
and Yahweh prophet is a matter of life or death. Jeremiah is also
attacked by the nabis who have been deported to Babylon. He had
heard that rallying cries about an imminent return were being
circulated there in Yahweh's name; and he had therefore written a
letter to the exiles, in which he warned them against premature hopes
for a return, and called upon them to build houses, plant gardens,
beget children and behave loyally to the victorious power (29.1ff.):

Seek the welfare (*šālōm*) of the city,
   pray to Yahweh on its behalf!
For out of its welfare (*šālōm*) shall arise
   your welfare . . .
(Only) after a fulfilment for Babylon
   of seventy years
   will I visit you and raise up over you my word [. . .]
   bring up back
   to this place.

The letter ends:

For I know the thoughts
   that I think abouut you,
Thoughts of salvation . . .
   to give you a future and a hope.

In spite of this conclusion, the letter evokes furious protest from the
rejected nabis. One of them writes to the high priest in Jerusalem,
reminding him that he has police power over every insane nabi, and
demanding that he should shut Jeremiah's mouth. But the era of a
priest like Pashur is past (see 2.5.2 above). The priest gives Jeremiah
the letter, and Jeremiah counters: because the letter-writer allows the
prisoners to put their trust in *šeqer*, no descendants will be left to him
'who will see the good that I will do to my people' (29.24–32).

Jeremiah cannot reproach the nabis of the Zedekiah period with
being unfaithful to Yahweh, like their predecessors; and yet he has to
reproach them with seducing the people to a lie. This dispute becomes
the theme of an imprecatory writing, which is perhaps the last writing
we have from the hand of the prophet himself (23.9–14). The group

Jeremiah attacks is usually unjustifiably described as 'false prophets'
by scholars, or even 'prophets of salvation', although a prophet
certainly never existed who felt able to proclaim nothing but salvation
(and if he had done so, he would have lost his hearers' excited attention
to the oracle). These nabis rather proclaim salvation, *šālōm*, for this
particular hour in history. They appeal to the ancient divine promises
given in the cult, assuring Israel that God would never give up his
people; and from this they deduce an imminent saving turn of events.

The conflict that broke out over this went deeper than any other
dispute into which Jeremiah had been drawn earlier; for what was at
stake was two opposing positions, each of which claimed God's direct
inspiration, while denying genuineness to the other. But Jeremiah's
God asserts:

> I did not send the prophets,
>   yet they ran;
> I did not speak to them,
>   yet they prophesied (23.21).

What chance does a non-prophetic listener have of judging, when
intuitive mantic confronts intuitive mantic in this way, and when both
parties claim the subsequent insight of their listeners? In this case
Jeremiah does not venture to offer a historical proof. What occurs to
him is a moral one. He maintains that an over-hasty proclamation of
salvation to the Judaeans will hinder their repentance, which is
essential (23.14, 22). But ever since the beginning of Zedekiah's reign,
Jeremiah too has talked repeatedly about a future turn for the better,
and has in this context called his hearers to repentance – even if he
sees the matter in the long term, and not as immediately imminent.
Consequently this argument has only limited cogency. So he makes
his main criterion the special nature of his inspiration. The others are
reporting hallucinations, figments of their own brains (vv. 16, 26);
they are appealing to dreams. But a prophet should mistrust dreams.
Forced by the requirements of the moment, Jeremiah begins to cast
doubt upon what had always been considered in Israel, ever since the
time of the patriarchs, as a legitimate way of experiencing a divine
message. (It was also a mode of communication which was still to be
claimed by prophets later on as well.)

> The prophet who has his dream,
>   let him tell his dream!
> But let him who has my word
>   speak my word truthfully.
> What has straw in common with the corn? murmur of Yahweh's.

Is not my word like fire . . . like a hammer which breaks the rock in pieces? (23.28f.)

It is not the person who falls into an ecstasy and begins to prophesy who receives Yahweh's genuine *dābār*. It is the person who is able to discern Yahweh's word attentively, the word which he speaks in his heavenly council (v. 18) and which therefore enjoys the certainty of a supernatural origin.

It is not completely clear what different types of secret experience stand behind this distinction. Apparently Jeremiah receives his *dābār* in a non-ecstatic, meditative way, even though it is embedded in a highly mythological framework of ideas. What he says is founded on a conviction about the all-embracing vastness of the deity:

Am I (only?) a God at hand . . .
   and not (also?) a God afar off? . . .
Is it not the universe that I fill? (23.23f.).

Whereas the optimistic nabis insist on the nearness of God, the prophet boasts that the God he has experienced is a far-off God; and he sees this experience as the objective one. But ultimately it is the assurance of the conscience subjected and committed to Yahweh's moral will which impels Jeremiah; this tells him that, in view of the severity of past misdeeds, the defeat of 597 (in which the people came off relatively lightly) cannot be the last word where Judah's downfall is concerned.

2.8.2 The call to desertion. In 590 the hesitant Zedekiah allowed himself to be persuaded by the Egyptian Pharaoh Hophrah and the war party at his own court to rise against Nebuchadnezzar. Jeremiah continued to adhere to his opinion that the wickedness of the past generation of Baal worshippers had still not found its end in the appropriate fate. These people made burnt sacrifices to the false god, so they themselves must burn. Resistance was not merely unreasonable; struggle for an independent Israel was now, paradoxically, a revolt against the God who directs history.

When the siege closes in on Jerusalem, the prophet is put in a dungeon and condemned to slow suffocation in a pit of mud. He is saved at the last minute by a negro. From this time on he is kept in the courtyard belonging to the palace guard. There the vacillating Zedekiah several times comes to him for advice, though each time he rejects what Jeremiah says. It is of course no wonder that the prominent men of Jerusalem should have looked on Jeremiah as a traitor to his country, since he cried mockingly to the defenders that, even if only cripples were left in the Babylonian army, they would be

quite enough to put the Judaean army to flight and to burn Jerusalem
(37.10). Because of Judah's guilt-laden history, God has put himself
on the side of the enemy and will turn the weapons of the defenders
against themselves (21.1–4). Whenever possible, Jeremiah tries to
weaken the army's power of resistance:

> Thus says Yahweh:
> Behold I set before you the way to life
>   and the way to death.
> He who stays in this city shall die
>   by the sword and by famine and by pestilence.
> But he who goes over to the Chaldaeans . . .
>   shall bring away his life as booty (21.8f.; 38.2).

Even when the king asks the prophet to make intercession for the
nation which is fighting for survival, Jeremiah refuses categorically.
The downfall of the last Israelite state has been resolved on by God,
once and for all. But there is alleviation and exemption for the
individual – for the negro, Ebed-melech (39.15–17), for Baruch
(ch. 45), and for the deserters. Anyone who is discerning and acts
accordingly will carry off his life as booty. More cannot be expected
in this hour of history. But the offer applies even to the king, provided
that he capitulates unconditionally:

> If you (king) yourself will really go outside
>   to the generals of the Babylonian king,
> then your life shall be spared,
>   and this city shall not be burned with fire (38.17).

But the king is not prepared to humiliate himself so far. And he has
never lacked defenders for his behaviour. Even the great sociologist
Max Weber characterized Jeremiah's call as 'an unworthy exhortation
to capitulation'.

In the end what Jeremiah has repeatedly proclaimed actually comes
about. The besiegers succeed in storming the city. The king is
overtaken by a dreadful fate. His sons are put to death before his eyes.
Then he himself is blinded and carried off to Babylon. The prophet,
with a whole crowd of prisoners of war, is made ready to march away.
Then he is removed from the group and liberated by an officer sent
specially for the purpose on orders from the very highest level. As a
member of the defeated enemy, he is given the chance of emigrating
to Babylon as a pensioner of the state, or of remaining in his devasted
homeland: 'See, the whole land is before you.'

The reader of the Bible may be put off by such a generous concession
to the Israelite prophet by the victorious heathen power. It is

understandable that seventy years ago the orientalist Hugo Winkler became suspicious and suggested that Jeremiah and those like him were paid agents of the Babylonians, a kind of fifth column. But the whole-heartedness with which Jeremiah risked his life for years for what he proclaimed puts him beyond any such suspicion. None the less, his political effectiveness must have been so considerable that it even became known to the Babylonian enemy.

The behaviour of Jeremiah's God would seem to be even more dubious than the behaviour of the prophet himself. What kind of Power is this, who expects preaching of this kind from his prophet and imposes it on his people? The French Jew André Neher has put forward a fascinating picture of Jeremiah. Its focal point is the accusation that here an arbitrary God is speaking, and a sinister God at that:

> Does God want man . . . to humilate himself, to dishonour himself, to sully himself, to take upon himself the triple crown of folly, cowardice and treason? Does life deserve to be won back at the cost of sacrificing one's country and elemental human dignity? The men of Jerusalem are no fools. They detect in this demand, a hundred times repeated, merely an ironic and cynical method through which God aims for the very last time to make people realize that in truth man has no area of free decision at his disposal, and that all that remains to him is to put his neck under the fateful yoke.[15]

But does Jeremiah really find God's way of acting so irrational? Does it really seem to him to be aimed at reducing reason *ad absurdum*? Does Jeremiah really accept that there is no area of free decision? Anyone who reads his book notices that he does indeed cease to admit this liberty of decision where his own lost generation is concerned – or if he does recognize it at all, then only to a very limited degree. But this is by no means true as a general proposition. Jeremiah is so inexorable in his political directives because he is convinced that a fateful aura of action, once 'produced', has metahistorical validity from one generation to the next.

2.8.3 The Israelite God and his Babylonian power. Jeremiah's admiration for Nebuchadnezzar grew in the degree to which the Babylonians intervened, disturbingly and destructively, in Palestine. The all-destroying enemy from the north was at first anonymous; but after Carchemish (605) he became personalized in the meteoric figure of the Chaldeans. From the time of Zedekiah, however, as the downfall of his own Palestinian state begins to cast its shadow ahead, Yahweh formally calls the great king, through Jeremiah's lips, his *'ebed*, which

can be translated as servant, but in this context means the general
administrator of the divine rule over the world. Yahweh's (political)
'ebed had previously been a title applied exclusively to David and his
dynasty. Jeremiah gives the phrase a universal connotation in a way
that was unheard of for Israelite ears. It is true that Amos and Isaiah
had viewed the Assyrian kings as tools of a destruction instigated by
Yahweh; but they did not see the foreign power as a positive ordering
force. Yet this is what Jeremiah stresses the Babylonian to be, even
though Nebuchadnezzar does not know Yahweh and manifestly
worships other gods. But in spite of the astral cult which was pursued
in Babylon almost as faithfully as in Assyria (though without the
burning of children), Jeremiah does not consider the Babylonian Bel
to be a Baal, and therefore dangerous. On the contrary. At Yahweh's
instigation the vessels from the Jerusalem temple have been tran-
sported to the temple of Babylonian gods; and with them part of the
divine glory has passed over into Mesopotamia.

In this context, and for the first time in prophecy, the metahistorical
reflections extend as far as *creation itself*:

> Thus says Yahweh Sabaoth, the God of Israel . . . :
> A Behold I have made the earth
> and the men and the animals . . .
> have *given* them (since time immemorial) to him
> who is righteous in my eyes.
> B And now: I *give* all these lands
> into the hand of Nebuchadnezzar [. . .], my servant.
> Even the beasts of the field
> I *give* to him, that they may serve him (27.4–6).

The underlying presupposition here is that there is only one legitimate
monarchy on earth, and that it is established by Yahweh. For centuries
the Jerusalem kings had claimed this position (Ps. 2), in defiance of
all reality. But the conflict with their own monarchy made the prophets
arrive at the conclusion that the Davidic dynasty had run its course.
Jeremiah now links the actual, present balance of power with
Yahweh's metahistorical objective (though he had previously denied
the connection, where Assyria was concerned, 2.18). This time a
world-wide empire – up to now never more than a plan and an
intention – is going to be implemented in actual fact. Every kingdom
that rebels against Nebuchadnezzar will be visited by Yahweh through
three active, mythical powers: sword, famine and pestilence. Yahweh's
kingdom will extend as far as distant Elam, and will bring down evil
on evil men through the agency of the Babylonian troops (49.34–39).
But anyone who places himself under Nebuchadnezzar's yoke will

thereby gain the freedom (*m⁽nūḥā*) which will secure his survival (27.11; cf. the giving of the land to the poor, 39.10).

The significance of Jeremiah's utterances for world history can hardly be put too high. What he says replaces what had previously been held to be a matter of course: that Yahweh was closest to his chosen people, not merely religiously, but of course politically too. This 'Israelite dogma of election . . . had now been corrected by Yahweh through his guidance of history'.[16] From this time on, faithfulness to Yahweh was one thing, political rule another – though this did not mean a surrender of the metahistorical categories of moral causality. In Deuteronomy we saw how the requirements of *ṣ⁽dāqā* came to be relativized, where these were applied to natural and original forms of community (cf. 1.4 above). Here we can observe the same thing in another guise. The distinction between 'church' and state begins to make itself felt for the first time (cf. also the section on Ezekiel, 4.5.2 below).

But what made Jeremiah hit on Babylon, of all places? The only definite thing we are actually told is that dominion is part of creation, and that rule over the earth ought to be undivided, and hence monarchical. But Israel had an ancient tradition according to which the beginning of monarchy on earth began in Babel, in the cities of Erech, Accad and Calneh (Gen. 10.10 AV). Is Jeremiah going back to this? Is there to be a reversion to those primaeval conditions? This would fit in with Jeremiah's view of history, according to which the salvation history that was to begin once more after the catastrophe was to run parallel to the first salvation history of former times (Gen. 11.27ff.), and would therefore have its genesis in Mesopotamia.

Impressed though Jeremiah was by the achievements of the Babylonian power, he announced its limitation in the same breath. After seventy years (probably an unlucky number for the Babylonians, for some reason connected with their astrology) Babylon is going to sink into oblivion through Yahweh's visitation, and none of its inhabitants will remain (27.21f.; 51.59ff.). For rule inevitably leads to injustice and wickedness; the wider the dominion, the more self-destructive it becomes. It is only after seventy years that Israel can reckon with a turn for the better, with a new covenant and a ruler from the dynasty of David.

2.8.4 The new covenant. The darker the clouds on the political horizon, the more major the key of Jeremiah's poems on behalf of his people. For the first time his predictions go beyond the immediate future, and think in terms, not of years, but of decades. After the Babylonian era there is to be a new beginning for Judah-Israel. During the Babylonian siege of the city, Jeremiah purchases a piece of land in order to demonstrate symbolically that one day the fields will again be planted and that the settlements that have been destroyed will be built up once more (ch. 32). He proclaims a saviour king from the house of David who will reunite the two parts of the nation, will himself practise faithfulness to the community as *ṣᵉdāqā*, and will mediate this faithfulness to the people (23.5f; 33.15f.). History is a twice broken line, divided into three stages: *(a)* salvation history; *(b)* the history of disaster, down to Israel's downfall; and *(c)* the new eschatological history of salvation. This picture is at the back of Jeremiah's thinking, as it was for the prophets of the Assyrian period (cf. Vol. I, section 7.6.3). Certainly all the exaltation is missing. There is no wondrous victory over the Babylonians, let alone any subsequent peace in the animal world, such as we find in Isaiah. 'This picture of the future is almost disappointingly sober.'[17]

Only in one respect is it possible to perceive that what has existed up to now is to be surpassed in the future, and that to this extent Jeremiah's prophecy does contain an eschatological element. This one element is what he says about the new covenant. We find this in three places in the Book of Jeremiah: 31.31–34; 32.36–41; 50.4–7. The promise of a new divinely conferred covenant was to play a fundamental part centuries later in the development of the Christian church, which set itself up as the community of the New Covenant, cutting itself off from Israel, the people of the Old. When today the Christian section of the Bible is given the name New Testament, this term (by way of the Latin translation) is a reminiscence of, and reference to, passages in Jeremiah.

By virtue of its genre and language, the second passage has the best claim to Jeremiah's authorship (although generally 31.31–34 is given the preference, without any particular discussion – perhaps because it is more reminiscent of the New Testament?).

> Thus says Yahweh, the God of Israel, to this city, of which [you say]:
> A 'It is given into the hand of the Babylonian king,
>   to the sword, to famine and to pestilence.'
> B Behold, I will gather them out of the [land],
>   I have driven them there . . .
>   I will let them return (*šūb*) to this (cultic?) place,
>   I will let them dwell in safety.
>   They shall be my people,
>   I will be to them their divinity (*ᵉlōhīm*).
>   I will give them a single understanding (*lēb*)

and a single way (*derek*) . . .
I will make for them a covenant for incalculable time,
  [. . .] I will not (any longer) turn away (*šūb*) from them . . .
I will put my fear (*yir'ā*) in their understanding (*lēb*),
  no longer to depart from me!
I shall rejoice to do them good,
  and I will plant them in this land . . . (32.36–41).

The prophecy offers precisely what might be expected, if it is seen as a prolongation or development of Jeremiah's prophecy of disaster (always supposing that it is not pressed into the Procrustean bed of an alleged prophecy of judgment). There will be repentance, the people who have been deported will return and, from that time on, will dwell in the promised land once more. The fact that, in the future, history is going to take a more favourable course, and will never again bend away from salvation to disaster, presupposes a change in what hitherto had been considered anthropological constants enjoying general validity. Through a mighty encounter with the God who, in his hiddenness, contains within himself all reality, the Israelites are to be welded together into a nation and inspired by a common will, which will be translated into corresponding deeds. These deeds will then in their turn lead to a common, healthful destiny (*derek*). The 'covenant formula' (cf. also 30.22; 31.1), 'They shall be my people, and I will be their divinity', presupposes a change in Yahweh himself as well. Up to now he has apparently not yet been this divinity. What does this mean? Significantly enough, we never read: 'Then I shall be their Yahweh.' The designation *ᵉlōhīm* can surely only mean a divine power that fills 'the body politic' – the nation as a whole (perhaps analogously to Immanu-El, Isa. 7.14?), which raises this people above the normal human level and confers on it the quality of holiness. It is only in, with and among the people that Yahweh 'realizes' – or 'materializes' – as it were his *ᵉlōhīm* aspect. So in the great eschatological turning point God and his people will both find their self-realization.

It is possible for God to enter into a permanent alliance with a people that comes before him as a unity in this way. 'To conclude' a covenant (*bᵉrīt*) means literally 'to cut it'; what was probably meant was a rite in which the two partners passed between the divided parts of dead animals, with the self-imposed, conditional curse of being cut apart themselves if they broke the covenant they had made (34.8ff.; Gen. 15.7ff.). This resulted in what was more than a contract; what came into being was a form of community which, in its binding character, was the equivalent of the blood relationships which were so important for semitic peoples. But there was no equality in this covenant. It was conferred by the stronger partner. He established it or gave it (*hēqīm, nātan*), and as 'master of the covenant' (*ba'al*) he remained the dominant partner from that time on as well.

We find alliances of this kind quite frequently in the ancient East, between individuals. But they were also concluded, and were of special importance, in the context of the 'constitutional' relations between the major kings and their royal vassals. Up to now it is only in the case of Israel that we have certain evidence for the use of the term to express a relationship between a deity and the group of his worshippers – although the usage was probably taken over from a Canaanite El cult in Shechem (Judges 8.33; 9.4, 46). In Israel the word came in the course of time to develop into the essential key to the relationship (based on mutual agreement) between the one nation and the God Yahweh, who was certainly efficacious far beyond the borders of this single nation but outside Israel was always anonymous. Israel's bond with this God was not forged by a mythical series of ancestors; on the contrary, the tie came into being on a single occasion, in a particular historical context; and as such it was the pride of the nation, which knew itself to be elevated above all the polytheistic neighbouring religions by virtue of its worship of the One God.

The idea of the covenant probably developed in Northern Israel (cf. Vol. I, section 5.4). It seems to have penetrated into Judah only in the seventh century. Up to then there had been frequent talk there only about a *bᵉrīt* between God and the house of David. When an Israelite used the word *bᵉrīt*, he was not merely maintaining a historical theory, or propounding an aetiology to explain the special character of Israel's relationship to God. For the first conferring of the covenant, in salvation history, had to be renewed on extraordinary occasions, in the framework of the cult – as when Deuteronomy was introduced by Josiah (II Kings 23; or perhaps at regular seven-year intervals?). Hosea had presumed that, where his fellow-countrymen in North Israel were concerned, the covenant between Yahweh and Israel had to all intents and purposes lapsed; but he believed that it would be renewed in an improved form in the era of salvation (Hos. 2.18–23). Jeremiah picks up these sayings of Hosea, and therefore talks about the renewal of the gift of the land conferred on Israel, but also about an anthropological re-structuring – a renewal of man himself. The fear of God will then become man's second nature, and this will mean that a deviation from the way, from *derek*, as the straightforward, purposeful line for living, need no longer be anticipated.

The Little Book of Consolation for Ephraim, which probably dates from Jeremiah's early period, also now closes with a promise of a covenant (31.31–34). In the form in which we now have it, it is part of a prose C fragment. But we cannot exclude the possibility that an earlier poetical version did in fact appear on the scroll, which was composed for North Israel. Reminiscences of Hosea are stronger here, and this would fit in with the early Jeremiah period. The devastating judgment is pronounced that Israel has broken (*hēpēr*) the covenant. Before Jeremiah, there had occasionally been talk about transgressions against the covenant; but no one had dared to talk about its being broken (though see 11.10; 22.9; here Jeremiah sets himself in diametrical contradiction to Deuteronomy, where election to the covenant counts as irrepealable). But the prophet looks further, to a fundamental renewal, beyond the ending of the relationship. Let me try to reconstruct the decisive lines:

> [Behold I] . . . make with the house of Israel
> a new covenant . . .
> And I will put my *tōrāh* within them,
> write it in their understanding (*lēb*).
> I will become to them their God,
> they will become to me my people.
> Not from henceforth will one teach the other . . .:
> know Yahweh!
> For they will all know me,
> from the least to the greatest.

Similar anthropological changes to those described in 32.36ff. are associated with the conclusion of the new covenant. This time the fear of God is replaced by the divine directive, the *tōrā*, which in pre-exilic times was related to the priestly distinction between the holy and the unclean, between behaviour which was to be seen as good or evil in the context of the cult. But even earlier, in Isaiah (1.10), *tōrā* had already begun to apply to the whole sphere of moral behaviour, because all actions that were sacrilegious and contrary to the interests of the human community made people quite simply incapable of community with the holy, whereas the person who practised *ṣᵉdāqā* could be newly endowed with holiness from above.

The background here is the conviction of a threefold form of the divine word (18.18; the third form, Wisdom, need not concern us here). As prophetic *dābār* it both predicted and provoked the future course of history, and was created and established (*'āśā/hēqīm*) by God. As a directive, or *tōrā*, on the other hand, it issued from the mouth of the priest (2.6–8) and was then created and established when it was acted upon by an individual Israelite. In the future era of salvation, this distinction was no longer to apply. The *tōrā* was then to be as stringently cogent as the *dābār*, though it was still to be mediated by human agency. As soon as the Israelites spontaneously do what is right, teaching institutions (which had previously characterized Israel, or had at least been necessary) will no longer be required. For unlike the *dābār*, the *tōrā* does not propound a unique word about the immediate historical moment; it is designed to fit all situations in life. It is meant to be enunciated regularly, repeated, imprinted on the mind. But among the people affected this leads to domination on the one side and subordination on the other; and this brings the divine instruction under suspicion of being a law imposed from outside, a form of compulsion. In the eschatological future, God and man will come close to one another in spirit and discernment – so close that the divine will that creates community and fellowship will be freely accepted by the mind of every individual and will be followed understandingly. This will be the beginning of conditions which will rule out any future repetition of the frightful catastrophes of Israelite history.

This change in the *lēb* means the transformation of the most important part of a human being – the point where an act originates and where the foundation for the correlation between action and destiny is laid. Jeremiah saw the depravation of the understanding (*lēb*) through one's own fault as the real root of evil (cf. 2.7.4 above); but he never makes Yahweh responsible for it. Now he proclaims that in the future the *lēb* will be regenerated – and for this he does make Yahweh responsible.

In accordance with Jeremiah's sober view of man and the world, we have to assume that when he talks about the new covenant he really does visualize a splendid feast on Zion (31.23ff.; 50.4–6); and that in proclaiming the enduring 'internalization' of the Torah in the spirit, he was thinking of an actual priestly recital, which would remain ineffaceable because of the eschatological hour in which it was proclaimed. But although the prophet's predictions of disaster had, to an astonishing degree, been fulfilled to the letter, no date for the fulfilment of his hope for salvation could be put forward in the context of Israel's history. Even in Isaiah, the messianic hopes were already characterized by a mistiness and ambiguity very different from the statements about military entanglements. In Jeremiah and the later prophets, this difference between very much more realistic predictions of disaster and apparently vague prophecies of salvation continues – even though the prophecies of salvation are meant to have a much more fundamental significance.

The Christian church appeals to Jeremiah to support its assertion that Israel was once the people of God, but that – according to the word of its own prophet – its covenant was broken; and that the new covenant announced here was concluded through Jesus Christ. This assertion is a general one, in spite of a few modern voices. Is its appeal to Jeremiah justified? Or are the Jews right when they insist that the whole of the Old Testament, to the very end, presupposes the uncancelled covenant between God and Israel, and that Jeremiah is therefore not to be taken as meaning any so fundamental a breach? Seen historically, both points of view are wrong. Jeremiah really does see the covenant between God and his people as having been broken – even though almost all the later writings of the Old Testament presuppose its continuance. On the other hand, Jeremiah had in mind the restoration of Israel *qua* state. He is not thinking even remotely of a covenant that is to reach out beyond Israel's borders. But the conflict cannot be resolved by an investigation of historical origins; rightly or wrongly, it is connected with a long 'reception' history, lasting from Jeremiah to the beginning of the Christian era, during which the idea was not merely taken up but also modified and interpreted. But it is impossible to enter into that here.

2.8.5 The Gedaliah episode and the deportation to Egypt. After 586 the Babylonians installed a Judaean, Gedaliah, as governor. He took up residence in Mizpah, and Jeremiah supported him as far as he could. But after only a few months Gedaliah was murdered by a group of nationalist guerillas. Panic seized the rest of the population. They were afraid of a Babylonian counter-stroke which would put an end to them altogether. Jeremiah was asked for a word from Yahweh.

This time the prophet is as if transformed in what he says. Don't be afraid! Yahweh is still fully resolved, and Israel's destiny has taken a completely new turn (42.10):

> If you . . . continue to live here,
>   I will build you up.
> I will not pull you down
>   and will not root you up.
> For I am sorry for the evil
>   which I had to bring upon you.

Only the guilty will be punished. Nothing will stand in the way of the country's reconstruction. It is astounding to see how, in this hour of catastrophe for his people, Jeremiah is convinced that the cup has finally become full, and that from now on things are going to improve, whatever dark times may still be ahead. For the first twenty years of his life he had announced that after the downfall of the Assyrians an even more terrible enemy was going to invade the country from the north. In 605 Nebuchadnezzar emerged and conquered the Near East; and for Jeremiah it seemed obvious that this was the enemy from the north. But the Babylonian conquest of Judah was by no means yet the year of visitation which he had announced. After an initial rebellion against the Babylonians, Jerusalem was captured in 597. The ruling classes were deported and the temple plundered. Jeremiah remained firm: even this was not yet the terrible requital which Judah must still expect to come upon it from the north for the evil of an erroneous pseudo-cult. Ten years later, forty years after Jeremiah's first prophecy, Jerusalem really was reduced to dust and ashes, and the kingdom vanished. For Jeremiah this hour meant that the era of disaster had been brought to an end at a stroke. Even if murder and anarchy continued to reign in the country, from now on things were going to take an upward trend. But whereas the people as a whole had been optimistic up to the very last minute, now their terror knew no bounds.

Jeremiah's soothing words after the assassination of Gedaliah had no effect. Although in fact no punitive Babylonian expedition did follow, every Judaean who had the chance now fled into Egypt. Jeremiah was forced to go with them. In Egypt the ancient conflicts flared up once more. Jeremiah's fellow-countrymen remain firm in their 'hardness of understanding' and tell the prophet to his face: 'We will burn incense to [the queen] of heaven. Since we left off burning incense to [the queen] of heaven (since Zedekiah?) we have perished by the sword and by famine.' Jeremiah steadfastly continues to counter this with his metahistory. Nebuchadnezzar, he prophesies, will fall upon Egypt too and

> will delouse the land of Egypt
> as a shepherd delouses his clothes;
> and he shall march back again in well-being.

Anyone who has fled to Egypt from Judah will never again return home (44.14). Down to the last phase of his life the prophet knows that he is part of the collective life of his people; and he does not expect to return home himself either. The Egyptian Pharaoh Hophra (= Apries), on whom the refugees pin their hopes, will be given by no less a one than Yahweh himself 'into the hands of his enemies who seek his life' (44.30). This is the last of Jeremiah's sayings that has come down to us. Probably Nebuchadnezzar really did attack Egypt afterwards, though without permanently occupying the country, and in 569 Apries fell, fighting against Egyptian rebels.

If we remember Jeremiah's predictions of disaster throughout the years, and if we make clear to ourselves how the prophecy which he had clung to for decades had in fact been fulfilled (for the deviations in detail only underline the genuineness of the sayings that have come down to us), then we can judge the achievement of the prophet's metahistory, and can understand the tremendous effect it had on later centuries. Even the seventy years he predicted for Babylonian rule were correct, if we see that rule as lasting from 605 to 538 BC, the year in which the edict of the Persian Cyrus ended prisoner status for the men and women in exile. The prophet has his ear to the pulse of history in an almost inconceivable way. He does not only possess a gift second to none for intuitive presentiment. Passionate though he is, he is never narrow-mindedly provincial. On the contrary, his horizon continually widens out to universal dimensions. He never appears on the stage as the stubborn prophet of judgment which Old Testament scholars occasionally brand him as being. But although he predicted history with an accuracy that hardly anyone else achieves, he reaped no gratitude for it, and to the end of his life he never won any recognition. The understanding which he hoped to the very end to find among his listeners never appeared. Today, a few hundred yards behind the famous stepped pyramid of Saqqara in the deserts of Middle Egypt, lie the ruins of the Jeremiah monastery where, according to tradition, the prophet died. Whether this place, which has largely been buried by the sands of the desert, really was the place where Jeremiah's life came to an end or not, it is symbolic of the fate of the prophet, whose traces have disappeared in the Egyptian sand.

2.9 Jeremiah's metahistory

2.9.1 Secret experience which runs counter to external history. On the downfall of the Assyrian power Jeremiah's fellow-countrymen heaved rapturous sighs of relief. But the young Jeremiah became aware through vision and audition that there was no reason for hope. For behind the collapse of Assyria signs could be seen of the rise of a still more terrible enemy. At the same time it became clear to his 'mind's eye' that intercourse between Yahweh, the fundamental force of history, and his people was still profoundly disturbed. The people were not as devoted to Yahweh as they appeared. On the contrary, they had abandoned their God by interpreting him in the light of an outlook on the world based on the movement and influence of the stars. The secret experience given to him alone compelled Jeremiah to announce and, through his words, to evoke the new disaster that was brewing up. After the Babylonian emperor had really devasted Judah in 587/6, burning down Jerusalem, together with the temple, and after everyone had become convinced that Judah's sands were running out, Jeremiah heard with his inward ear the announcement of the contrary – the

prediction of coming salvation and a new covenant which was to surpass everything that had hitherto existed.

In each case, therefore, Jeremiah proclaimed the exact opposite of what public opinion expected and what political calculation had worked out. And yet he is not just a grouser who contradicts on principle. The astonishing, sharp reversal in his predictions from the first inexorable plunge downward to a new, upward trend later is not the expression of a sudden turn from pessimism to optimism. In both cases it is prepared for a considerable time previously, so that the prophet can see what he proclaims as a logically cogent new turn of events. He himself knows that he is fundamentally called and empowered to subsequent insight into what has initially been given to him intuitively; and he believes that in that in the case of his listeners this subsequent insight is possible and reasonable. Certainly the insight does not always emerge automatically. The Confessions show that in certain hours perceptive understanding fails even the prophet. When it is missing, its absence torments him terribly. The idea of a divine inscrutability to which man has to submit plays no part in his thinking; nor does he insist on the necessity of faith where reason fails. On the contrary, he complains and cries out; for not to understand God and history means being totally exposed to meaninglessness.

For Jeremiah, this state of mind is exceptional; we find evidence for it only during the Jehoiakim period. Otherwise he is fully aware of being in a position to understand why God acts in this particular way, and no differently. But this inevitably presupposes that a particular conviction about the relationship between present, past and future underlies his proclamation. For this I have coined the term metahistory. If we try to reconstruct this metahistory, it emerges that the theory behind it remained to an astonishing degree the same for Jeremiah throughout all the years of his preaching.

2.9.2 A reconstruction of Jeremiah's metahistory. By metahistory we should understand a theory which – while presupposing a knowledge of actual political and military events (and the recording of these in narrative reports) – interprets the whole trend of history in such a way that collective human life appears to make sense, both in the course it takes in the present and in its future development. In order to avoid misunderstanding, let me say explicitly that not a single one of the prophets ever discursively expounds metahistory as a theoretical complex, or sets it apart from the history of actual and visible events. None the less, the poetry of the literary prophets is a highly reflective poetry – a poetry of thought – marked in particular by the artistic skill with which prophecy as a genre is constructed, the indication of

situation (A) and the prediction (B) generally being clearly differentiated and yet bound together by key or link words. And this poetry,
contemplative and intricate as it is, presupposes that the prophets
have in their mind's eye a total view of reality as a happening that is
also a process. What the prophetic sayings propound is formulated in
exceedingly concise terms; for these sayings are designed to impress
the mind and to be easily committed to memory. The aim is not a
didactic exposition. Nevertheless they presuppose in both the speaker
and the hearer an underlying knowledge which has of course no longer
been explicitly preserved for us; so the interpreter is forced to build
up the underlying teaching by fitting together a whole series of little
mosaic stones. If we are not prepared for this, not a single prophetic
utterance is really comprehensible.

All this means that, under the superficial structure of historio-
graphy, the prophets are searching for a 'structure in depth'.

(a) The external, visible, datable, 'wordly' link between cause and
effect is explained by reasons and rules which above all presuppose
that there are auras of action that create destiny, and that these allow
the course of history to be correlated with the moral behaviour of men and women.
The human subject does not only create in history what he or she
plans and intends. At the same time, through his everyday behaviour,
he more or less unconsciously and unintentionally evokes conditions
under which life, from then on, will either be calamitously constricted
or healthfully opened up and expanded. But the correlation between
action and destiny is only one aspect of metahistory.

(b) It also includes the insight that the moral life is not something
self-evident, and that the capacity for doing what is good must in
human beings continually be evoked anew. Here factors play a
part which go beyond the independent actions of men and women
themselves. Here contingency rules – contingency which surely has
to come from the foundation of history itself, that is to say from
Yahweh.

(c) But God does not act directly on the course of history. He makes
use of active powers such as the *ṣedeq* which confers salvation, or the
'wrath' that is seen as an objective force.

(d) With a premise like this, the sphere which the modern mind
distinguishes from nature and calls history is necessarily transcended;
here nature and history form a single whole in a connected, total
process of reality. History appears as prolonged creation, and creation
means nothing other than the provision of the conditions that make
history possible (cf. Vol. I, sections 4.9 and 7.8).

To a modern historian, the prophetic search for metahistorical
categories may seem like the childish efforts of an age entangled in

mythology. Anyone who, in his contemplation of history today, is not prepared to accept the admissibility even of trans-subjective forces such as divine providence, or a 'national spirit', will be still less willing to accept a moral causality according to which good or evil acts have a whiplash effect on the person responsible, issuing in a correspondingly favourable or unfavourable destiny. But has modern historical scholarship not paid too high a price for its allegedly 'objective' view of history? While renouncing the right to judge historical phenomena as good or evil, or to search for the effects of a corresponding moral guilt, it finds it difficult to escape from a positivist fetishism of pure power (unless, that is, it has recourse to some ideology or other).

2.9.3 Graduated monotheism. It is a matter of course, not only for Jeremiah, but for his listeners too, that only a single God is worthy of worship and adoration. To this extent they all pay homage to a practical monotheism. There is no divine being comparable with Yahweh (2.11). But this does not mean that they ascribe to Yahweh either omnipotence or omni-causality. It is only to a limited degree that evil in the world can be traced back to the God – only in so far as (in the form of an evil fate) it represents the backlash of some wickedness for which a human being has been responsible. It can in no case be traced back beyond the human author to evil as an act of God in creation itself. This means that there is no need for a theodicy. (In fact an explicit notion of creation hardly plays any part in the pre-exilic prophets in general. Where we do come across the idea in Jeremiah, in connection with the commission given by Yahweh to Nebuchadnezzar, it does not imply *creatio ex nihilo*, a creation out of nothing, without any presuppositions.)

What Yahweh primarily brings to pass are contingent decrees in the process of history. Jeremiah is concerned above all with the impending new turn of national history, which he, like the other prophets, expects will bring a transition from the conditions of the present, now intolerable, to a future which will have a totally different direction. This turn of events will be evoked through Yahweh's power, in two different ways: through word and through act. First of all God utters his historically efficacious *dābār* through the prophet's mouth. This means a first, anticipatory speech event which cannot in principle be recalled before it has materialized in a corresponding 'factual' event. A *dābār* issues from God's purposive thinking, which is always directed towards man (29.11); or it may spring from some profound hurt (*kā'as*) by which he has been touched. Once a *dābār* has gone forth to the earth, Yahweh watches over it until it has been fulfilled (1.11f.). God speaks and can also be spoken to: for both Jeremiah and for Israel in general this is an indisputable axiom. (And this axiom is connected with a second: that all reality is ultimately communicated through speech. It is not by chance that *dābār* also means 'fact' or happening.)

God later fulfils what he has said by approaching, or 'visiting', the group of people touched by the impact of his divinity. This personal divine approach (*pāqad*), leads to a salvation among the righteous that is the manifestation of their faithfulness to the community. It leads, that is to say, to the completion of their aura, their sphere of good deeds and salvation (29.10). But since the righteous are few in number, visitation usually evokes an activation of the spheres of sin, both in Israel (14.10) and among the Egyptians (46.25) or Moabites (48.44). Such a disaster can even come upon the sinner, however, through the very fact of Yahweh's withdrawal from him, through the divine abstinence. Where human beings have turned away from him, God hides his face (33.5), departs from his house, and abandons man to his own devices (12.7; 23.33).

But the real turn of events which Jeremiah expects is not catastrophe, but the salvation that succeeds it. The positive turn of events goes far beyond anything that can be contained within the coherences of act and outcome: for example, God offers his saving help in bringing back home again the men and women who have been deported (31.7f.); or he brings about a decisive turn in the people's destiny (*šūb š'būt*, 30.3; 29.14) without any preconditions, as far as human action is concerned. Where the divine will appears as the ultimate impetus behind history, Yahweh is described in personal categories. His character as conscious mind is stressed, as well as the communicative aspect with which he turns to man.

But God is experienced personally, especially by the prophet himself. Jeremiah is convinced that he quite clearly hears actual Hebrew words with his physical ear; and that he feels the nearness of the speaker, who has to be the familiar God of his people. He for his part calls upon God in intercession and is convinced that, as prophet, his prayers have more prospect of being heard than those of other people, and that he is listened to directly. (Admittedly God sometimes forbids him to intercede for his people, 7.16; 14.11.) He experiences God in the most varied ways: as a pressing compulsion that lies heavy on him, in the Confessions; and as an overflowing compassion, when God laments the fate of the people whom he himself has to bring up out of captivity.

But the personal aspect of the deity is not the only one. For Jeremiah, as for the prophets of the Assyrian period, Yahweh intervenes in human history for the most part through mediatory agencies. The effective *dābār* is already one of these. *Dābār* is more than the imparting of information; it is the power that shatters the rocks of the 'real' political forces which confront it (23.29). In and together with the word, constructive, restorative potencies are also roused into activity. Jeremiah thinks especially of *šālōm* as the sphere which confers welfare, security and confidence on the country (12.5; 13.19; 25.37; 29.7; 33.6, 9). On the other hand, destructive potencies also proceed from Yahweh; and, because of the conditions of the time, Jeremiah has to evoke these even more frequently. The elements of the divine wrath must be mentioned here first of all. For these the prophet uses the paired concepts 'breathing fire and white heat' (*'ap* and *ḥēmā*). These words are not merely intended to indicate emotional reactions on God's part. They are actual powers issuing from the centre of the divine being, Yahweh himself, with the purpose of moving upon human associations and alliances and pouring themselves out on them. These powers evoke an unquenchable fire (7.20), which does not withdraw until it has carried out the divine intention (30.24). This pair of wrathful powers are served on earth by the three or four deadly and evil entities, famine, sword, pestilence (and imprisonment, 15.2). These forces are set in march by the energy of *'ap* and *ḥēmā* (34.17–20; cf. 21.5f.; 15.15f.), and they make the Babylonian army their instrument. Through them the sword of Yahweh moves with a relentless and devouring force from one end of the earth to the other, ending *šālōm* for every living thing (12.2). But before the forces of wrath prevail in the events of history, they procure expression for themselves in the prophetic *dābār*. That is why Jeremiah is sometimes so overwhelmed by them that he cannot contain himself (6.11). He can then, in an anticipatory speech event, adopt a very old surrender formula from ancient oriental oracle practice and proclaim that Yahweh has given 'people and state and king' 'into the hand of the king of Babylon'. The evil three, sword, famine and pestilence, then put themselves at Babylon's disposal (32.3, 28, 36; 38.2f.). The forces of disaster are therefore clearly gradated. But the end and purpose of them all is to reduce Israel to ignominy and devastation. (It is surprising to find that these hidden and interrelated metahistorical forces of activity differ considerably from those of the Isaiah period. For the prophet of the Assyrian period, famine, sword and pestilence had not yet become independent entities. Instead Yahweh's glory, his plan and his work played a decisive role; cf. Vol. I, p. 266).

When he is considering Yahweh's rule in history, Jeremiah offers an additional viewpoint which was previously unknown: the concept of temporal laws. Above (in section 2.7.3) I pointed out how Jeremiah rejected the view of the world based on astrology and instead put

forward the idea of natural laws which are 'etched into' (*ḥōq*) the stars.
The laws for sun and moon and the cycle of the seasons are related to
temporal forces, to the alternation of day and night, and the progress
of the weeks. When he is talking about the imminent world catastrophe
he often points to the *day* of disaster, the *year* or the *time* of visitation
(48.44; 46.21). Does the law presuppose more extensive periods of
time which are bound up with these laws? Jeremiah evidently gave
considerable thought to the question of firmly established epochs,
ordered according to law and number. When in 604 BC Nebuchadnezzar acceded to his Judaean kingdom, Jeremiah prophesied seventy
years of devastation for Judah and for Jerusalem (25.1–14; cf. 29.10f.).
After that, events were to take a more favourable turn once more.
(The seventy-year epoch was known to the Babylonians, too, as a
special period established by the gods. It corresponds, that is to say,
to a concept of the epoch familiar at that time.) So Jeremiah points
forward to the years round about 535, according to our chronology.

He comes back to the same period twenty years later, in a dramatic
event dating from Jerusalem's final years. While the Babylonians
were besieging the city, a year of jubilee – a year of general liberty –
fell due, according to the cultic calendar (*dᵉrōr* = every forty-ninth or
fiftieth year). Beleaguered as they are by a superior army, the besieged
decide to celebrate this occasion by a renewal of the covenant, and
they resolve, at the same time, to carry out a Deuteronomic edict
(15.1ff.) applying to the seventh year (every *dᵉrōr* also being a sabbatical
year); this edict required the liberation of any Hebrews who had been
enslaved for debt. But the former slave-owners soon afterwards repent
of their pious resolve and reimpose the yoke of slavery on the people
who have just been freed. Jeremiah's God reacts to this with the
extremest severity. Instead of the slaves, he will give their masters the
'freedom' granted to someone in a *dᵉrōr* year – but what a merciless
freedom: a surrender to famine, sword and pestilence (34.8ff.)! What
is announced here almost twenty years after the first 'dated' prophecy,
as being promised after forty-nine (or fifty?) years, brings us down to
about 538/537. It therefore presupposes the same temporal 'skeleton'
or framework. (For a corresponding calculation by Ezekiel, see Ch.
4.) Will it be permissible to deduce from clues such as this that
Jeremiah was concerned – far more than the few definite statements
that have come down to us would suggest – with the question of how
the history guided by God is structured in epochs of numbered years
(fifty; seventy, etc.)?

Whatever the answer to this last problem may be, one thing is
certain: in Jeremiah's monotheism, the name of Yahweh by no means
denotes merely a personal power who has to do with individuals.

Yahweh is a power who moves history, who intervenes in world events, even if in a highly differentiated and 'graduated' way; though he is also the One God whose name Israel alone knows and uses. In view of the multiplicity of powers and forces of activity employed, I would suggest talking here about a *gradated* monotheism. But what this term means will be fully discernible only when we set it beside the understanding of human existence that went along with it.

2.9.4 Concentric monathropology. For the critical prophets, men and women are responsible for what happens on earth – with the exception of the heavenly bodies which order the times and seasons, and wondrous and contingent interventions by divine powers. There is not really any such thing as 'nature', if this means something that unfolds itself automatically, of its own accord, in the earthly sphere. Whether a field brings forth fruit or not depends primarily on the owner who plants it – and whether he has acted, largely speaking, in a way that accords with loyalty to the community, or the reverse. The face of the earth is shaped and conditioned by the correlation between human action and destiny. (One might almost call man – especially in the form of 'the total self' or the king – the 'little God' of the earth.) Among all created beings, it is man alone who strikes out a path for himself, a *derek*. Unlike animals or stars, human beings form their destiny through what they do. This view – the view that human beings play this decisive role in the earthly sphere – I term *monanthropology* or *monanthropism*. A term like monotheism only seems appropriate for the prophetic understanding of God if one talks in a complementary way about monanthropology. God and mankind are the essential poles of reality, both of them fermenting forces in the process of events, and both linked together through a field of force that itself has a highly complex structure.

It is of course true that there can be no question of equality of rank between the two forces. The monotheistic pole is far and away the more powerful and comprehensive. It creates the potentialities that make it possible for what is human to develop in a truly human way, to this end conferring the *šālōm* and the blessing of the earth, and also the dependability of the times and seasons. It is this pole that lets evil recoil on the head of its perpetrator, in order to free the earth from the spell of evil's calamitous effects. The more distinctly monotheism of this kind develops in the prophets, the firmer too their monathropology.

The monanthropology is conceived of *concentrically*, in two different ways. On the one hand, man himself, with the sphere of his actions, establishes his own life and that of his house (both in the sense of his household and his dwelling place); to a lesser degree his fields and vineyards are also affected, and to some slight extent the rest of the land (the desert and the sea not at all). But the monanthropology is concentric, secondly, in that, although all dwellers on earth share a common destiny before Yahweh, yet Israel-Judah knows itself to be the centre of mankind and closest to the source of life, with special responsibility, but also with especial opportunities for salvation. Israel-Judah is surrounded by neighbouring peoples who are also touched by the prophetic *dābār*. Foreign nations, on the other hand, appear at most anonymously, as attendants of the enemy from the north.

Israel itself also has a concentric structure, the centre (towards which the rest tends) being the king, and the outer spheres the elders, priests or ministers. The prophet has a special position. He is certainly in no way the centre of the people's corporate personality, like the king, or perhaps the priest; and yet, even more than king or priest, he is the mediator between heaven and earth. He has the task, which is otherwise God's alone, of testing the paths of men and women (6.27f.). Nowhere do the monotheistic and monanthropological poles of history touch one another so closely as in a prophet's words. Jeremiah can tear out and tear down nations and kingdoms, or can build them up and establish them (1.10 – a later interpolation?). He almost outgrows his adherence to any one single nation.

We have already described Jeremiah's precise views about the structure of man, and the hope he puts forward for an eschatological transformation. A person's life as *derek* is formed according to the devices of the understanding (*lēb*), by what have become habitual ways of behaviour (*ma'alālīm*, twelve times). This behaviour may be righteous or wicked – there is no intermediate possibility. God rules over this process as the one 'who searches the understanding . . . to give (the destiny) to every man according to his *derek* and according to the fruit of his *ma'alālīm*' (17.10). Through his analysis of a person's mental and spiritual state, God can therefore ascertain the character of his corresponding conduct and way of life. For Jeremiah, acts no longer seem to hover round the agent like an aura; they also actually affect at least the doer's *lēb*. A divine scrutiny can at all events deduce the character of a person's destiny from his 'heart'. Where Jeremiah's contemporaries are concerned, the result can only be that the understanding has become 'incurable' (*'ānuš*, 17.9) – that is, characterized by 'hardness' (*š'rīrūt*, see above). It is then incapable of comprehending what goes on in life. Here sin is engraved with an iron pen on the tablet of the heart (17.1). Jeremiah's contemporaries are talking and living in deception (*šeqer*); through objects of horror (*šiqqūṣ*) and the worship of other gods, they have given themselves up to a counter-world which is dragging them down to their downfall. Where this perversion of the human spirit and human 'nature' comes from is not explained. Moreover it is superfluous to enquire; for one day, within the reality of history, God will prevail and will call better people into being. Jeremiah has no hope that this will happen in the immediate future, but he no doubt expects it to come about in the era following Babylonian rule. It has to be said, however, that in this respect Jeremiah's metahistorical prognosis would seem to have been denied fulfilment down to the present day . . .

Is this metahistory, or is it a *juridical* interpretation? Instead of metahistory, scholars often talk about the proclamation of judgment in Jeremiah, as in the other prophets. They assume that the prophet conceives of his God primarily as a personal, transcendent judge, who once upon a time gave Israel commandments and law, and who now watches to see that these are being meticulously observed. Where there is disobedience, God resolves on punishment; and it is this that the prophets of judgment have come to proclaim. For this the course of previous history is of no essential importance. And the eschatological salvation of the future will be the effulgence of pure grace – grace which the divine judge is able to bestow. But this too stands outside any historical continuity.

Can this juridically determined interpretation be deduced from the Jeremianic texts? It seems to me to be more in accordance with the restricted viewpoint of a Western understanding of God, which increasingly sets him over against all history, as pure transcendence, and only permits him rule over the universe on the level of the condemnatory and redeeming word. It must be admitted that it is difficult to reconstruct the metahistorical ideas of a prophet. But an underlying metahistorical view of the kind I have suggested is more in accord with the complex wording of the text than the apparently simple, juridicial interpretation, which rests far more on the Latin or English translation of the text than on the original Hebrew.

3.   Babylon and Her Satellite Edom: Habakkuk and Obadiah

3.1 Habbakkuk

Habakkuk was a younger contemporary of Jeremiah's, and his prophecies were uttered under the shadow of the rising Babylonian power.

B Lo, I am rousing the Chaldeans,
    that bitter and hasty nation,
  who march through the breadth of the earth,
    to seize habitations not their own.
  Dread and terrible are they;
    their *just order* (*mišpāṭ*) and sovereignty proceed from them-
    selves (1.6f.).

There is no withstanding their assault. They are striking at Judah
because violence rules in the country, and the just order of society has
been turned upside down, as the prophet's deeply felt lament shows.
His social criticism – especially in the accusations underlying the
poems of lament (2.6b-19) – in no way falls short of Amos or Micah
in ferocity. According to these laments, the person who is so unbridled
a profiteer that his debtors threaten to rebel is doomed to die. The
prophet attacks the man greedy for gain, in whose house the very
stones groan under the weight of the evil deeds brought into it; or the
person who builds his city with blood guilt. Originally these laments
contained no indication of all of a divine intervention. The only thing
they stressed was the firm connection between a person's act and his
subsequent destiny. Is the target here one particular ruler, perhaps
King Jehoiakim (Jer. 22.13ff.)? Or is the singular collective form being
used, the object of the attack being the property-owning classes in
Jerusalem?

After the invasion of the Babylonians, social criticism is embodied
in sayings which are now built into the framework of a prophetic
liturgy, and reinterpreted accordingly. What was originally meant to
apply to the man of violence in the homeland is now transferred to
the foreign tyrants, the Babylonians (1.12–17):

Yahweh, you have installed him for a *just order* (*mišpāṭ*),
  O rock, you have established him as judge . . .
Why dost thou look on the robbers and art silent,
  when the wicked man swallows up those faithful to the
    community?
You have let men become like the fish of the sea,
  like crawling things that have no ruler . . .
Therefore he sacrifices to his net,
  burns incense to his seine . . .
Is he then to keep on emptying his net for ever
  by mercilessly slaying nations?

It is worth stressing that crimes against the nations in general are
condemned here, not merely the injustice done to Judah – though this

was by no means a matter of course among the Israelite prophets. The book ends with the vision of a divine theophany, couched in the form of a hymn. From his age-old dwelling place in the southern mountains, Yahweh storms up against the enemy power. The hymn closes triumphantly:

Thou tramplest [his] horses into the sea,
into the sand of the mighty waters (3.15).

This is a reference to Yahweh's victory over the Egyptian army during the exodus from Egypt, in primeval times (Ex. 15). What happened in salvation history is given a new contemporary form, with Babylon as enemy.

Today the little book resembles the Book of Joel more closely than anything else, in form and outline. Twice the prophet begins with a lament in the first person. However, this is not meant personally. It is intended to give voice to the people's 'total self'. In both cases an oracle of assurance follows, expressing confidence that the complaint has been heard (1.5–11, following 1.2–4; 2.1–5, following 1.12–17). A series of 'woe' laments (2.6ff.) come next, and these are succeeded by the final hymn (ch. 3). This would fit into the pattern of a liturgical ceremony. We may imagine it as belonging to an Israelite ceremony of lamentation. However, scholars are divided as to whether it was Habakkuk himself who incorporated his original sayings into a self-contained anti-Babylonian liturgy, or whether this was the work of a later hand. Since it is impossible to show any differences in the language, I myself am inclined to assign the revision to Habakkuk himself. In this case the prophet changed from a prophet of doom into one prophesying salvation for Israel. (This can only seem surprising to anyone who cherishes the cliché that the pre-exilic (cultic) prophets proclaimed salvation and only salvation, with complete consistency. But this view is refuted by Hos. 6.5, Micah 3.5 and Jer. 28.8.) Habakkuk's social criticism – his first phase – was probably voiced between 609 and 605, shortly before Judah was annexed and incorporated in the neo-Babylonian empire. If this is correct, his second period of proclamation, which was directed against Babylon, would have been about 600 BC.

Habakkuk is one of the few literary prophets who is actually introduced as nabi in the book's title. This probably means that he was a institutionalized cultic prophet (cf. Vol. I, 4.1, on Amos 7). This fits in with remarks scattered throughout the book – for example that Habakkuk went up to a watchtower (in the temple?) in order to keep a look-out for a vision, and that Yahweh answered him there (2.1f.); or that his whole body trembled during his ecstatic reception of the word (3.16). In addition, the essential components even of his social criticism suggest that this belonged within a liturgical framework (cf. 1.2–11). However, there is one objection to this classification. If the Jewish man of violence whom Habakkuk rebukes so sharply was the king of Jerusalem, this makes it difficult to see the prophet as a nabi; for would criticism like this have been tolerated in public worship?

One passage in the Book of Habakkuk has become particularly famous: 2.3bff.

A ... If it (the fulfilment of the vision) delays, wait for it,
   for it will surely come and will not be removed.
B Behold [the one who is puffed up], the power of his life will not
   remain upright (= bringing salvation, *yšr*) in him,
      but the man faithful to the community (*ṣaddīq*) will through
      his trust (*'emūnā*) gain life.
How much more will (riches) deceive?
   The arrogant man [. . .] will not achieve his goal.
   [. . .] He has made the power of his life as wide as the
   underworld.

In the rendering 'the just shall live by faith' (which comes through the Greek) the passage was later to become a pillar of Pauline theology (Rom. 1.17; Gal. 3.11), providing evidence that people are justified before God by faith alone, and not by good works. Now, it is true that *'emūnā*, the Hebrew word used here, can occasionally mean 'faith'. But in the present context it is parallel to 'waiting for' the fulfilment of a particular prophecy (v. 3). It therefore points to the kind of trust which Isaiah also demanded at a particular moment in history (7.9, cf. Vol I, section 7.4). So the statement does not as yet express any kind of general principle of religious behaviour. Paul's generalization was admittedly already anticipated to some extent in the Habakkuk' Commentary' found twenty years ago in the caves near the Dead Sea; for there the prime religious duty is 'faithfulness to the Teacher of Righteousness' (the founder of the Qumran community); and this is deduced from Hab. 2.4 (1Qp Hab VIII 1–3).

3.2 Obadiah

The shortest book in the Old Testament probably also goes back to a cultic prophet, this time one who proclaimed Yahweh's *dābār* at ceremonies of lamentation to the people who had remained behind in the homeland after the fall of Judah and Jerusalem in 587/6. Biting threats are directed against the Edomites, Judah's 'relations' south of Palestine, because they had consorted with the people who had seized Judah for themselves. The Day of Yahweh will bring down Edom's deeds on its own head in disastrous fulfilment. This Day is now imminent, and Obadiah yearns for it on Israel's behalf, seeing it in the context of a popular eschatology (an interpretation which Amos had rejected; cf. Vol. I, section 4.6.1). In a second daying, Edom's doom is linked with a victorious Israelite advance against all the nations which had robbed them of land (vv. 16–18). A later addition describes in detail the regions which are going to be recovered. This addition is worth mentioning because it closes wit the expectation that Yahweh will manifest his royal dignity on a renewed Mount Zion (vv. 17–21). This expectation emerges for the first time in the middle of the sixth century, and is an early form of the later hope for a manifestation of the kingdom of God on earth.

4. Ezekiel ben Buzi

4.1 A strange visionary among the exiles

4.1.1 The proclamation of doom in the situation of the exile. The Judaeans who were carried off to Babylon in 597 were settled on the great irrigation canals in Mesopotamia. They were presumably condemned to forced labour under Babylonian surveillance, their function being to keep the canal system between the Tigris and the Euphrates in repair; and they were given camps or village settlements of their own. If the conditions in Tel Abib which the Book of Ezekiel describes were typical, the exiles were allowed a limited degree of self-administration as well as their own worship. Ezekiel ben Buzi, the son of a former Jerusalem priest, was apparently exempted from forced labour; and from time to time – perhaps in the evenings, after work? – the elders (the quasi-cultic representatives of the exiles) met at his house to prepare lamentation rites (cf. Ps. 137), or in order to wait for a *dābār* from Yahweh which would reveal the future.

We know from Jer. 29 that in the early years many nabis emerged among the deported people, and that these nabis ecstatically proclaimed that the people would soon be returning home. The Book of Ezekiel begins in 593/2 BC, five years after the deportation. Now nothing more is said about an imminent return home. The priest, who now comes forward as a prophet, is entirely at one with Jeremiah in his conviction that the Babylonian domination is going to last for years. Like Jeremiah in Jerusalem, Ezekiel proclaims among the *gōlā* (the deportees) that the guilt of Israelite and Judaean history has piled up to such an extent over the centuries that the defeat of 597 – in which Judah really came off lightly – and the (first) deportation cannot yet be viewed as the end of the correlation between misdeeds and disaster. The real downfall is still ahead. It will come about through a new Babylonian conquest. In the homeland Jeremiah was threatened with death when he put forward this interpretation of history. But Ezekiel, preaching the same message, did not face actual hostility, though he certainly met with resistance among the captives. Although his listeners sympathized with the people of Jerusalem in their revolt against Babylon, they came back to Ezekiel's house again and again, sat at his feet and listened to his teachings.

It is noticeable that, in spite of very different social conditions, Jeremiah in the homeland and Ezekiel in exile take a surprisingly unanimous view about the past and future of their people, and apply a similar metahistorical framework. At the same time, Ezekiel stresses certain lines of thinking more forcibly, and draws conclusions which Jeremiah hints at but does not dare to think through to the end. One of these more stringently pursued ideas is Yahweh's assertion of himself and the majesty of his 'name' in history; another is the importance of individual human repentance as the turning point of destiny. It is only when he comes to the role of the divine commandments and edicts in events as a whole that, as we shall see, the Jerusalem priest takes a different line from the priest's son from Anathoth.

We may assume that Ezekiel had received news of Jeremiah's prediction of doom. One or two allusions suggest this. However, it is hardly likely that he possessed anything in writing; there are no direct quotations. Moreover Ezekiel pursues his argumentation quite independently, and is much more strongly influenced by an ethic rooted in priestly modes of expression; so there can be no question of what he says being a mere echo of Jeremiah. He certainly makes it easier for his fellow-countrymen to assent to what he said than Jeremiah did. For it is only exceptionally that Ezekiel censures the behaviour of the men and women who had been deported with him. He devotes all his fervour to condemning the way his fellow-countrymen are behaving in far-off Judaea, and their attempts to rebel against Babylon, which are a breach of the oath sworn before Yahweh. Again and again he stresses the calamity of a misguided history, which weighs on the home country just as much as on the *gōlā*. Ezekiel would not be a prophet if he did not occasionally criticize his listeners. The deportees are cherishing their little idols (perhaps amulets? ch. 14), even though they cannot be accused of actual leanings towards Babylonian religious practices. Nabis and women prophets are criticized for proclaiming *šālōm* although no *šālōm* is in prospect. But this seems to be really a retrospect on past activities, or on conditions in the home country. Of course there are wicked people, and behaviour

which infringes the interests of the community in the *gōlā* camp too
(ch. 18). This will mean the downfall of individuals, but hardly doom
for the *gōlā* as a whole.

Ezekiel gets a bad mark from many Old Testament scholars because
he seldom makes any direct appeal to his listeners, and because his
dābār is much more didactic than the words of the earlier critical
prophets. 'He is completely lacking in poetic inspiration,' said Duhm,
'a man of cold intellect and sober calculation.' But this can only be
the judgment of someone who completely ignores the Hebrew way of
viewing kindred and people as a total self, a corporate personality,
which is the real, active subject. Ezekiel knows he is a branch on the
tree of his national community, and he knows too that he is woven
into events in his home country as well. Like his discouraged fellow
deportees, he is unable to settle down to things as they are. Even when
he talks about the holy city, which is continually in his thoughts, far
away though it is, or when he ponders the course of past history, he
does not forget for a moment that what is in question is a collective
derek, which includes his own past and his own, highly personal future.
The passion, even the apparently bloodthirsty cruelty with which he
sometimes wishes death and destruction on Jerusalem – for example
in the sinister cry for the sword in 21.8–16 – is only the reaction of a
deeply wounded heart which has to live through the misery of Israel's
final hour. He knows that his commission as nabi is not merely to
enlighten and predict future events to his fellow exiles. He actually
has to embody the fate of the house of Israel's 'total self' – embody it
physically, in a way that borders on the pathological. Amos is perhaps
the most inexorable of the critical prophets, Isaiah the most mighty
eloquent, and Jeremiah the most sensitive; but Ezekiel is the strangest
of them all. And that is saying a great deal, for they all go far beyond
the bounds of decent bourgeois behaviour (cf. Vol. I, sections 5.2 and
7.1).

4.1.2 The opening of the heavens and the presentation of the book. Ezekiel is
designated for prophetic activity by an inner vision which is already
highly unusual in its content. Chapters 1 to 3 report a bizarre, not to
say monstrous, vision of a richly furnished chariot of state which
rushes up through the air from the north, driven onwards by the active
force of the *rūᵃḥ*, and surrounded by a marvellous aura.

> Behold a rushing of the spirit of the storm coming out of the north
> as a great cloud, fire and brightness round about it, flashing forth
> here and there. In its midst it shone like a ring of electrum (brass?)
> (v. 4).

As it approaches more closely, four strangely compounded creatures emerge from the ring, carrying a crystal slab above their heads. Each of them has four wings, human hands, a bull's foot, made of metal, and four faces – the faces of a man, a lion, a bull and an eagle. In each case the foot is bound to a wheel, which can turn in all directions and the spikes of which are studded with eyes. Above the crystal slab, which is called 'the firmament' (*rāqī̆aʿ*), towers a throne of lapis lazuli, on which a figure sits with 'the likeness as it were of a human form', from the hips upward like electrum, but downwards like fire, the whole figure totally surrounded by its own radiance. 'This was the appearance of the form of the glory (*kābōd*) of Yahweh,' Ezekiel adds in explanation, and goes on that he thereupon fell to the ground unconscious.

The vision goes beyond anything we can find in the visions of earlier prophets. Centuries later it provided the starting point for Jewish *merkābā* (chariot) mysticism and became the occasion for such extensive speculations about the appearance and appointments of the heavenly world that the rabbis forbade these chapters to be read in public. Recently they have provided inspiration for the burgeoning fantasies of Däniken and others about space travel in the ancient world. The details of the description are still obscure in certain respects. This has tempted painters like William Blake to grandiose portrayals. The vision did not appear quite so strange to Ezekiel's own hearers as it does to the modern reader. Yahweh's throne above the firmament, borne up by composite figures, was an entirely familiar feature of the language used in the Jerusalem cult; and so was the rushing approach of God in all his glory, in a theophany, during religious festivals (Ps. 29). It is true that hitherto it had been thought that Yahweh, with his *kābōd*, appeared in a theophany in order to ascend the throne in Jerusalem, because it was there that it towered above the earth (Isa. 6). It was certainly new and surprising for Ezekiel to find the divine throne moving into a foreign land, or – probably more exactly – to discover that Yahweh's *kābōd* had a throne of its own (apparently a reflection of Yahweh's throne in heaven) with which it moved into Babylon. According to traditional beliefs, the divine *kābōd* could certainly shine out over heaven and earth, but it none the less had its centre and goal in the holy city of Jerusalem (Ps. 24.7ff.; 97). Now, however, it has its destination in the non-Palestinian 'unclean' land where the Israelite *gōlā* are living. (The story in the Priestly writing of the wanderings in the wilderness dates from about the same period, and this too shows the *kābōd* as flashing forth at will in the desert, Num. 16.19; 16.42.) Now the *kābōd* is personified to such a degree that it actually takes on human form (cf. 10.4), and acquires an uncanny, roaring voice. Babylonian and Assyrian influences are probably making themselves felt here. In this form the *kābōd* is reminiscent of the glory surrounding the gods, which was thought of as an aureole or a garment of flame.[18] The Babylonian sun god sits on a throne above the disc of the firmament.[19] The head of a man, a lion, a bull and an eagle – these very four, probably representing the four corners of the earth (they were later symbols of the four evangelists) – can be found a hundred years later on the pillars supporting the roofs of the palace in Persepolis. There, too, they were no doubt intended to be a copy of the firmament. We also find a mention of chariots used by the gods among the Persians. Both these examples probably go back to Mesopotamian influence.[20]

What was the purpose of this display – this overwhelming manifestation? It comes to a halt just in front of Ezekiel, and he falls to the ground. But the rushing spirit which has driven the chariot forward enters into him and makes him stand up again, so that he may receive his prophetic charge. According to the context this charge is the only reason for the whole phenomenon. However, commentators are generally of the opinion that the phenomenon was really directed to the whole exiled community, and was intended to proclaim the fact that the *kābōd* – which up to then had been thought of as having its sole presence in the temple in Jerusalem – was now taking up its dwelling among the exiles in impure Babylon. But there is no indication that the glory was going to remain among the exiles, even though the priest must certainly have been surprised that the *kābōd* should appear in Babylon at all. It is true that the theophany experience meant casting to the winds a fundamental axiom of the dogma Ezekiel had learned; for it taught him that Yahweh's radius of movement was far wider than the spell of a narrow-minded national religion had hitherto allowed him to believe. But the stress does not lie on a new discernment about the *kābōd*. The throne hardly ended its journey in Babylon just to console the exiles. The purpose was more probably to show that from now on Babylon was to become the focus of world events, which had to be seen in a metahistorical context; and that the man charged to proclaim and evoke the *dābār* was therefore now to be chosen from among the exiles. Like Jeremiah at the same period, Ezekiel sees God's providence as assigning a key role to Babylon and Nebuchadnezzar. So it is in Babylon that the *dābār* that lays the foundation for history has to be heard, and it is here that the nabi is appointed.

The position of the prophet as such shows signs of being somewhat reduced in stature, in spite of the splendour of the happening itself. Earlier prophets knew that they were listening directly to the heavenly council, and were onlookers there (I Kings 22; Isa. 6; still Jer. 23.18). But Ezekiel is fully conscious that he is still on earth. The distance between him and the heavenly Lord remains immeasurable; and what he beholds is merely the reflection of God in the *kābōd*. It is in accordance with this perception that the voice should speak to him without using his name, addressing him as 'son of man' (*ben 'ādām*); and it is worth noting here that the collective word *'ādām* has an underlying note of helplessness and frailty, though there is also a suggestion of monanthropological universality. It is significant that Ezekiel is not addressed as 'son of Israel', but as a specially marked out example of the species human being in general. It is in keeping with this that he has to proclaim the future to the other nations on earth too (cf. chs. 25–32).

According to the present text, the first vision was soon followed by a second one:

> I looked and behold a hand was stretched out to me,
> and lo, a written scroll was in it.

This scroll includes laments for the dead, and whimperings, and wailings. A voice summons the seer to eat the scroll, which he does: 'and it was in my mouth as sweet as honey.' Then he is sent to proclaim the words to the people, which is a refractory people, hard of brow and face. But by virtue of the *dābār* the prophet receives the ability to prevail: he is himself given 'a hard brow' (2.9ff.).

The book solemnly brought down from heaven contains the destinies determined by God; but these require human mediation if they are to be fulfilled on earth. A new page of history is turned. But what it shows is not encouraging. After five years of imprisonment, it merely allows the exiled people to be told that things will go on as before, and indeed will get worse.

The vision presupposes that prophecy is already in existence in written, book, form. This suggests that Ezekiel wrote down his message from the very beginning and knew that he was actually charged to do so. (We may contrast Jer. 36, where the prophet is only forced by circumstances to take up his pen.) But Ezekiel remains convinced that Yahweh's effective *dābār* will take objective form in the historical events which are to follow. Indeed he even heightens this idea by seeing the prophetic book as a kind of transcription of a fate laid down in heaven (a Babylonian idea). Many scholars have taken a disapproving view of the high estimate he attaches to the book as such. Ezekiel has been put down as a 'writer', and belittled compared with his predecessors, who had been men of authoritative speech. But the disparaging judgment is unjust in itself (has a writer less genius than an orator?) and also fails to grasp the change in social conditions. Ezekiel can come forward with a spoken message only to the people belonging to the community of his camp. This he undoubtedly did, according to chs. 14; 20. But if he wanted to exert any wider influence, he had to write down his message. The degree to which he here preserved the tradition of prophetic speech is shown by the way he keeps the genre of prophecy in most of his sayings, with an indication of situation followed by a prediction. But he very noticeably renounces the poetic form. Was poetic language no longer indispensable for a prophet in exile? Or was the written version deliberately a prose one, because the poetic form was unnecessary for a text designed to be read?

4.1.3 The acted-out siege and destruction of Jerusalem. Again Yahweh's *kābōd* rushes upon the prophet, this time giving his commission a specific form (3.22–5.17). Ezekiel's lips will be paralysed in the period immediately ahead. Then he has to scratch the ground-plan of the city of Jerusalem on a brick in front of his house, to make a model of a siege wall and to lay himself down on the ground as if he himself were the besieger. He has first of all to lie for 390 days on his left side, in order to illustrate the weight of sin (*'āwen*) in Israel as a whole; and then he has to lie for forty days on his right side, in order to represent the guilt of Judah. During this period he has to ration his bread and water; and he is initially told to bake his bread on human excrement. In response to his appalled objection that he has never used anything so unclean, he is permitted to use cow dung. But this is the only alleviation. At the end of the given period he has to shave off his hair, burning a third of it in the fire, cutting a third of it into small pieces with a sword, and throwing a third of it to the winds. He is told to catch some of the last third, and again to burn part of that. Only a tiny fragment remains. This is what the fate of the people is going to be.

In spite of all the peculiarities, even this very first symbolic act shows that Ezekiel uses quite familiar metahistorical categories. The number 390 plus 40 comes to 430; and this corresponds to the reigns of the Jerusalem kings, from the building of Solomon's temple to the beginning of the exile, according to the chronology of the Books of Kings. (Modern historical chronology is different.) The presumption seems to be that the kings belonging to the Davidic line were kings of the house of Israel – which means the nation as a whole – down to the death of Manasseh (642 BC). Only after that was their government restricted to Judah (cf. II Chron. 33.11?). From the beginning of the building of the temple – that is to say, from the time when a centre of salvation was established for the people in the cultivated lands – Israel's sphere of guilt had continually increased, centring in this very capital. Since then its God has had to lay siege to it, until the guilt matured and he could march to the attack.

With considerable skill, Ezekiel weaves the different metahistorical aspects together into a prophecy which brings the description of the symbolic act to a close. He ignores the level of practical politics – the Babylonian danger – though he does mention the correlation between act and destiny, which is the initial factor explaining the course of actual political affairs. The nation has heaped up the mass of guilt in which it will one day inevitably putrefy (4.17). Then its bread and water will come to an end. But even the connection between act and destiny is a superficial way of looking at things. For this itself is part of a much wider plane of divine activity and purpose:

A The matter is thus: you have defiled my sanctuary with all your detestable things and with all your abominable acts (*tōʿēbā*).
B So I too. I will cut you down, my eyes will not spare, and cherish no pity.
A third part of you shall die of pestilence and be consumed with famine in the midst of you;
a third part shall fall by the sword round about you; and a third part I will scatter to all the winds and will unsheathe the sword after them.
The breath of my wrath (*ʾap*) shall vent itself, my white heat (*ḥēmā*) will come to rest (. . .),
C And they shall know that I am Yahweh.
I have spoken in my zeal, by letting my white heat be vented upon them (5.11–13).

If we consider this final saying, which is a commentary on the symbolic act illustrating the siege of Jerusalem, we find a weft of metahistorical ideas very similar to those in Jeremiah. The human misdeed has its gravest consequences when it is connected with the defilement of the sanctuary; for then it infringes Yahweh's private sphere, as it were. When the connection between misdeed and disaster is thereupon consummated in the guilty person, this is also the work of a pair of divine wrathful powers. The two expressions for wrath do not merely refer to the psychological reactions of a transcendent power; they represent a metahistorical and mythological entity, which proceeds from Yahweh, moves towards men and women, and only finds its end when they too are destroyed. The breath of wrath and white heat take material form, on a lower level, in three evil forces: pestilence, famine and sword. These are evoked in other passages in Ezekiel as well.

They hasten mysteriously over the earth and can manifest themselves
in the Babylonian power (7.3–9; 11.9–12; 16.38–41). This all adds up
to a stroke of destruction unparalleled in history. Wherever a group
of people continually engages in evil behaviour, deadly mechanisms
begin to interlock. At the bottom of the pyramid come the spheres of
act and corresponding destiny, which are now consummated. Above
them are the active powers such as pestilence, famine and sword.
Higher up still are the entities of wrath and white heat. And finally
comes the burning-glass itself – the personal focus in Yahweh who, in
his desire to be known, intervenes in history with ardent zeal and
without compassion. Except for the goal 'to know Yahweh', which
we shall be considering in a moment, the metahistorical concepts
correspond to the Book of Jeremiah. But in other passages Ezekiel
brings a different level into play: Yahweh's edicts and laws. We shall
have to consider this new emphasis later.

4.1.4 Ezekiel – a pathological or parapsychological case? After his first vision
at the Chebar canal, Ezekiel loses his ability to speak for a week,
because he feels Yahweh's hand heavy upon him (3.14f.). The
overwhelming experience he has just, for the first time, undergone
may perhaps make this explicable. But the reader is none the less
surprised that the prophet should lose his power of speech a second
time, and that he has later even to be tied up by other people (3.25f.;
cf. 33.22). It is also astonishing that he should lie, incapable of
movement, for 390 days on his left side, and then 40 days on his right
(4.4–6). Israel was used to strange behaviour enough on the part of
its prophets. But Ezekiel goes far beyond other prophetic eccentricity.
For he tells of 'journeys through the air' from Tel Abib, the prisoners'
settlement, to the bottom of a valley, or even to far-off Jerusalem,
hundreds of miles away. In hours like this he feels as if the wind of the
Spirit (*rūaḥ*) has seized him by the hair and kidnapped him – and has
brought him back again in the same way at the end of the vision (chs.
8.11; 37; 40.1f.). All this has encouraged interpreters to try to apply
medical diagnoses. Generally the verdict is catalepsy, a rare form of
muscular paralysis which has psychological causes. The philosopher
Karl Jaspers even thought that he could show that these were the
typical symptoms of schizophrenia.[21] But it is difficult to deduce a
case history with any degree of certainty from a document two and a
half thousand years old. Whatever the medical opinion may be, it
must be said that at no point do Ezekiel's mental powers appear to be
in any way clouded. The general tendency of his proclamation agrees
so much with that of his contemporary Jeremiah that it does not seem

advisable to look for an explanation in any special pathological predisposition.

It would be surprising if so curious a figure had not tempted people to look for psychoanalytical interpretations. Anyone who is determined to do so may, for example, like Arlow,[22] interpret the man-like figure on the throne in the first vision – who is pure fire from the hips down – as being the figment of a phallus fascination; and he may think of *fellatio* in connection with the written scroll which is handed to the prophet and which he swallows. (It must, however, be said that adventurous speculations of this kind make the interpretations of someone like von Däniken seem positively serious.)

Another problem is the precise knowledge of Jerusalem conditions which Ezekiel brings back with him from the journeys on which the *rū^aḥ* takes him in his ecstatic state. He expounds this new-found knowledge to his fellow-countrymen in the *gōlā*. In a second, far-ranging vision (chs. 8–11) the prophet finds himself on the square in front of the temple in Jerusalem. There, in a gateway on the north side, he sees 'an image of jealousy' – that is to say, an idol. In a closed room there are pictures of animals scratched on the walls (probably signs of the zodiac), to which the elders of Israel are burning incense, while outside, in the forecourt, men are worshipping the sun.

What is described here fits in with conditions during the final years of Zedekiah. Astral worship and the heavenly Baal are officially censured; that is why Ezekiel does not mention any priest as being involved in the condemned rites. All the same, leanings of this kind were once again widespread among the laity and found expression in the less prominent parts of the temple. Deuteronomy evidently still possessed authority, but its provisions were undermined. Ezekiel is even able to name some of the people involved, prophesying their downfall (8.11; 11.1). In his vision, this prophecy is immediately fulfilled: 'And it came to pass, while I was prophesying, that Pelatiah the son of Benaiah died' (11.3).

This precise knowledge about events in Judah has led scholars to propound the theory that Ezekiel was active in two different places – for a time in Jerusalem and for a time in Babylon. According to this view, the stories about journeys through the air were later attempts to preserve past experiences, after the Jerusalem phase had been forgotten. But is this not an illegitimate rationalization? At all events, no support for any such theory can be found in the text; and most scholars have therefore abandoned it. But then how are the descriptions of Jerusalem to be explained? Did the prophet have informants, messengers from the home country whom he could question? Other passages show that he evidently had reliable information about conditions in Phoenician Tyre and far-off Egypt. But if news from Jerusalem had got through, Ezekiel's listeners would have known about it, too, and there would have been no need to enlighten them by means of prophecies. So here, as with other prophets, even a sober observer is compelled to consider the possibility of extra-sensory perception. One day the prophet hears the inward message: 'Son of man, write down the name of this day, this very day. The king of Babylon has thrown himself upon Jerusalem this very day' (24.2). The date actually proves to be correct: the prophet has perceived the beginning of the siege far away beyond the wide Syrian-Arabian desert. What possible explanation is there for anything like this? Or when he tells his listeners in the morning that his wife, 'the delight of his eyes', is going to die, and in the evening she actually lies dead (24.15ff.)? Our modern rational way of looking at things may protest as it likes: the parapsychological riddle of prophetic clairvoyance can only be eliminated from this writing at the cost of an exegetical act of violence.

Where the prediction of future events is concerned, there is more ambiguity, although here it is important to remember the prophetic understanding of what a *dābār* is; for in the prophets' view the dynamic aspect of the word, which calls forth historical events, is more important than the dianoetic information it contains. Consequently the wording cannot be pressed too literally. For example, when a *dābār* directed against the island city of Tyre is not fulfilled there, Ezekiel can actually 'redirect' it to Egypt, without proving himself wrong (26.7ff.; 29.17ff.).

4.2 Israel's failure in the light of the divine law

4.2.1 Social criticism. Looking back to the era of the old covenant, Paul writes (Rom. 5.20) that in the salvation history of the Old Testament the law 'came in'. The apostle rightly sensed that commandments and laws played no part at the beginning of the history narrated among his people – the history between the one God and the men and women he had created. But he still assumes that the law already 'came between' with Moses, and had from that time on been of essential significance for the relationship to God. In reality it was only much later that the law became of decisive significance; and even then this did not happen overnight. It was a process lasting many centuries. Ezekiel implants the first germ of this trend, in a similar way to Deuteronomy. He does not as yet aim at a religion of the law, but in his social criticism he does feel compelled to point to laws as providing the standard for right conduct.

Up to the catastrophe of 587/6 – which is to say throughout the first five years of his activity – the prophet was incessantly engaged in castigating conditions in his far-off Judaean homeland and in proclaiming to her that her downfall was inescapable. At the same time, however, he deprived his fellow deportees of the hope that a return to their own country would be an improvement. His indictment agrees largely with the reproaches of Jeremiah, who was active in Jerusalem at the same time, although Ezekiel displays a more emphatically priestly judgment about good and evil acts. The temple in Jerusalem and Yahweh's name are being desecrated by idolatry, by sacrifices in unlawful high places, by the burning of children, and by the eating of meat from which the animal's blood has not been completely drained. Sexual misdemeanours also provide grounds for reproach, and here adultery and sexual intercourse with menstruating women are put on the same level. In a third group Ezekiel lists social transgressions, especially financial manipulations designed to exploit poor people and strangers, as well as usury and the seizure of goods for debt. All these things create auras of blood guilt which will result in the destruction of the evildoer's own 'blood', in accordance with the correlation between act and destiny (22.1–4).

But it is not only conditions within the country itself which are in complete disharmony. Foreign policy is being pursued in an irresponsible way, too. The king in Jerusalem, Zedekiah, is criticized particularly bitterly. Whereas Jeremiah shows a certain amount of sympathy for him, the prophet in exile sees Zedekiah as 'pierced through with wickedness . . . whose day has come, the time of your final punishment' (21.25). For through his rebellion Zedekiah has broken his oath of fealty towards his Babylonian overlord, and this oath was sworn before Yahweh. So not only has he broken the pact with the Babylonians; he has also broken Yahweh's oath and covenant, thereby breaking away from the realities of that covenant. Yahweh, the lord of the covenant, will therefore bring him to Babylon and there judge his unfaithfulness (17.19–21).

4.2.2 Ḥuqqōt and mišpāṭīm. In his criticism of the king, it is the broken oath which Ezekiel denounces as a flagrant violation of the all-embracing order of the covenant. Similarly, the offences of the people of Jerusalem are judged against the just ordinances (*mišpāṭīm*) which Yahweh had once established or wanted to call into being through the edicts of his word. Ezekiel goes beyond any specific accusations, again and again attacking the infringement of God's decrees and just ordinances. The same edicts which the people are violating so culpably will become the basis for Yahweh's impending, forcible intervention.

This brings a new complex of arguments into prophecy, into which we must look more closely.

The symbolic game about the siege and starvation of Jerusalem contains another prophecy, as well as the interpretative one we have already discussed. This second prophecy was added later, either by the prophet himself or by the editorial hand of a pupil. It no longer talks in terms of mythical powers like forces of anger, or a huge invisible sword. Instead it reveals another metahistorical factor:

A The matter is thus: you behave more anarchically (*hmn*) than the nations round about you.
   You have not walked in my *statutes* (*ḥuqqōt*).
   You have not *given effect* (*'āśā*) to my *just ordinances* (*mišpāṭīm*).
   Even to the *just ordinances* of the nations that are round about you, you have not *given effect*.

B Therefore, so has the Almighty Lord Yahweh spoken:
   Behold, I will attack you . . .
   And in the midst of you I will *give effect* to the *just ordinances* in the sight of the nation:
   I will *effect* in you what I have never yet *effected* and what I will never more *effect* in this way . . .
   I will *give effect* to judgments (*šepeṭ*) on you, and scatter the whole remnant of you to the winds (5.7–10).

The keywords used here are 'statutes' and 'just ordinances', which are a pair of legal concepts. This pair is used twelve times after this passage, and serves as a general key to an understanding of the catastrophe which is about to descend inexorably on Israel. In Ezekiel's opinion, these traditional rules show clearly whether someone is or is not living as *ṣaddīq*, which means acting in faithfulness to the community and being potentially destined for salvation (18.9; 17.21f.). The two linked concepts do not mean the same thing. *ḥuqqōt* is always associated with the human duty of 'walking in them' (*hlk*). These are therefore already given paths which a person can certainly leave, to his own detriment, but which he himself can do nothing to shape. Keeping to these paths is expected to be so much a matter of course that a positive action-destiny correlation is apparently not even called into existence. Jeremiah had assigned natural laws (*ḥuqqīm*, masc.) to this category; and the same will have been true of Ezekiel, although he gives us no direct evidence of the fact. He does at all events see the institutions of the cult as falling under this heading. These do not originate in human choice, and the form they take can hardly be judged by purely rational criteria. The ceremonies for the consecration of an altar (43.18) and the daily sacrifice (46.14) both belong to the category of *ḥuqqōt. mišpāṭīm,* on the other hand, are actual deeds which have to be performed by people, or which 'have to be heeded and given expression to' (*šmr* and *'āsā*). These are therefore regulations, for every day particularly, which are supposed to be observed and the performance of which communicates an aura of salvation to the doer. But this does not exhaust the full meaning of the word. *Mišpāṭ* (the singular form) is one of the most difficult concepts in the Hebrew vocabulary. Its many shades of meaning cannot be conveyed by any one modern word. (For a further discussion of its significance, cf. Vol. I, section 4.5.2.) It comprises:

(*a*) The unassailed, healthful existence of a person, group or institution (e.g. the rooms of the temple, 42.11), in which the bearer of *mišpāṭ* can live in *šālōm,* fulfilling his social role, and where he is completely accepted by the human community which sustains him. A *mišpāṭ* like this is never statically existent, once and for all. It has continually to be renewed through the person's own behaviour, as well as through the assent of the community. The expression is essentially positive in content; but Ezekiel occasionally uses it analogously for some evil way of life which has become customary and which the community has to eliminate: he talks about the *mišpāṭ* of the adulteress and the murderess (16.38; cf. 7.23).

(*b*) An *action* to support or restore the *mišpāṭ* condition of other people is called *mišpāṭ,* too. In this sense the word is also associated in Ezekiel with the duty to be faithful to the community (*ṣedāqā;* 18.5–9). This duty cannot be summed up in precisely formulated tenets.

(*c*) *Judicial proceedings* count as *mišpāṭ* (19.9, 22; Deut. 25.1), because they are to a marked degree an action designed to fulfil the correlation between act and destiny in both the plaintiff and the accused. They therefore restore *mišpāṭ* as a condition or state.

(*d*) In the plural the word means precisely formulated *casuistic legal edicts* deriving from Yahweh (Ex. 21.1). They regulate procedural and political acts which are designed to guard the *mišpāṭ* of both the national community and its individual members. By Ezekiel's time, the distinctions between casuistic law for 'the community in the gate' and sacral apodictic law (cf. 1.1.3) had long since disappeared. Where the prophet lists a number of *mišpāṭīm,* he is presenting what was originally an apodictic series in the casuistic framework: 'A man, if he does this or that . . . ' (ch. 18).[23]

(*e*) The person who rejects the principles of Yahweh's *mišpāṭīm* strays into the aura of an abominable act (*tō'ēbā*). Through his rejection he compels God to give realization to his *mišpāṭīm* all by himself. This God does in a demonstratively world-wide act of divine 'judgment' (5.7–10). Then he judges (*špṭ,* 16.38; 18.30) the deviators according to their own hollow *mišpāṭîm* (7.27), completing their evil path (39.21) in order to make the way free for a new, better *mišpāṭ* on earth.

(*f*) Doing *mišpāṭ* presupposes *knowledge*. Because they are designed to make it possible for human beings to live together without conflict, *mišpāṭîm* should manifestly make sense; there is nothing irrational about them. Indeed reason (*lēb*) is actually required if *mišpāṭîm* are to be realized. But because the *lēb* of Ezekiel's contemporaries is confused, the people have become incapable of realizing *mišpāṭ*. So in the eschatological turn of events, Yahweh will first of all give the Israelites a new *lēb* and a new *rūᵃḥ*. Then they will at last walk in *ḥuqqōt* and perform Yahweh's *mišpāṭ* (11.20; 36.27; 37.24). Only after that will a new covenant between God and people become possible.

Although he is a priest, Ezekiel no longer shows any signs of maintaining the sacramental mediation of the capacity for doing good which is still at the root of the idea of *mišpāṭ* and *ṣᵉdāqā* in Amos and Isaiah. Instead, another idea comes to the fore: the essential part played by language in the relationship to God. There is no longer any talk about the divine *ṣedeq* in Ezekiel, and all the words connected with the royal predicates of Yahweh recede completely into the background. Instead, enunciated words of God are in the forefront of religious interest. However, these words of God do not touch on any commandments about the conduct of life which are in themselves new in kind. What are presented as divine edicts have nothing to do with a catalogue of the virtues required for individual salvation; nor do they offer instructions as to how to acquire particular religious merit. What Ezekiel appeals to might rather be called the common law of past centuries, which the exiled community has now gathered together in the form of set principles. Ezekiel himself sometimes formulates *mišpāṭîm*, but his intention in doing so is merely to reduce to a common denominator what ought to have been a matter of course from time immemorial (14.13–20). In cases of conflict, *mišpāṭîm* clarify what it means to act in accordance with the community between God and human beings, and the community of men and women with one another. They also initiate a favourable correlation between action and destiny. God has communicated these *mišpāṭîm* so that through them men and women may find life (18.9, 22). Every nation possesses its own *mišpāṭ*, and as a rule the nations act accordingly, because this is the reasonable thing to do. How much more should Israel be obedient to its just order, which is better than that of the other nations! Yet for some mysterious reason Yahweh's own people despises this way. They are so anarchistic in their attitude that they do not even fulfil the rough and ready *mišpāṭîm* of their neighbours (5.7).

4.2.3 Turning religion into law? Christian theologians – particularly Protestant ones – have made a practice of lamenting that with the exilic period, by way of Ezekiel and Deuteronomy, the observance of divine laws became the essential characteristic of Israelite religion. They believe that here a fatal path was chosen – one leading to the Jewish righteousness of works with which Jesus and Paul had later to wage a life-and-death struggle. Here, they maintain, is the beginning of the legalism which has always been, and still is, in strict opposition to faith and Christian liberty. Ezekiel is considered to be 'the father of Judaism'; and K. Budde, to take one example, links this assumption with the observation: 'We cannot fail to note a severe religious retrogression here. Amos, Isaiah and Jeremiah had all perceived that God is spirit and desires to be worshipped in the spirit . . . But in the case of Ezekiel . . . stress lies on the correctness and purity of religious practice, on the *opus operatum* of an external fulfilment of the law.'[24] Is this an accurate judgment? Or do the conditions of the exilic period force us to arrive at a different historical evaluation?

(a) Sociologically, it was at that time essential to establish rules of behaviour, if Israel as a nation and a community of the covenant was to retain its identity, and if the fundamental principles of earlier Israelite ethics were to be preserved. Clan, tribe and monarchy – the 'natural' forms of community – had broken down under the strains and consequences of war. As a result the spontaneous feeling of solidarity lacked clear points of reference for behaviour which would bring about salvation and be in accordance with the nature and needs of the community. There was danger that arbitrary group interests would be put forward as *ṣedāqā*, opening the door wide to corruption and nepotism. The anthropological necessity of law becomes the subject for reflection as soon as a social order with a long tradition begins to crumble. We see this 1,200 years earlier under the first ancient Babylonian dynasty, when the Code of Hammurabi came into existence; and we find it again, 150 years later, in Greece, when Plato and the Sophists quarrelled about the validity of the *nomos*. Ezekiel does not stress the law in order to crush the liberty of men and women; his aim is to save the freedom of them all if possible. (About the same time, in Iran, Zoroaster began to proclaim the True Law, *asha,* as divine goal, while in India Buddha started to 'turn the Wheel of Law or Righteousness', *dhamma.* Are these the general constellations of a particular hour of world history?)

(b) There is no trace of any heteronomous compulsion in the appeal to the law. Although Ezekiel is certainly not thinking of a natural law, innate in all human beings, he does assume as a matter of course that the human *reason (lēb)* can grasp the point of the divine law, and accept that its function is to promote life.

(c) The determining function of laws as Ezekiel sees them is not to lay down gradated punishments for the people who break them; nor do laws talk about the retaliation that falls on the guilty person from some outside source. What they do is to stress *the alternative of life or death.* The person who gives effect to *mišpāṭ* creates the room to live for himself and his society. We are told of the person who fails that 'he shall surely die' *(mōt yūmāt* – death will fetch him), and his blood – the quintessence of serious transgression – will be upon his own head (18.13 and frequently elsewhere). The new stress on just divine ordinances therefore by no means contradicts the ancient traditional view of the spheres of action which bring about personal destiny. The new emphasis aims to give a clearer explanation than was previously possible of the way this correlation works.

(d) Yahweh is preparing *to judge (špṭ)* Israel and the nations. It is in Ezekiel for the first time that this word is emphatically used as a metahistorical term. People will be judged according to their ways, and their abominable deeds will react on themselves (7.3, 8; cf. 16.18; 18.30). Does this mean that the prophet is translating the biblical understanding of God into juridical categories for the first time? But in Ezekiel's view God's intervention has nothing forensic about it. There are no 'court proceedings' with plaintiff and judge. Nor does God intervene mainly in order to punish the wicked. The purpose of his intervention is to purify the earth from spheres of evil deeds, and to make a new, unburdened human existence possible. When Ezekiel talks about the impending divine judgment, he is already thinking about a new state of salvation beyond the catastrophe (20.36). Judgment means the contingent enforcement of just ordinances (e.g., 5.7–10), which God had long since infused into Israelite history but which hitherto had not really been fulfilled. Yahweh is retrieving what men and women have neglected. But he does so only in order that other people may pick up the *mišpāṭîm* afterwards, and lay active hold on them. So laws are only part of a great metahistorical cohesion of activity which – as a cross-section of history – looks more or less as follows:

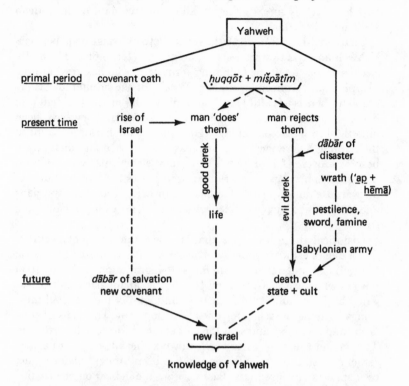

The foundation is a primal speech event which sets salvation history in motion. When, later, Israel is required to act, it brings about the history of doom. God reacts with words which increasingly prevail in the external world. The great final death is still to come; but so is the renewal of Israel in an eschatological future.

The knowledge of Yahweh is therefore the final goal of history.

But what kind of knowledge is this? And how can it be communicated by any kind of history?

4.3 The crisis of history and the eschatological knowledge of Yahweh

4.3.1 Forfeited salvation history. Ezekiel only occasionally denounces the failure of his listeners, i.e. the community of the exiled people. He more usually criticizes the failure of the people who have remained in the home country. However, the indications of situation in his prophecies often turn into historical flashbacks, and stress a failure which can be shown to go back generations. The essential metahistorical turning points in national history are concentrated in chs. 16, 20 and 23, telescoped in order to show the inescapability of the cata-

strophe which is surely going to fall on the remnant of the Judean
state in the homeland.

Chapters 16 and 23 pick up the concept of a marriage bond between
Yahweh and the two sections of the people (Jer. 3.6ff.). In ch. 16,
Ezekiel writes about the foundling Jerusalem, who has grown into a
nymphomaniac queen; while ch. 23 tells of the adulterous sisters
Oholah ('hers is a [cultic] tent') and Oholibah ('my [cultic] tent is in
her'), these sisters being Samaria and Jerusalem. They have been
unfaithful from the beginning. 'They played the harlot in Egypt in
their youth. There they let their breasts be touched and their virgin
bosoms squeezed.' Jerusalem's behaviour is particularly scandalous.
She spreads her legs for every man who passes by. Even pictures of
men arouse an unquenchable passion in her. Egyptians, Assyrians
and Chaldeans all have to sleep with her, and are even paid for doing
so.

Historical allegories of this kind are the summing-up of a century
and a half of critical prophecy. The sexual rites criticized by Hosea;
the political and religious attempts at ingratiation with the great
powers which were attacked by Isaiah; the fateful astral cults casti-
gated by Jeremiah – seen from the standpoint of the exile, all these
things lie along the self-same line of development. The transgression
is one and the same, and so is the lack of metahistorical discernment.
The foreign rule which has borne down so heavily on both parts of
Israel ever since the eighth century has been brought about by her
own spheres of wickedness. Passing from the indication of situation
to the prediction, the prophet proclaims a divine act of judgment
(*šāpaṭ*). Yahweh lets the way Israel has chosen recoil on her own head
(16.43); he lets the content of evil auras vent itself on the perpetrators
of the deeds. In this way the prostitute Jerusalem becomes fair game
for all. Her former lovers are called together; they tear her clothes and
jewels off her, strip her naked, rob her of her children, burn her houses,
and make her the 'blood guilt' which in secret she has long since
become. They consummate in her the divine wrath and zeal, enforcing
on her the *mišpāṭ* for adulteresses and murderesses (16.38; 23.45). In
the end the woman is left naked and bare, as she was at the beginning.
The nation's history has failed to achieve its goal. Does this mean that
it was superfluous? Not entirely. The end makes that clear: 'You shall
know that I am Yahweh' (23.48f.).

The survey of the abortive history of the covenant in ch. 20 presents
the same picture, this time without any allegory. Beginning with the
exodus, attention is drawn to the communication of God's laws to
Israel. The purpose of this communication was to elucidate Yahweh's
initial revelation of himself, after the community of the covenant had

been promised in the foundation oath: 'I, Yahweh, am your God.' Soon the people rebel, refusing to see that the purpose of the divine edicts is to further life. Yahweh thereupon reflects whether he will pour out his wrath and anger upon Israel. But he does not do so, because he does not wish to bring his name into disrepute before the nations. But even then he already resolves upon the exile, and that one day Israel shall be scattered among the nations. In addition, he communicates to the people *'ḥuqqīm* that were not good, and harmful *mišpāṭīm'*, so that Israel might defile herself by sacrificing her first-born (or perhaps by sacrificing the first-born of animals – does Ezekiel already view this kind of sacrifice as senseless?). In spite of this marred relationship, God gives the people the land which becomes their home. The giver is ill-repaid. For the increased potentialities of the cultivated lands lead the people to practise idolatry on every hill and beneath every leafy tree, while they neglect their relationship with Yahweh. Again Yahweh swears an oath. What is left of Israel shall be fetched out of every corner of every land and driven into the wilderness of the nations, 'and there I will dispute with you face to face'. The people who are refractory will be eliminated, and a remnant will be led into the bond of the covenant once more. This remnant will worship Yahweh, and Yahweh alone, on the holy hill in Jerusalem. 'And you shall know that I [am] Yahweh; when I deal with you for my name's sake, not according to your evil ways' (20.44).

It is hard to find any document in the literature of the world which presents the history of its own people so unfavourably, as a history of guilt. Israel is described as an assembly of human beings who from the very beginning foolishly and obstinately reject their own salvation. It is a people which never fulfils the wise and intelligible laws of its God, and which has behaved worse then all the other nations on earth; for these other nations have at least observed their own *mišpāṭīm*, inadequate though these are.

Here Ezekiel is unmistakably picking up the view of history shared by the critical prophets as a whole – history as a line broken in two places: salvation history at the beginning is followed by a history of increasing degeneracy, and then, in the end, by a better, eschatological salvation history (cf. Vol. I, pp. 139f.). At the beginning Jerusalem lay there naked. At the end it will be the same. Both times Yahweh comes to the rescue (16.7, 39, cf. 59ff.). At the beginning Yahweh confers a covenant. At the end the people will be received into the covenant once more. In spite of this, for Ezekiel history as a whole takes a more strictly linear course than it did for earlier prophets. It no longer displays the sharp breaks which are otherwise characteristic of the prophetic picture. Salvation and disaster run parallel to one

another from the very beginning. What emerges is what von Rad calls
'a travesty of salvation history'. To talk about Israel's history means
talking about something abominable, *tō'ēbā* (16.2; 20.4). *Tō'ēbā* is an
infringement of the holy, which does not merely evoke a sphere
pregnant with disaster round the perpetrator of the deed, but at the
same time attacks God personally and challenges him directly. The
prophet already 'judges' simply by presenting history as a history that
has miscarried. He convicts the guilty, which means the community
to which he is none the less inseparably bound. By virtue of the
effective *dābār* which he proclaims, he sets in motion the stone which
finally buries the broken pieces of wasted historical opportunities
(20.4; 22.2).

4.3.2. 'I, Yahweh'. Although the history of the covenant has miscarried,
Yahweh has been able to prevent one thing: the total desecration of
his name. Because his name has been linked with Israel ever since the
Egyptian period, he has refrained from immediately pouring out his
annihilating wrath on this people (20.9, 22 [39]). For the sake of his
name, Israel will rise anew at the eschatological end (20.44). In
historical interpretations of this kind, Ezekiel shows a jealous zeal for
the majesty of his God which is reminiscent of a Calvinist fighting for
the absolute glory of God, beyond any kind of human salvation. What
is the significance of the Name?

The ancient East was never inclined to ask, like Shakespeare's
Juliet, 'What's in a name?' On the contrary, the name was viewed as
an intrinsic part of the person who bore it. To proclaim the name
means to evoke its efficacy. (That is why the commandment not to
misuse Yahweh's name is so important.) But in Ezekiel's case it is not
the name itself which is the point at issue; it is the estimate in which
it is held, and the position assigned to it by human beings. The pointer
to the Name as the divine principle guiding events in history cannot
be separated from the formula according to which men and women
will one day 'know that I [am] Yahweh'. The phrase occurs 72 times,
generally at the close of a prophecy. The general sense is that the
eschatological turn of events will compel the people involved to
recognize that Yahweh has brought it about. History therefore
becomes a proof of God – though admittedly it is only at the end of
history that this emerges. W. Zimmerli, who has gone into the formula
in detail, explains it as 'God's self-introduction'. But it is questionable
whether this is sufficient. Israel had long known that its God was
called Yahweh. In Babylon, Ezekiel was for the most part surrounded
by people who spoke Aramaic; and in Aramaic (unlike Hebrew) the
word 'Yahweh' has a quite precise meaning: 'I will call into being'

(causative) or 'I am present/am coming into being' (qal). This would suggest that Ezekiel associates a meaning of this kind with the markedly stressed 'I, Yahweh' (though this does not necessarily imply that that was the original meaning of the name). Knowing that Yahweh *is* means recognizing him as the One who, in any event, will ultimately prevail. The act of human knowledge does not merely imply theoretical insight. It involves modified practical behaviour as well; for the Hebrew word for knowing, *yāda'*, does not mean objective and detached observation. It means arriving at an understanding of something through use and association.[25] In Ezekiel, this knowledge does not become the common property of eschatological Israel alone. It is given to the other nations as well (36.36; on the knowledge of God, cf. Vol. I, section 5.5).

4.4 The individualization of the correlation between act and destiny

Chapter 18 begins by quoting a sarcastic proverb which went the rounds among the Israelites after the downfall of the state (v. 2);

> The fathers have eaten sour grapes and the children's teeth are set on edge.

In plain language this means that the exilic generation has to pay the price for what their ancestors have done. In earlier times a conclusion of this kind would not have seemed surprising to anyone in Israel. It was still considered a matter of course that children were simply a continuation of their parents' existence, and that they therefore carried on the link between action and destiny in their family (cf. the 'motive' clause in the Decalogue: 'For I visit . . . to the third and fourth generation', Ex. 20.5). Even the Deuteronomistic History (Joshua to II Kings), which was written at the time of Ezekiel in the home country, still detects the continuing influence of fateful spheres of action as it looks down through past ages. The Deuteronomists see this as the only way of interpreting the course of history, and its end in the catastrophe of the exile. But the bitter *māšāl* which Ezekiel quotes is a rebellion against this kind of logic. The old notions of community have broken down. The deported people have been torn out of their local communities and their clan associations, while those left behind in the homeland are living under conditions of oppression. These people impeach God. They find it outrageous and unjust that later generations should have to bear the misdeeds of their fathers. We discovered the first stirrings of an individual awareness in Jeremiah, in the Confessions; now the same awareness makes itself felt here, in non-prophetic circles.

Ezekiel by no means brushes aside this viewpoint as lack of faith.

On the contrary, in a sense he and his God are on the side of the inward rebels. With a solemn oath, Yahweh makes Ezekiel proclaim (18.3f.):

> As I live . . . this proverb shall no more be used by you in Israel. For all vital power (*nepeš*) is (directly) mine. Like the vital power of the father, so the vital power of the son. The vital power that is sinful, that alone will die.

According to these verses, it is impossible for auras of action to spring from one individual to another. So it is out of the question for salvation or disaster caused by any individual agent to radiate to the group. However, the temporal reference of the oath is not perfectly clear. Is Ezekiel (like Jer. 31.29) referring to an eschatological future, with different anthropological conditions? Or is he thinking of his fellow exiles? Does he mean that anyone who has personally tasted the bitterness of the annihilating stroke of 597 no longer needs to accept responsibility for the fate of the group? Or is this the expression of a general law – that the father has never had to answer for the sins of the son, or vice versa? This last interpretation can probably be excluded: it would not only be inconsistent with the Hebrew tenses used; it would also contradict everything that Ezekiel had previously expounded in his pictures of history.

Where individuals are concerned, the prophet still clings to the prolongation of human acts through a corresponding personal destiny. In the long run, the wicked man is going to die. He will then die in his guilt and sin (*'āwōn/ḥaṭṭā't*, 18.17f.; 24.26). The sphere of disaster will have its effect in what it breeds. Conversely, the righteous man will arrive at life in his *ṣᵉdāqā*. The *ṣaddīq*'s faithfulness to the community 'will come into being' upon him – that is to say, it will be translated into life, just as the evil deed of the *rāšā'* will 'come into being' upon him too, so that he dies.

It is also a matter of course that Yahweh, too, is at work in every correlation between act and destiny. The 'day' of consummation comes about for the doer of the deed when Yahweh 'remembers' his spheres of action. Remembering, *zākar*, is not merely a mental act. It is also an act of will which takes some material, outward form. Moreover Yahweh himself will be a cause of stumbling (*mikšōl*) for evil-doers. The auras of their sin come into conflict with his holiness (which is multivolipresent on earth; cf. Vol. I, section 4.9.2), and are thereby transformed into the corresponding destiny. Yahweh's way (*derek*) comprehends every human path, and the correspondence between act and destiny which prevails there (18.25ff.).

God sums up every human life and then makes his decision, with the aim of establishing orderly conditions on earth. Deciding means *šāpaṭ*, which is generally translated as 'judge': 'Therefore I will judge you, everyone according to his ways' (18.30). God's 'judgment' is the same proceeding which causes a wicked person to die in his sins; that person is harnessed to the sphere of his sin once and for all, as it were. In the same way, a *ṣaddīq*, in his faithfulness to the community, achieves life. So judging does not mean dealing out rewards and punishments, in the sense of some eternal requital which could be separated from a person's way of life and the aura of his personality. God is a judge only in the sense that he brings to light whatever already invisibly characterizes a person's nature.

However, God's way is not merely a reaction to the ways of men and women. It is the doing of *ṣᵉdāqā* and *mišpāṭ* which determines what a good human *derek* is. But the elucidation of what these terms actually mean is to be found in an ancient, traditional series of commandments (18.5ff.).[25] Thus legal instructions become the standard for conduct, this conduct in its turn being understood as an inseparable cohesion between act and personal destiny. The commandments are therefore part of the divine way.

What is new is not merely the reference to laws, but also the individual limitation of the correspondence between act and destiny. This limitation cannot be found in Israel at any earlier period. The prophet tests against individual cases what he has discovered as being the standard for God's future behaviour. The son neither has to carry the load of his father's sins, nor is he able to inherit his father's faithfulness to the community. In his eagerness to confute any notion of collective guilt, Ezekiel even goes so far as to divide up a single life into different parts. 'The wicked man, as soon as he turns away from all his sins . . . keeps all my statutes and does what is lawful and right (*ḥuqqōt, mišpāṭ*), he shall surely live; he shall not die' (18.21). And the reverse is true as well.

The people addressed are to be wooed to repentance (*šūb*): that is the motive underlying the casuistic dissection and the unequivocal limitation of the link between action and destiny. For the first time in prophecy, the individual is urged to repent. And this repentance is linked with a promise (cf. 14.12ff.; 33). Accordingly Ezekiel sees the care of every individual soul as his responsibility. It is surely not by chance that this point of view should emerge for the first time within the limited scope of an exiled community (3.16ff.). Chapter 18 closes with an invitation:

Repent, let yourselves be turned from all your rebellions . . . Get yourselves a new reason (*lēb*) and a new spirit (*rūᵃḥ*)! Why will you die, O house of Israel? For I have no pleasure in the death of those given over to death, murmurs Yahweh, the almighty God.

How is this radical individualization to be judged? It had its effect in the years that followed, influencing for example the Chronicler's History. But it is hardly ever articulated with the rigour we find here. That is all too understandable. It may seem right and just that each individual alone should bear the fruits of what he does; but none the less, general human experience tells us that children also have to suffer when their parents suffer. The ties between the generations, and collective liability, cannot be entirely abrogated, even in a nation. (We only have to remember, for example, the intensive discussion that went on after 1945 about the collective guilt of all Germans; or today's anxiety about the burdens laid on future generations by our present treatment of the environment.) If we take this everyday experience into account, does not Ezekiel go too far? (The lack of justice which individual thinking people sense when they are faced with the web of collective guilt was later to lead Old Testament apocalyptic to link an individual connection between act and destiny with the expectation of a resurrection of the dead. That is to say, apocalyptic prolonged into an eternal life the link between the deed and its personal outcome.)

But the individual aspect is not the only angle from which Ezekiel views the future. He has the restoration of his people just as much at heart, if not more.

4.5 Eschatology, a transformed humanity, the new covenant and a social revolution

4.5.1 The resurgence of Israel and the renewal of the covenant.

In the twelfth year of our exile, in the tenth month, on the fifth day of the month, a man who had escaped from Jerusalem came to me and said, 'The city has fallen' (33.21).

At this point the Book of Ezekiel begins a series of proclamations centring on the coming era of salvation instead of on doom, as hitherto. The prophet senses that the downfall of Jerusalem has brought about a decisive turn of events. Up to now his task has been to accelerate the downfall through the *dābār*. But it is now time to proclaim a *dābār* which predicts and provokes a radical change to better things. In what he says he almost entirely ignores the level of military affairs and foreign policy. He certainly announces that Israel is going to be liberated from foreign rule; but how it is going to happen, and why

Babylon is going to fall, remains unsaid. What he promises is a reunion of the two parts of the nation, Israel and Judah, after the people who were once deported have returned to Palestine.

In a splendid vision (ch. 37), the prophet sees a valley full of dry bones. At the command of the *dābār*, these bones come together again and cover themselves with flesh, blood-vessels and skin. As the wind of the Spirit is breathed into them, they finally come to life again. The meaning is explained to him: 'Son of man, these bones are the whole house of Israel . . . you shall know that I [am] because I open your graves.'

The passage was later seen as a promise of the resurrection of the dead. But this is not what the prophet himself means. His intention is merely to proclaim the 'resurrection' of his people as 'total self'. This is in itself the miracle of miracles, made possible by a uniquely extraordinary intervention of the divine life-giving wind of the Spirit in history.

The book has already explained that Israel's previous shepherds, the kings, have proved themselves incapable, and will not return (ch. 34). Instead, David – the first and best of the kings, according to the Jerusalem view – is going to be raised again (34.23, *hēqīm*, later an expression for resurrection, and perhaps already so here, with reference to an individual man of God?). A monarchical constitution is therefore not totally renounced. But Ezekiel avoids applying the word 'king' (*melek*) to the future ruler, merely calling him shepherd and *nāsī'*, a man 'lifted out' of the ruck of the people. *Nāsī'* was a title used in the prenational period by the heads of tribes. It may perhaps have characterized the ruling person as being the embodiment of the corporate personality of the whole people. The divine law will still provide the guideline for faithfulness to the community in this coming era too – indeed it will really prevail for the first time. The returning David, as shepherd of all, will ensure that 'they shall follow my ordinances and preserve my statutes (*ḥuqqōt*) and perform them' (37.24). He will probably bring this about, not through any externally coercive methods but through his example, which will have an evocative influence.

Both passages which talk about the returning David also prophesy that on his accession to power a new covenant will be made between Yahweh and Israel (and that a new temple will then be built in Jerusalem, 37.26).

> I will make for them a covenant of salvation
>   and banish wicked beasts from the earth . . .

I will give them and those round them my hill (Zion) as [a source
      of] blessing
   and will send down the rain in due season . . .
The tree of the field shall yield its fruit
   and the ground shall yield its increase.
They shall live secure on their land
   and shall know that I [am] Yahweh.
By breaking the cords of their yoke
   I will deliver them from those who enslaved them . . .
And they shall know that I [am] Yahweh, their God with them.
   and that they are my people, the house of Israel (34.25–30).

The conviction that Yahweh's covenant with Israel has been broken
and requires a fundamental renewal, picks up statements made by
Hosea (2.14ff.) and Jeremiah (31.31–34, and frequently elsewhere).
Hosea already suggested that a better – and at all events more effective
– covenant in the future will be closely linked with the increased
fertility of the soil. But Ezekiel also shares Jeremiah's hope that the
characteristics of men and women themselves would be remoulded.
For the fruitful earth only opens itself for the person who acts in
accordance with the interests of the community, thereby creating for
himself the corresponding auras of action. The capacity for this has
hitherto been insufficient among the Israelites.

I will sanctify my name, my great name,
   which among the nations has been by you profaned . . .
I will take you out from among the nations
   . . . and bring you into your own land.
I will sprinkle clean water upon you,
   and you shall be cleansed from all your uncleanness . . .
A new heart (*lēb*) I will give you,
   so that I may put a new wind of the spirit (*rūᵃḥ*) within you.
I will take out of your body the petrified heart (*lēb*)
   and give you a heart of flesh,
   so that I may put the wind of my spirit within you.
I will cause you to walk in my statutes,
   and preserve my ordinances of salvation and perform them.
You shall become to me my people
   so that I shall become to you your God (*ᵉlōhīm*) (36.23–28).

The passage ends with what is known as the covenant formula. A
statement of this kind frequently appears in association with a
covenant as a statement of its purpose. Through the extraordinary
institution of the *bᵉrīt*, both partners arrive at their 'identity' or

authenticity. Yahweh is not truly a God until he is surrounded by a people faithful to him. And Israel cannot really call itself a people as long as it is not continually and entirely governed by the divine power which guarantees its continuance and solidarity as a people, beyond any injury it can suffer.

The new covenant does not merely give the human partner a new relationship to law and duty. It actually changes his *lēb*. This time I have retained the metaphor 'heart' in the translation, because otherwise the image is obscure – even though, in our modern language, 'heart' can lead to the misunderstanding that what is meant is feeling rather than consciousness. At the decisive moment of her history, Israel's calcified heart will be cut out, as if by an operation, and a supple, pliable heart will be implanted instead (cf. 11.19). Underlying this image of a 'heart transplant' is Ezekiel's view that, as the history of doom has progressed, the Israelites as human beings have increasingly strayed into a *cul de sac*. They have become so entangled in the spheres of their misdeeds that escape is no longer possible (cf. 24.6ff.; 35.6; 36.18). More: the misdeeds recoil on those responsible for them to such an extent that their capacity for discernment has become increasingly obscured. The very first vision on the Chebar canal reveals to the prophet that his people has degenerated into 'the house of rebellion' (*bēt mᵉrî*); this term is repeated twelve times. The rebellion is directed against Yahweh's ordinances, and exceeds every conceivable rejection of those ordinances by non-Israelite nations (12.16). The revolt shows itself in rigidly obdurate behaviour, which is the expression of a hardened or stubborn *lēb* that no longer allows world history to be discerned for what it is. At the same time the people affected let the 'trashy things' (*gillūlîm*) of idols rise up in their *lēb;* and this also affects their capacity for discernment (11.21; 20.16). The concept of a degenerate reason is therefore a theme that permeates Ezekiel's anthropology. And it is just this degeneracy which will be remedied in the eschaton. Unfortunately the prophet does not explain more precisely how he thinks this is going to happen – perhaps sacramentally through a covenant sacrifice?

'Why did not Yahweh give the Israelites the proper heart and his Spirit from the very beginning, so that the whole 'defilement' was impossible?' asks Duhm derisively.[27] The question shows how little even so notable a scholar knows how to allow for prophetic monanthropology. None of the prophets are interested in metaphysical questions about ultimate and abiding causes. What they are concerned with is metahistorical reflection about the reasons for the evil prevailing at the present moment. Who is responsible for the shattered conditions in the home country, and for the misery of the men and women

who have been deported? Since conditions have meanwhile become
unendurable (which had not always been the case) the prophet feels
bound to suppose that the capacity for perception and reason among
the people responsible has continued to degenerate. And by the people
responsible he does not mean the Babylonians. Ezekiel does not utter
a single word against them. Nor is it Yahweh. It is true that the
prophet fights passionately for the uniqueness of his God and the
divine power that moulds history. But the idea of a primordial creation
ex nihilo, without any preconditions, is not one of the premises of his
monotheism. On the contrary, God's creation is still in the process of
becoming. It is establishing itself against resistance, just as at the
beginning it prevailed against the sea of chaos and the darkness (Gen.
1; 2).

We can talk about monotheism here only if in our thinking we
simultaneously add 'monoanthropism' as a complementary concept.
For it is human beings who are primarily responsible for earthly
events. They are certainly comprehended and embraced by the God
who is conceived of in monotheistic terms; but not in any deterministic
sense. Man's ability to devise evil is in no way excluded. It is true that
Yahweh advances victoriously, impelling his *derek* onwards and
outstripping all the ways of human beings. According to Ezekiel's
hope, Yahweh's advance is so inexorable that he will one day remake
man's 'reasonable nature', providing him with a changed modality of
being which will essentially diminish the probability of his falling a
victim to evil, sin and unreasonable behaviour.

4.5.2 The draft constitution. The Book of Ezekiel ends (chs. 40–48) with
a series of visions in which the prophet – after a new 'journey through
the air' to Jerusalem – sees the fundamental features of a reunited
Israel. The people who have been raised up in the home country will
take their bearings from Zion, their cultic place. An accompanying
angel tells the prophet the precise measurements for the layout of the
sanctuary that is to be built there. These instructions also delineate
the ordinances for a cult which in the future will succeed in establishing
and guaranteeing for ever the link between man and God. At the
centre stands the altar, the place of purification and atonement,
through the blood of an animal. This will finally eliminate the
evil aura of national history, with its misdeed-disaster correlation.
Significantly enough, atonement can only take place after the *kābōd*,
the glory of Yahweh, has come back from the east to the Zion it had
deserted before the destruction of the sanctuary (chs. 8–11). The *kābōd*
now returns, to become 'the place of my throne and the place of the
soles of my feet, where I will dwell in the midst of the people of Israel

for ever. And the house of Israel shall no more defile my holy name'
(ch. 43).

In a second section (chs. 44–46), three 'estates' – priests, Levites
and princes – are installed in their rights and duties. Like the
Deuteronomic law, the draft aims at a separation of powers at the
head of the nation. In the future there will be two classes of priests.
The 'sons of Zadok' (apparently descendants of the pre-exilic Zion
priests to whom Ezekiel belongs) constitute the first group: they did
not participate in Israel's aberrations (a judgment to which Jeremiah
would hardly have subscribed!), so they will 'stand' before Yahweh,
carrying out the cultic ceremonies which serve to establish direct
contact with the deity. They are to be responsible for instructing the
people with *tōrā*. However, to prevent them from exploiting their
privileged position, they are forbidden to inherit land, and are merely
given a place where they can live. They are to exist solely from cultic
offerings. The Levites are distinguished from 'the sons of Zadok'.
They have participated in Israel's aberrations, and will in future assist
the Zadokites as minor clergy. (We find the twofold division of the
priesthood in the cultic law laid down by the Priestly Writing at about
the same period. The division played an important part in post-exilic
history.)

If this regulation was already a breach with Israelite tradition, the
position of the political leader is changed even more radically. He is
called *nāśī'* – an archaic title dating from the pre-national period. His
competences are even more stringently restricted than the powers of
the king in Deuteronomy (cf. 1.3.3 above). Jurisdiction is not in the
hands of the *nāśī'*; it is to be exercised by the priests (44.24). The very
first sentence in the passage dealing with the new ruler shows how
allergic the prophet is towards the monarchy, and how deeply the evil
role played by the pre-exilic kings sticks in his memory: 'My *nāśī'*s
shall no more oppress my people' (45.8). The buildings of the palace
are no longer to be connected with those of the temple, as they were
in pre-exilic Jerusalem; this earlier arrangement is now strictly
forbidden (43.7f.). Here we have the first indications of a separation
between spiritual and secular power (though a similar trend is already
to be found in Deuteronomy). Apart from the task of apportioning the
land to the different tribes, and standardizing weights and measures,
the *nāśī'*'s main function is to see that offerings are prepared for
the cult in its revived form. As the embodiment of the corporate
personality, he also has to represent the nation as a whole in religious
ceremonies on feast days. Above all, at ceremonies of expiation he has
to concentrate the guilt of the people in his own person, so that it may
then be wiped out by ritual means. The *nāśī'* is therefore a consecrated

person, like the priests. His land, right and left of the land lived in by the Zadokites and Levites, is – like theirs – a cultic oblation given by the people (*tᵉrūmā*).

The future possession of the land plays a decisive part generally in the draft constitution. After the temple and the various offices have been described, Ezekiel sees in his vision a mighty spring of pure water breaking out beneath the threshold of the temple. It flows eastwards and turns the Dead Sea into a fresh-water lake, and the desert surrounding it into fruitful land. So the whole country is guaranteed equal fertility; and this makes it possible to assign each one of the twelve tribes an area in which to settle which is more or less equal in size. Ezekiel's vision divides up Palestine with a tape-measure.

If we compare the plan with the historical areas of tribal settlement (see the maps usually to be found at the back of the Bible) a revolutionary feature emerges. A feeling for a strict equality and social justice makes itself felt which had hitherto been unknown to Israel. Even more clearly than in previous history, it was to be made demonstrably clear that Israel could exist only if it was more or less concentrically constituted round its cultic focus, Jerusalem. But the division of the land was too theoretical – too much a matter of paper-work. It could no more become historical reality than the triple offices could function in everyday, practical terms. And yet – or perhaps for that very reason? – the final chapters of the book became enormously influential, and in the late Israelite period led to continually new plans of an eschatological Jerusalem, such as we still find in the Book of Revelation in the New Testament.

One feature is common to all the prophets. We can see that their predictions of disaster were fulfilled more or less at the time foretold. But the same can hardly ever be said of the prophecies of salvation. Moreover these prophecies of salvation differ from the prophecies of doom in that they are couched in far more marvellous terms. Earlier theologians used to talk here about 'a contraction of the times': what the prophet predicted for the years immediately ahead was, in their view, fulfilled centuries later in Jesus Christ. But this was a dogmatic construction. (Is a just division of the resources of the earth not still one of the tremendous difficulties facing us today? And is not the elimination of forms of rule 'which oppress my people' our problem even now?)

4.5.3 Foreign policy. The land assigned to the resurgent twelve tribes includes the southern part of the present state of Lebanon, as part of Israel's patrimony. But it does not include the Negeb desert south of Kadesh, or the land east of the River Jordan. This means that in the

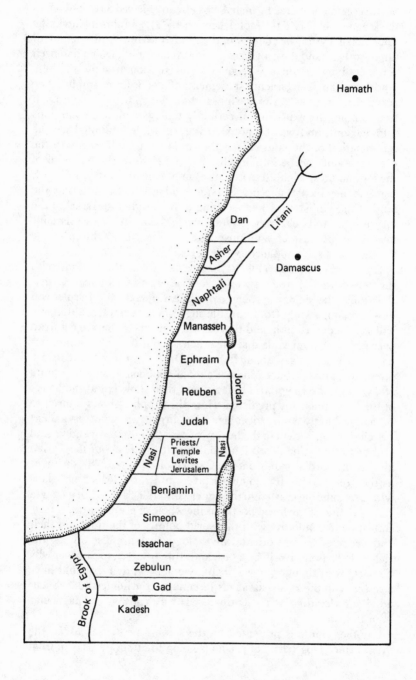

north a region is claimed which Amos already viewed as belonging to
the kingdom of David (cf. Vol. I, section 4.7.3); and this included the
Phoenician Tyre. The country of the Philistines is also incorporated.
On the other hand the provinces in the east and south which had been
conquered by David are renounced, even though some of these
lands were ancient Israelite settlements (Gilead, for example). The
surrender of this territory shows that, in spite of his utopian
programme, the exiled priest certainly took geopolitical conditions
into account, and was by no means an unbridled nationalist. The
renunciation of the land east of the Jordan can be linked with the
oracles about the nations in chs. 25 to 32. Here the downfall of
the Ammonites, Moabites, Edomites and Philistines is prophesied,
because they have rejoiced over Israel's adversity. But it is only the
land of the Philistines which is going to be assigned to Israel in the
future. The land belonging to Israel's neighbours in the east remains
inviolable, because of a promise given to them by Yahweh in the
framework of salvation history (Gen. 19; Deut. 2.4–23).

One further point connects the oracles about the nations with
the constitutional draft. In both cases there is no indication that
Babylonian hegemony is going to disappear. Israel's future ruler will
be a *nāśī'*, not a king. Does this title suggest that complete autonomy
will still be denied him, and that he will continue to be subject to an
overlord? It is noticeable that the oracles about the nations have not
an angry word to say about Babylon. On the contrary, threats are
directed against Nebuchadnezzar's main opponents, the island state
of Tyre and the Egyptian Pharaoh, and their downfall at the hands
of the Babylonians is predicted. Here the prophet shows himself to
be astonishingly knowledgeable. The dirge over Tyre as gallant
merchantman, perfect in the beauty of her appointments, and yet full
of the most cunning deception (ch. 27), the oracle about the Tyrian
king as primordial man from the Garden of Eden (ch. 28), or Egypt
as the great cosmic tree joining heaven and earth, which now falls
with a resounding crash into the underworld (ch. 31) – these passages
contain some of the finest poetry in the whole of prophetic literature.
But in their familiarity with the world politics of the time and their
knowledge of ancient oriental mythology, they are also among the
richest in content. It will be a task for future research to discover why
Ezekiel, even though he was in Babylonian captivity, should have
stressed with the same passion as Jeremiah in the homeland Nebuchadnezzar's legitimacy, as a figure raised up by Yahweh for a particular
hour in history.

Another riddle is presented by the sombre prediction about the
great prince Gog (chs. 38f.), who is going to attack Jerusalem from

the extreme north, with the support of many other nations. This is to happen after the conclusion of the new covenant, and when it is beginning to have its effect, but before the draft constitution has been implemented or the temple rebuilt. A frightful warlike intermezzo, led by a figure who is based on Gyges, the king of Lydia in Asia Minor (a figure known to us from Greek tradition), will interrupt the build-up of the eschatological people of salvation. Gog with his hordes will then be defeated on the mount of Israel, by means of a miraculous divine intervention. The bodies will provide a vast provender for the wild beasts, while the weapons that have been left behind will supply firewood for seven years. Only after that will Jacob's destiny take a final turn for the better. Ezekiel's reason for fearing another interlude of this kind in the future can be found in his commitment to earlier prophecies about the terrible enemy from the north (Jer. 1.13ff.; Joel 2.20). Unlike Jeremiah, Ezekiel is unable to view Babylon as the fulfilment of these prophecies. At the same time the Gog prophecy (which apocalyptic later elaborated; cf. Rev. 20.8f.) still quivers with the secret fear of the continual, unexpected emergence of brutal enemies from the north, a fear cherished for centuries by ancient oriental peoples. Ezekiel's aim is to bring this fear into the open once more, in order to get rid of it once and for all.

4.5.4 The dispute about the term 'eschatology'. For many years, there has been a dispute among biblical scholars as to whether the prophets' outlook on the future can be given the name 'eschatology'. The term originally meant a doctrine about the end of the world and its renewal; and in the context of Christian dogma it means teachings about the Last Judgment and the new creation. There is no need to go into this specialized discussion here.[28] If the word is used to mean a certain continuity – albeit an interrupted one – between final salvation, preceding history and creation at the beginning, the term can certainly be applied to the prophets. If the modern definition of eschatology excludes any continuity between the new age and previous world history, then the word cannot be employed in the exegesis of the prophetic books; for the prophets have no conception of eschatology as *the end* of history; nor do they expect a future in which human history will come to an abrupt end and an eternity, totally different in kind, will begin. What they do maintain is an eschatology *within* history. That is to say, they assume that there is going to be a revolution, after which history will continue to run its course, but in a new natural environment and with new anthropological, sociological and mythical conditions. This is nowhere so evident as in Ezekiel's draft constitution. Just because here Israel's salvation is painted with a detail we find nowhere else, the character of what the prophets expect of the future becomes clearly evident. Fundamentally speaking, the other prophets are just as utopian in their ideas, even if they are more content with hints and images.

The prophets are all permeated through and through by a sense of the relentless onward movement of everything that exists, and human existence especially. In this sense their orientation is a historical one. But in spite of its irreversibility and purposefulness, history is not for them a homogeneous continuum. The eras of Israel's salvation history, which ended with the settlement (or with the consecration of the temple on Zion), saw the foundation of the institutions belonging to past history. These eras displayed a different temporal quality from 'the present time' which followed; for in 'present time', divine contingent activity, while certainly not disappearing entirely, has nevertheless receded, so that a history of disaster has become possible. The new salvation history that is impending will be characterized by yet another kind of time. (The Hebrew language cannot convey time as a pure, 'empty' quantity; according to the Hebrew way of looking at the world, the movement of time and its content always coincide; cf. Eccles. 3.1ff.). The abrupt change of direction between salvation history and the present time (cf. Jer. 2.7a with 2.7b) will be parallelled by a similar 'bend' in the future as well. History, conceived of metahistorically, therefore emerges as a line broken in two places (cf. Vol I, section 7.6). If we remember this viewpoint when we are considering the prophetic view of history, it is entirely appropriate to use the term 'eschatology' for the prophets' expectation of the upheaval of the times, and the new evolution of the people of God which is to follow. It then becomes evident that the prophets never consider that a catastrophe (a 'divine judgment') occurring at any particular point in time is the one thing that matters. In their view, the impending collapse, even if it is of hitherto unknown dimensions, is only a transitional stage, during which the earth will be purged, as a preparation for a better human society. In this sense, eschatology is an essential aspect of the prophet's metahistory.

5. Deutero-Isaiah

5.1 The marvellous highway through the desert and the divine accession to the throne on Zion

5.1.1 Prologue: commands given by supernatural beings. A generation after Ezekiel, though still during the exilic period, a second prophet appears on the stage. Unfortunately we do not know his name. But a collection of prophetic sayings is appended to the Book of Isaiah (chs. 40–55) which is evidently the work of a particular individual. The distinctive language and characteristic images make that plain. For this prophet, scholars have perforce fallen back on the name Deutero-Isaiah – the second Isaiah.

Deutero-Isaiah evidently belongs to the closing years of the exile, for he refers to the destruction of Jerusalem, the rule of Babylonia over the whole inhabited earth, and Israel's captivity in Mesopotamia – but also to the rise of the Persian conqueror, Cyrus. Whether he also presupposes Cyrus' victory over the Lydian king Croesus in 547 or not, is open to discussion. At all events, the conquest of Babylonia by the Persians (539) is still in the future; so the prophet must be dated between 550 and 540 BC. Probably Deutero-Isaiah preached among the deported Judaeans in one of their Babylonian camps. This would explain his familiarity with Babylonian divination (43.13) and with the Chaldaean processional roads (40.3–5), and the ceremonial ships of their gods, which sailed along the Tigris and Euphrates at the great annual festival (43.14). On the other hand, he never goes into any detail about conditions in the home country of Judaea.

Deutero-Isaiah is one of the few prophetic books which is not preceded by any introductory heading. Was it perhaps omitted when the work was attached to the book of the first Isaiah? (Scholars have also considered whether Deutero-Isaiah intended from the very first to proclaim his message in Isaiah's spirit, and hence to write a sequel to his predecessor's prophecies. But the features which the two prophets have in common are few, and are restricted to the use of language deriving from the pre-exilic Jerusalem cult. Both prophets deliberately draw on this.) The book opens with a prologue spoken by a heavenly being (40.1–11), which is reminiscent of the beginning of other prophetic books dating from the Babylonian era (Jer. 1; Ezek. 1–3). With his inward ear, the prophet hears the cry:

> Comfort, comfort my people,
>   your God begins to say.
> Convince the heart (*lēb*) of Jerusalem, and cry to it that its forced
>   labour is ended,
>   that through the divine good pleasure the weight of its inquity
>   has been taken away.
> That it has received from Yahweh's hand
>   an equivalent for all the disasters caused by its sins.

The prophet hears this liberating message in the midst of his fellow deportees, who have already been cut off from their country for two or three generations, and who are the slaves of a foreign power. But he is not so much concerned with the conditions of the moment. His thinking is primarily political. This is shown by the fact that the supernatural voice does not first of all proclaim to him that a return home is immediately impending. The voice begins with the news that Jerusalem, the prophet's native city, is going to be free once more. Not a word of censure is uttered against the Babylonian oppressor! The passage opens with an affirmation of critical prophecy, which had announced that Israel's downfall was inescapable. But now there is a complete reversal of direction. The 'āwōn spheres of disaster have been Jerusalem's undoing. Under the pressure of the divine hand, a century-long correlation between act and destiny has been consummated once and for all. But the final word is no longer wrath, but the divine good pleasure. Forced labour under foreign occupation has come to an end. Is the writer thinking here of a prescribed period proclaimed by earlier prophets – perhaps a year of jubilee or a year of release, after 49/50 years (Jer. 34.17; Ezek. 40.1: 25 years as half-way point)? At all events, reasonable thinking (lēb) – entering with subsequent insight into the intutive message – finds every reason for expecting the imminent turn of events. The voice heard in the spoken message is not that of Yahweh himself (he is referred to in the third person); it is the voice of a mysterious mediator between the divine background of reality and its human foreground. This voice continues (40.3–8):

A voice crying:
  in the desert prepare the way (derek) of Yahweh!
Prepare in the valley
  a level highway for our God.
Every valley must lift itself up
  and every mountain and hill will lower itself.
The uneven ground will become level, and the hillocks will become
  a hollow.
Revealed will be the glory (kābōd) of Yahweh
  and all flesh shall see (it) together!
For the mouth of Yahweh has said it!
A voice saying: 'Proclaim!'. And [I] said: 'What shall I proclaim?
All flesh is grass,
  and all its continuance like that of the flowers of the field.
The grass withers, the flower fades,
  because the wind of Yahweh's spirit blows upon them [. . .]'
    (Answer)
The grass withers, the flower fades,
  but the dābār of our God comes true and will endure.

The first message heard by the prophet proclaimed Jerusalem's liberation. This time the invisible herald demands that a great highway be built right through the desert. According to vv. 1f., this is a road leading straight to Jerusalem. On this road the *kābōd* will appear – the mysterious radiance shed by the divine theophany, which mortal men and women can only perceive in those extraordinary moments in which God, emerging from his invisibility, demonstrates his presence in earthly history (Ezek. 1; before the exile at the New Year Festival, I Kings 8.10f.; Ps. 24.7–10). Yahweh enters liberated Jerusalem from the east (Ezek. 43.2). That is to say, he comes from the direction of Babylonia, right through the Syrian-Arabian desert. This unheard-of event creates a stir all over the world, and will turn the attention of the nations to a God who is at present known only to a tiny people. Who is to build the divine highway? Impossible for it to be the Israelites, condemned as they are to forced labour, and kept under supervision in their camps! The supernatural herald turns to those like himself – to supernatural spirits. None the less, the proclamation has to be made to men and women. And for this Deutero-Isaiah has been chosen. 'Proclaim!' he hears in compelling tones. Terrified, he raises objections (cf. Jer. 1.6). Through many years of captivity he too, as well as his fellow countrymen, has come to experience human transience and the destructive intervention of the divine breath. But the invisible partner to the discussion does not relent. There is no bargain to be struck about human transience. But the *dābār* is a power that does not only bring about something new; it also implants in the world something that endures. The person who hears the *dābār* has the opportunity to enter its orbit and so to acquire permanence himself. The prophet therefore abstains from further opposition and hastens to perform the task given to him. (The Latin translation of the final sentence, *verbum dei manet in aeternum*, suggests the view that the word of God has as its content eternal truths, which always remain the same, i.e., dogmas. But the original text is thinking of an utterance which materializes (*qūm*) in and through history.)

The message is not yet at an end. The invisible voice is heard again (vv. 9–11).

Climb up upon a high mountain,
　　Zion's messenger of joy!
Raise your voice with strength, Jerusalem's messenger of joy!
Raise it, do not be afraid! Say to the cities of Judah:
'Behold, [. . .] Yahweh is coming with [strength]
　　and his arm will rule for him.

Behold, his reward for labour is with him,
and its result is before him.
As a shepherd feeds his flock,
gathers it with his arm . . .'

This time a female figure is addressed who is apparently responsible, in the supernatural realm, for Zion, or for special messages of joy. (The word used here, *mᵉbaśśeret*, becomes *euaggelizomenos* in Greek; the messenger is the prototype of the New Testament evangelist.) From a mountain near by, the messenger of joy is to proclaim the return of its God to Jerusalem, which lies in ruins. God will not come alone, but will bring with him those for whom he has worked. This can only mean the group of exiles – Deutero-Isaiah and the rest of the deported people. Now, at long last, the people round Deutero-Isaiah are mentioned, at the very end of the message in which he receives his call. This first experience set its ineradicable mark on Deutero-Isaiah. He reverts again and again to the wonderful road running right across the desert. On the journey home there will be no need to take the long way round, along the paths taken by the caravans and the armies, up the Euphrates and through Syria. The people will soon be making their way as the crow flies, heading for their homeland as straight as a die. Then springs will break out everywhere in the desert, to quench the thirst of the travellers. Shady trees will grow on both sides of the road – everything brought about by the marvellous hand of Yahweh (41.17–20; 43.19f.; and frequently).

5.1.2 Yahweh will be king. But the unheard-of turn of events which is impending will not merely bring with it the restoration of Jerusalem. It also means that power over the whole world is going to be seized by Yahweh himself. A messenger of joy is called upon, and told to proclaim to Zion:

Your God has become king!

The people of Jerusalem will see with their own eyes the return of Yahweh to his holy mountain. And not only the inhabitants of Jerusalem:

Yahweh has bared his holy arm
before the eyes of all the nations.
And all the ends of the earth see
the saving help of our God (52.10).

A modern reader finds it a strange idea – even a displeasing one – that God should one day become king on earth in visible form. Deutero-

Isaiah evidently assumes that the idea is a familiar one. He is referring here to the cultic climax of the autumn and New Year festival of pre-exilic times. Then – accompanied by the jubilant cry of the multitude, 'Yahweh has become king' (Ps. 47; 93; 96–99), God moved into the Holy of Holies in the temple, entering invisibly in the visible ark, which was carried in by priests. In the Holy of Holies he ascended his throne, in order to create favourable conditions for a new year (or for a period of seven years). Deutero-Isaiah picks up the remembrance of this as a pattern for what he expects of the eschatological turn of events. (Some scholars dispute that Yahweh's ascent of the throne was part of the pre-exilic cult, since according to the Israelite view Yahweh had occupied his throne from time immemorial [Ps. 93.2]. But apart from the fact that here the passage from the psalm is wrongly translated, Deutero-Isaiah's prophecies are incomprehensible unless we assume that his listeners shared a traditional background of this kind.) Of course Deutero-Isaiah is also convinced that Yahweh has always been king. But the Hebrew verb *mālak*, 'to become king', has a wider meaning. In the ancient East, the king is not thought of in terms of a continually reigning administrator. Kingship is something different: a *melek* displays his kingliness when he implements public actions of which only a ruler is capable – and even then only when he has taken his place on the throne, for it is this that confers special authority on him. (What Deutero-Isaiah expects of the eschatological ascent of the throne, later became hope for the coming of the kingdom of God; and this then played the decisive role in Jesus' teaching; cf. 3.2 above, on Obadiah 21.)

Of course the prophetic saying is not concerned with a mere demonstration of Yahweh's might. In assuming his kingly function, God intervenes efficaciously in the design of earthly conditions on behalf of the people belonging to him. Tradition (Ps. 98.2) already presupposed that, once Yahweh had ascended the throne, his salvation, which was founded on faithfulness to the community (*ṣ°dāqā*), would be revealed to all nations – that is to say, would have an effect on the whole world. But Deutero-Isaiah goes a step further and has the ends of the earth actually included in Yahweh's saving help (*y°šū°ā*). ('See', *r'h*, often has the secondary meaning of inward or outward involvement.) The prophet, living as he was under the Babylonian scourge, broke all the confines of a restricted nationalism in his vistas of the future, and has the whole of mankind participating in Israelite salvation in a way that no other prophet before him had dared to do.

This does not mean that the special position of Israel and Jerusalem as cultic and spiritual centre of the world is thereby abolished.

Deutero-Isaiah paints the holy city – which from now on will be unassailable – in words and images just as marvellous as those he draws upon for the return of the *gōlā* and the entry of Yahweh. The city is not merely founded on the abiding *ṣedāqā* of those dwelling in it. It is furnished with indestructible walls built of sapphires and adorned with rubies, and its gates sparkle with precious stones (54.11–17). (The picture of the new Jerusalem is infinitely more poetical than the description in Ezekiel's ideal constitution; cf. 4.2 above.)

5.1.3 Eschatological ṣedeq. But Deutero-Isaiah is less concerned than Ezekiel with the external restoration of the state. What he has much more at heart is that the Israel of the future should be equipped with a new *ṣedāqā*. Unlike Jeremiah and Ezekiel, he dispenses entirely with prophecy about a change in the nature of man. Instead his hopes revolve round an eschatological transference to the people concerned of the divine sphere which would make it possible for them to act in accordance with the needs of the community (*ṣedeq*); this transference was presumably conceived of in sacramental terms.

> Shower, you heavens, from above,
>   and you clouds, let *ṣedeq* gently fall,
> Then the earth will open and let saving help [blossom forth]
>   and *ṣedāqā* [spring up] also.
> I, Yahweh, have created it (45.8).

Like Hosea (10.12) and Isaiah (1.21 and frequently elsewhere), he thinks of *ṣedeq* an an entity which sinks down from above, allowing salvation to appear in the world among human beings, but with faithfulness to the earthly community (*ṣedāqā*) as its corresponding manifestation. So when Yahweh becomes king he confers on his subjects a new capacity for moral action.

The divine gift presupposes readiness for it on the part of the human person. Quite unlike all the prophets who preceded him, Deutero-Isaiah tries to win over his listeners. He softens every authoritative, demanding or threatening tone in the *dābār* which he proclaims. With this purpose, he even tries to avoid the genre of prophecy, though this was used as a matter of course by the prophets before (and after) him. He prefers another textual form: the oracle of assurance, declaring that the petitioner's prayer has been heard; before 587/6 this had been used on Zion to express a divine response to a human song of lament. One characteristic of this kind of oracle is the change-over to an address to the people concerned; there is a call, 'Fear not!', and an assurance of support (introduced by 'for') which points to God's special relationship to the person in distress. Chapter 41.8–13 is an example:

> You, Israel, my servant (*'ebed*),
>> Jacob, whom I have chosen,
>> offspring of Abraham, whom I love (who loves me?)!
> him whom I snatched up from the ends of the earth,
>> from its furthest corners I called him.
> I said to him: 'You are my servant!
>> I have chosen you and not cast you off.'
> Fear not! For I am with you.
>> Be not dismayed, for I am your God.
> I will strengthen you, I will also help you,
>> I will as well uphold you through the right hand of my *ṣedeq*.
> Behold, put to shame and confounded will be
>> all who are incensed against you.
> They shall be as nothing, shall perish,
>> the men with whom you must contend.
> You will seek them and no longer find them . . .

Is this not noticeably different in tone from the way in which, a generation earlier, Ezekiel had slated the same group of exiles as a 'house of rebellion'? Here no more is said about anger, or white heat and the fateful results of sinful deeds. There is only reassurance and consolation – though certainly not cheap consolation, but comfort based on argument. This people has nothing to fear from God, but everything to hope for from him. Here we see the first beginnings of a refashioning of the idea of God (see below).

But unlike Ezekiel, Deutero-Isaiah is talking to people some of whom have sunk into a paralysing hopelessness. It is true that they still cling to their religion, but they do so with the despairing complaint: 'My way (*derek*) is hidden from Yahweh, my existence (*mišpāṭ*) passes him by' (40.27b). The marked use of the cultic language of the psalms has made people suspect that Deutero-Isaiah belonged to the group of the singer guilds, who had served on Zion before the exile. The assumption would then be that he was one of the singers who took part in festivals of lamentation among groups of exiles (Ps. 137), though at the same time, as 'cultic prophet', providing the response. The hymnic utterances come easily to him, because he is accustomed to singing the psalms. But this by no means explains everything. It certainly in no way accounts for the fact that his prophecy is almost entirely dominated by a sense of the positive active powers of the God who manifests himself as the One who inclines towards Israel.

But let us return to the passage quoted. Deutero-Isaiah does not believe that Yahweh's compassion for Israel is a momentary mood. The past was already determined by a similar attitude on God's part. Ezekiel, Deutero-Isaiah's older companion in misfortune, described Israel's history as an era of sin and deterioration (see 4.3.1 above). Here the same history is judged positively, from its very beginnings. Ever since the patriarchs, Israel has been called to a world-wide political mission, and has been designated the servant of God; and this is as true today as it was in the past. The title, which means something like trustee of divine interests on earth, was coined earlier, for David; and it was applied by Jeremiah to Nebuchadnezzar (see 2.8.3 above). Here it sums up Israel's existence in the light of an ultimate divine purpose which as yet has not nearly attained its goal, and which therefore represents the promise of a future. But if this national vocation is to be reactivated, an explicit endowment with energies deriving from God himself will certainly be necessary. Deutero-Isaiah generally prophesies *ṣedeq*, which will again sink down upon the people from above. Occasionally he also talks about the outpouring of the divine spirit (*rūaḥ*), which in individual Israelites will arouse the awareness of being bound to Yahweh in an indissoluble bond (44.3).

Outside the national framework of Israel, the eschatological spheres of salvation will become efficacious among the 'survivors of the nations', who escape when the Babylonian empire falls. At present they still 'carry about their wooden idols' in processions. But one day they will gather round the one God who is mighty in history, and who will become their saviour also (45.22–25):

Turn to me and you will be helped,
    all the ends of the earth!
For I am God (*'el*) and there is no other.
    By myself I have sworn:
there goes forth from my mouth *ṣᵉdāqā*
    as *dābār* that shall not return,
so that to me every knee shall bow,
    and every tongue affirm:
'Only in Yahweh is there for me,'
    he will say, '*ṣᵉdāqā* (plural) and strength.'

The gift of an enduring capacity for doing good will therefore spread among the nations – no doubt starting from the temple in Jerusalem – and will lead to the universal worship of Yahweh (cf. Isa. 2.2–4, a later interpolation). Brilliant though the colours are with which the prophet paints his picture of future salvation, what is still of decisive importance for him is the new relationship of people with one another and with their God; an increased loyalty to the community; and improved moral standards.

5.2 The downfall of Babylon and the messiah from Persia

5.2.1 The end of the great capital and its wisdom.

The resurgence of Israel and the universal spread of the divine aid towards salvation (*yᵉšū'ā*) will only begin after the Babylonian empire has fallen. This, too, is explicitly announced in Deutero-Isaiah's *dābār*. In ch. 47, he mockingly invites the virgin Babylon to descend from the throne and sit down in the dust, calling upon her from now on to perform the most menial of labours: grinding with the hand mill. Her wickedness will recoil on her own head, since she boasted, 'I, and no one else'; and moreover it will be wickedness increased by the demons of barrenness and widowhood. The prophet stresses with particular passion the uselessness of the world-famous Babylonian divinations, which by then had already been built up on the foundation of astronomical knowledge (v. 13):

> Let them save you, those who [divide] the heavens,
>   the star watchers,
> who at the new moons are used to predict
>   what shall befall you.

In spite of living for decades in Babylon, Deutero-Isaiah does not entertain the least respect for the Babylonian science of auguries, which at that time even the Greeks – who were otherwise so critical – looked up to reverently. What counts for him incomparably more is his secret experience of the inner voice of Yahweh, which was of course verified by Israel's history. In the immediately impending future, Yahweh will send Bel and Nebo, the chief gods of Babylonian futurology, into shameful captivity (46.1f.). (Surprisingly enough, the king of Babylon is never attacked. Deutero-Isaiah certainly shows no signs of the positive view of Nebuchadnezzar shared by Jeremiah and Ezekiel; but he does not utter a word of criticism about him.)

5.2.2 Cyrus.

The prophet was not interested in the actual way the Babylonian power was to be annihilated, in military terms. But he did foresee – and rightly, as history was to show – what man it was who was going to bring down the kingdom of the Chaldeans: Cyrus, an equestrian prince from the southern Iranian highlands, who had been quite unknown outside his home country until a few years previously. Shortly before the middle of the sixth century BC, Cyrus defeated his Median overlord and overran his empire, far into Asia Minor. He crossed the Halys and in 547 subdued the kingdom of

Croesus of Lydia, with his legendary riches. Deutero-Isaiah became
an enthusiastic supporter of Cyrus. Yahweh had raised up the Persian
king in the east, and endowed him with special *ṣedeq*; that was why he
was hastening victoriously over the earth, so swiftly that his feet barely
touched the ground (41.1–5). Nowhere in the Bible is a foreign king
praised so unreservedly. (The Greek historian Herodotus takes a
similarly positive view of Cyrus.)

The prophet turns directly to the Persian conqueror with an oracle
of assurance, conferring on him the title of messiah, the anointed one,
which had hitherto been the supreme religious predicate for Israelite
kings (45.1–7):

> Thus has Yahweh spoken to his messiah,
>   Koresh I have taken by his right hand.
> To subdue the nations before him,
>   I have opened the girdles of kings . . .
> It is I who go before you
>   and level [mountains].
> I breach gates of bronze
>   and strike off iron bars.
> I give you treasures of darkness,
>   and hidden hoards,
> that you may know that I, Yahweh,
>   am the one who calls you by your name [. . .]
> For the sake of my servant Jacob
>   and Israel, my chosen one,
> I have called you by your name,
>   conferred honour upon you, though you did not know me.
> I am Yahweh and there is no other,
>   except me there is no God . . .
> That they may know from the rising [. . .] and the setting,
>   that there is nothing except me.
> I, Yahweh – there is no other
>   who forms the light and creates darkness,
> makes *šalōm* and creates evil.
> I, Yahweh, do all this.

The exciting thing about the saying is that Cyrus's continued
victorious progress is supposed to move him to recognize Yahweh,
i.e., to acknowledge the uniqueness of the Israelite God and to offer
him cultic worship. Cyrus' rule is even supposed to evoke the worship
of Yahweh all over the world. Did Deutero-Isaiah expect that the
Persian king would actually be converted to the Israelite religion? Or
did he merely anticipate that Cyrus would officially permit the

Yahweh cult? Did the Israelite prophet perhaps know something about the Iranian religion, which under Zoroaster (and even apart from him?) displayed a monotheistic tendency not unlike Deutero-Isaiah's own? Did he identify the supreme Iranian god Ahura Mazda with Yahweh?

It is noticeable that the prophet talks about God's creating darkness and evil, using a verb (*bārā'*) in connection with these negative forces which implies divine creation without pre-existent conditions. This, particularly, has made scholars suspect connections with Iran, even though Deutero-Isaiah would then immediately like to make a differentiation. In spite of the monotheistic character of their religion, the Iranians were dualists in assuming the existence of a counter world of evil and a darkness which was militantly opposed to the supreme God. Was Deutero-Isaiah dissociating himself from dualism of this kind in the closing lines of the passage we have just quoted? Even if he is supposed to have been familiar with the Iranian religion, he will hardly have felt the need to enter into a detailed dispute with it. It is much more likely that the prophet was aiming at his Israelite listeners. In their ears the statement must also have sounded provocative. For not a single Israelite writer had previously maintained that evil in the world had its origin in Yahweh's will. (In Gen. 1.2–5 the darkness is not created by God. It is pre-existent as a chaotic power, and is only tamed by giving it a name. On evil and God 'doing it', according to Amos 3.6, see Vol. I, section 4.9.8.) A consistent monotheism of this kind really means the abandonment of the prophetic monanthropology. Once the premise has been formulated that Yahweh creates absolutely everything, human activity no longer represents an independent pole, parallel to the divine centre, in the total movement of reality. In strict terms, this means the determination of all human happening. But this can hardly be the prophet's serious opinion, since in the history of his people he sees his God struggling with the burden of human guilt (see below). The statement therefore seems out of place, like what geologists call an erratic block. (Nor is its function clear in the context.)

To return to Cyrus: enthusiastically though Deutero-Isaiah praises the impending turn of events, he remains true to prophetic metahistory by including political dimensions as well. God's redeeming activity also has political and military effects; and, conversely, every political phenomenon of importance has a connection with the divine reality. Unerringly the prophet foresees that one day Cyrus is going to conquer the Babylonian capital. This actually came about a bare ten years later, when Cyrus entered Babylon without unsheathing his sword, the gates of the city opening to him as if of themselves. Cyrus also

supported the little group of Israelites and their religion (which was
by no means a matter of course); and in 538 – in the edict which was
of such unparalleled importance for the history of Israel – he permitted
the temple in Jerusalem to be rebuilt, as well as, in all probability,
abolishing the prisoner-of-war status of the *gōlā* in Babylonia (Ezra 1;
6.3–5). This pointed the way to the restoration of Israel after the exile.
But Cyrus was not converted to Yahweh; not did his victory draw the
attention of the nations to Israel's God. One greater than even
the most magnanimous Persian conqueror was needed, before the
paticularist barries of the Israelite religion could be broken down, and
the salvation contained within them spread to the ends of the earth.

Surprisingly enough, the Cyrus cylinder[29] tells us that, after he had
seized power in Babylon, Cyrus really did ascribe his victory to the
hand of a great God – though this God was Bel Marduk, not Yahweh!
The text of the inscription is astonishingly like the oracle just quoted
from Deutero-Isaiah. The supreme God of the Babylonians is praised
in the following terms: 'He scanned and looked (through) all the
countries, . . . searching for a righteous ruler. He took him by the
hand,[30] he pronounced the name of Cyrus . . . pronounced (his) name
to be(come) the ruler of all the world . . . He ordered him to march
against his city Babylon . . . going at his side like a real friend . . .
Without any battle, he made him enter his town Babylon.' The
essential themes coincide: the god takes Cyrus by the hand, gives him
his name, and confers universal rule and a marvellous victory. The
cylinder goes on to praise just such a solicitous care for the worship
of the Babylonian God as Isa. 45.1ff. prophesied for the worship of
the God of Israel. We almost get the impression that the Babylonian
priests who drew up the text for Cyrus copied Deutero-Isaiah's oracle.
But it is more probable that both texts go back to earlier Babylonian
descriptions of the ideal king. Deutero-Isaiah, elsewhere too, is
extremely well versed in Babylonian culture. He has no scruples about
claiming for his own Yahweh ascriptions of sovereignty made in the
context of the Babylonian religion. (Even the highway for the divine
procession to the sanctuary – 40.3ff. – is picking up a Babylonian
religious custom.) What he would have said about a document like
the Cyrus cylinder certainly remains a matter of conjecture. It would
seem that Deutero-Isaiah did not live to see the entry of Cyrus into
Babylon. (Some scholars think that he would have found Cyrus a
bitter disappointment. Or would he have seen the Bel praised in the
cylinder as one of Yahweh's active forces? For although the prophet
strictly dissociates heathen gods from Yahweh, he does not deny their
existence.)

5.3 Polemic against the gods: the argument from prophecy and creation

5.3.1 Heathen gods. When the prophet asserts that it is actually the God of his little group of exiles who sets in motion the machinery of world politics – a God whose sole sanctuary has been destroyed and whose cult has been abolished – he has to stretch his metahistorical framework far beyond the bounds accepted by his prophetic predecessors. Even though they often looked further afield to the world beyond Israel, the earlier prophets were still able to restrict themselves to their own national history when they were considering the significance of events and the meaning of existence. For there was an independent state and an intact cultic community to act as the vehicles of history. But for Deutero-Isaiah, Israel was no longer available as 'tangible' historical subject. The daily news bulletins reported the movements of foreign nations and kings; and Judah, as a remote Babylonian border province, played a highly insignificant role. But if Judah's God is the only God of power, and if he directs the fate of his own people by means of anonymous and collective forces, then he is bound to do the same for the other nations, too, even though these nations themselves ascribe their destiny to polytheistic deities with outlandish names. This view seems to imply that behind the gods there are hidden powers who have an influence on their particular worshippers which resembles the effect of Yahweh's arm or hand – or his *kābōd* and *ṣedeq* – on Israel. On the other hand, these forces must then be appropriated to Yahweh, and do not possess nearly the power which the Babylonians erroneously ascribe to their Bel or the Egyptians to their Osiris. When Deutero-Isaiah wants to stress that Yahweh is the fundamental power behind all positive reality, he has to demonstrate the impotence of the heathen gods. He offers this demonstration by way of disputations between the gods, in which Yahweh (perhaps as prosecutor in a supernatural trial?) contends with his rivals and proves their futility. Cf. 41.21ff.:

> Set forth your case, says Yahweh,
>> Bring your proofs, says the King of Jacob.
> Bring them and tell us
>> what is going to happen.
> The primordial things – what have you told of them?
>> That we may take it to heart (= admit it).
> Let us know their sequel
>> or let us hear what is to come.
> Tell us future things (*hā'ōtiyyōt l'āḥōr*),
>> that we may know that you are gods.

Do something good or something evil,
  that we may perceive it, astonished!
Therefore: you are less than nothing
  and what you produce is less than chaos,
  he who chooses you will become an abomination!
I stirred up (Cyrus) from the north, and he came.
From the rising of the sun he was called by his name . . .
Who declared (it) from the beginning (*rōš*), that we may acknow-
    ledge it,
  from earlier times, that we may say: '(You are) right'?
But there is none who declares it, there is no spokesman,
  there is none who hears words from you . . .
Therefore: you are all disaster,
  futile your works,
  wind and confusion your images of cast metal.

The statement that the gods are 'nothingnesses' by no means
implies that they are mere figments of the imagination – that they do
not exist at all. On the contrary, the scene is intended to be taken
literally. Yahweh actually talks to these beings, even though his
intention in so doing is to convince them of their lack of importance.
The main argument is the inability of those addressed to give any
information about the course of history, either history of the primordial
period, or history in the future. For Deutero-Isaiah, everything
culminates in the proof offered by prophecy. The emergence of the
victorious Persian king is an excellent example. Why had Yahweh
prophesied him from primordial times? The prophet's Israelite
listeners will have recalled cultic hymns which had long since been
given an eschatological interpretation – the hymn about the sun-hero,
for example, who hastens across the earth from the east to the end of
the world (Ps. 19.5f.). But they will also have remembered prophetic
predictions about the Medes who were going to destroy Babylon (Isa.
13.17; Jer. 51.11). No other deity was able to utter prophecies in so
cogent a form.
    At this point Babylonian soothsayer priests would object that their
gods also revealed the course of destiny, through the inspection of
entrails and the cuneiform script of the stars; they too had undoubtedly
concerned themselves with Cyrus. But Deutero-Isaiah looks down
contemptuously on all inductive divination by way of auguries (44.25,
cf. Vol. I, section 2.1). The inductive divination with which God
inspires him can certainly not be substantiated by way of external
objects, like the Babylonian science of omens. But since it takes place
through the sensory medium of language, it reveals the reasons

for the event, and its purpose. It embodies inner metahistorical significance. On the other hand, a prediction arrived at by 'technical' methods announces a mere fact, which remains meaningless for listeners. So whereas the Babylonian rivals tell fortunes, the Israelite prophet expounds prophecy.

The idols which adorn the Babylonian temples so lavishly are for Deutero-Isaiah also nothing more than the work of human hands. It seems to him ridiculous to symbolize the ground of all reality through an image resembling a human being, and then to ascribe sacramental significance to it – supposing, for example, that when it is carried round in procession it radiates blessing on everything round it. 'To whom will you liken me? With what would you like to portray me?' asks his God ironically (40.18; 46.5). For the enlightened prophet it does not make sense to suppose that any human artefact, however beautiful and however masterly it may be, can ensure the divine presence.

This attack on idols became a precedent and led later Israelites to pour scorn on the foolishness of heathen religious practices (44.9–20, a later interpolation; Epistle of Jeremiah, etc.). The main reason for their concept was not, as people used to suppose, that the Israelites were governed by the idea of God as a pure transcendent spirituality that debarred any material representation. For God's *kābōd* is undoubtedly manifested visibly in the world (40.6). What is rejected is the notion that God is at the disposal of human beings, and that this disposability can be sacrificially appropriated by means of an idol – the idea being that every artefact has to be thought of as dependent on its maker. A parallel argument for Deutero-Isaiah is the fact that images are speechless (46.7). In the Israelite view, history and speech event interlock so closely that every external turn of events which is of decisive importance inevitably requires a *dābār* of Yahweh's to evoke it; if this *dābār* is not directly known, it has to be postulated (hence the *vaticinia ex eventu*, Gen. 49; Deut. 33, and frequently elsewhere). But this makes every symbolization of the deity by way of a non-verbal medium seem inadequate from the outset; for it is unable to represent what is actually the essential feature of divine existence.

5.3.2 The cosmological proof of God. When Yahweh allows a prophecy to be heard, he becomes creatively active. To this degree the proof offered by prophecy shows, not only that God is omniscient, but also that he brings forth everything that is of essential importance in human history. For prophecy does not merely predict; it also provokes. The dynamic character of the *dābār* is stressed particularly by Deutero-

Isaiah. He paints it as an active force, hastening from heaven to earth.
He does not in any way see it as an abstract power (55.10f.):

> For as the rain
>   or the snow comes down from heaven
>   and returns not thither,
>   but waters the earth
>   and makes it fertile and sprout,
>   giving seed to the sower and bread to the eater.
> So is my *dābār*, which goes forth from my mouth;
>   it shall not return to me empty,
> but accomplishes that which I purpose,
>   brings about successfully the thing for which I send it.

Because the word of God is characterized by this effective power, the
proof offered by prophecy does not only make evident Yahweh's
surpassing insight, but also his supreme power of changing the course
of the world by means of free, contingent interventions.

It is not merely the correspondence between prophecy and
fulfilment in history which shows Yahweh to be incomparable. Even
the sphere which we in the Western world call 'nature' serves as
evidence of the unique, fundamental power of this God. This is
expounded to the Israelites, as well as the gods, in a debate (or
'disputation saying') with a concluding 'Therefore' (*hēn*):

> Who has measured the waters in the hollow of his hand?
>   Fastened the heavens exactly on the span?
> Recorded the dust of the earth with a measure?
>   Weighed the mountain with the scales [. . .]? (expected answer:
>   Yahweh's *rūaḥ*)
> Who has made fast the wind of Yahweh's spirit (*rūaḥ*)?
> Who gave him knowledge as his counsellor?
> With whom did he consult, who enlightened him,
>   taught him the path of the word's order (*ōraḥ mišpāṭ*)
>   and instructed him in [. . .] the way (*derek* = course of the world)
>   full of wisdom?
> Therefore: nations (are only) like a drop in a bucket . . . (40.12ff.).

The universe runs its course according to law and rule. Human
beings guess that this order conceals numerical constants, even if they
are not able to calculate what these are. There must be an agency
behind everything which plans all this. For an Israelite, the divine
wind of the spirit, the giver of life and the potency of the divine word,
seems the obvious answer (though this is supported by Yahweh's
hand, 48.13). It is also characteristic of Hebrew thought that the

writer's gaze should immediately turn away from the apparently static cosmos, back to universal history, which is conceived of as the *mišpāṭ* order which embraces both nature and human beings. That is why the passage concludes with the nations who determine events at the present moment, stressing how relative their importance is. If 'nature' has its measure, history must have it too. Babylonian rule weighs like a nightmare on the people who are touched by it. But against the backcloth of the meaningful structure of the universe, the Babylonian giant seems the merest dwarf, a drop of water which will soon evaporate. Creation takes place in order to provide the conditions which make history possible. A protological interest, which treats creation as a singular divine disposition, carried out thousands of years previously, is remote from Deutero-Isaiah's thinking. Every new historical event can go back to a creation without any preconditions (*bārā'*); this is particularly true of the genesis of Israel (43.1; cf. 44.21), but it also applies to the people who will be liberated anew in the eschaton (43.7). The cosmological proof of God, which was to play so important a part in the philosophical and theological debate in Europe, is therefore already maintained by Deutero-Isaiah. But he supports it in the sense that the proof presented by creation converges on a proof offered by history, which permits human beings living here and now to see what happens to them as having a meaning. It is this that the line of argument is aiming at, not an abstract doctrine of God.

5.3.3 Monotheism. Again and again, Deutero-Isaiah introduces into the text statements in which Yahweh himself asserts his uniqueness: 'I am the first and with the last', or 'I am Yahweh and there is no other, besides me there is no God' (41.4; 44.6f.; 45.5, 18). About the same time, in Iran, Zoroaster praised his God as 'the first and the last . . . the founder of a just order' (*Yasna* 31.8). For the prophet, Yahweh is the One who has unique power of speech. Because God can express himself more efficaciously than any other subject, he has called forth the world as it is (45.7) and is able to put it at the disposal of human beings as the starting point for history. The ethical monotheism which the nineteenth century celebrated as the great achievement of prophecy (cf. Vol. I, section 2.5) emerges more clearly in Deutero-Isaiah than anywhere else. His earlier colleague in exile, Ezekiel, was no less zealous for the uniqueness of Israel's Yahweh; but he saw human discernment of this uniqueness as something still belonging to the future (see above, 4.3). For Deutero-Isaiah, on the other hand, a convincing proof that Yahweh is the unique, fundamental force of positive reality is possible now, in the present. None the less, his monotheism is also futuristic, in that the full implementation of the

divine will and the divine power is still to come, and will be perceptible
only in the great eschatological revolution (52.7ff.).

It must also be said that here, too, we are still confronted with a
graduated form of monotheism. The prophet conceives of God in
highly personal terms. He is bound to men and women by ties of
tenderest intimacy, and to his chosen people especially. But it is
considered a matter of course that he should be associated with a great
network of active powers which mediate between the focus of his
divine self and the world (cf. below). In a certain sense, the so-called
gods of the heathen belong to this group of forces too. Prophetic
monotheism never aims at an exclusive transcendence.

5.4 The Servant of Yahweh liturgies

5.4.1 References. In four passages Deutero-Isaiah dispenses with his
more usual practice of announcing the coming upheaval of earthly
conditions through the medium of oracles of assurance or disputations.
Instead he adopts a liturgical framework for what he has to say about
a mysterious servant (*'ebed*) who is intimately connected with Yahweh
and who is going to assume religious functions in the new eschatological age – functions which are apparently of decisive importance for
the people involved. (The translation 'servant' has become generally
accepted, and I am therefore retaining it here, although in these
passages the term *'ebed* is used for a function which is unique and has
nothing to do with 'menial' work. 'Plenipotentiary' would be a more
appropriate rendering.)

The liturgy begins in 42.1ff., where Yahweh presents (to people all
over the world?) the person in whom he reposes trust. The presentation
resembles the way in which ancient oriental kings were accustomed
to install their viziers:

> [Behold] my servant, I uphold him,
>   my chosen, who has my good pleasure.
> I give him the wind of my spirit (*rū*^a*ḥ*),
>   he will bring *mišpāṭ* to the nations.
> He will not cry and shrilly draw attention to himself,
>   nor will his voice be heard in the street.
> A bruised reed he will not break,
>   a dimly burning wick he will not quench.
> He will faithfully bring forth *mišpāṭ* . . .

The solemn presentation is followed by an oracle of assurance
addressed to the person who has just been entrusted with world-wide
functions (vv. 5–9):

Thus has the deity Yahweh spoken.
Creating the heavens and stretching them out,
  increasing the earth and its vegetation,
giving breath to the people on it,
  wind of the spirit (*rūᵃḥ*) to those who walk on it.
I, Yahweh, have called you in (my) *ṣedeq* power,
  taken you by your hand.
I have formed you and installed you
  to be the covenant of a people, and the light of nations,
to open the eyes of the blind,
  to bring out the prisoners from the dungeon . . .

Surprisingly enough, the figure who has been installed is set in the
context of creation. What takes place when he is appointed has the
same status as the creation of heaven and earth. Everyone experiences
the efficacious power of the *rūᵃḥ* through the breath within him (it is
to this that the Hebrews trace back a person's spiritual mobility, Ezek.
36.26); but this power rests on the *'ebed* in concentrated fullness. His
chief task is to establish *mišpāṭ* all over the world.

What the term *mišpāṭ* means here is a matter of dispute among
scholars. It seems to me essential to arrive at its meaning in the context
of Deutero-Isaiah himself, and to link it with the path of the *mišpāṭ*
(40.14, see above) which, as divine *derek*, has run through time ever
since creation and – in the form of a meaningful world-order – arrives
at man, who is conceived of in monanthropological terms. What is
stressed three times as *mišpāṭ* in the presentation of the servant (vv. 1,
3, 4) is declared by the oracle of assurance as being the 'covenant of
a people, the light of nations'. What is probably meant is that, once
the plenipotentiary has liberated the prisoners from their dungeon
(i.e., has brought them home again from Babylonian captivity), he
will conclude on their behalf the new covenant prophesied by Jeremiah
and Ezekiel. He does not conclude this covenant merely in an executive
capacity, but as the embodiment of Israel's corporate personality,
which from now on is to enjoy a better future because of the covenant.
But the Servant does not merely introduce a cultic and national
restoration. In some measure – though this is not closely defined – he
will shine as a light to the nations. That is to say, he will serve as
guarantor of a peaceful order that will extend to the whole world; for,
in Hebrew, light is also a metaphor for life and peace. It tells in favour
of Deutero-Isaiah's political judgment that apparently he could not
imagine a renewed Israelite society which was not outwardly secured
by the cessation of all the warlike entanglements which had made
oriental history so sombre a picture. The divine *mišpāṭ* of a transformed

era of history therefore takes traditional concentric monanthropology into consideration, in the sense that in the new age Israel is going to dwell at the centre of the nations, with rights and duties conferred through a special order of the covenant. But at the centre of Israel is the *'ebed*, who represents as it were the heart of the covenant. An outer circle, composed of all the nations of earth, corresponds to this inner circle, its existence being prototypically represented in the existence of Israel.

For such a wide-ranging office, the *'ebed* needs not only the wind of the spirit, but also forces of salvation from God himself. That he is called 'in Yahweh's *ṣedeq*' also means that this sphere of activity passes over to him. He is therefore, as person, placed 'in *ṣedeq*'. His capacity for acting in faithfulness to the community differs from all the sovereignty known to current history, because he renounces force and is most concerned with the people whose rights have been snatched from them – the powerless, the broken reed and the dimly burning light. So the *'ebed* takes the opposite course from the warlike Cyrus.

In 49.1ff. the enigmatic Servant of Yahweh presents himself to the people: 'Listen to me, you (far-off) islands!' He tells of different stages in his life. Called by Yahweh from the womb and given a name, crowned with the gift of efficacious speech, he was first of all installed as plenipotentiary for Israel, 'to raise up once more the tribes (= tribal organization) of Jacob, and to bring to repentance the surviving Israelites'. But in fulfilling this task he is threatened with failure:

> I thought, I am labouring for nothing,
> I am spending my strength for confusion and wind.

But the inner voice of Yahweh which claims him does not give up; on the contrary, it expands his field of service even further: 'I designate you to be a light to the nations, so that my saving help may reach to the ends of the earth.'

Again an oracle of assurance follows, this time even a double one (vv. 7, 8–12), directly addressed to the *'ebed*. Although at the moment he is 'abhorred by the people, a servant of rulers', he is promised that one day kings will rise to their feet before him, and that they will all prostrate themselves in front of him 'for the sake of the Holy One of Israel who has chosen you'. Whereas this promise foreshadows an international sphere of influence, the second part of the oracle points to the *'ebed*'s function within the nation itself. It is true that at the moment both his situation and Israel's seem hopeless, but this will not continue for long:

In a time of good pleasure I will answer you,
  in a day of saving help will aid you.
Then I will transform you and make you
  a covenant for the people.

The *'ebed* then has to guide the return home of the deported people,
along the marvellous highway through the desert. He will then finally
– like Joshua in times past (Josh. 13ff.) '(newly) apportion the
inherited lands (*naḥ*ᵃ*lā*) that were forsaken'.

In 50.4ff., a psalm of confidence (similar e.g. to Ps. 23) is voiced by
a speaker who does not identify himself. It is recited to listeners who
know Yahweh – that is to say, to an Israelite congregation. The
speaker acknowledges proudly that the Almighty Lord has given him
'the tongue of a disciple' and wakes him 'morning by morning' with
spoken messages (?). This gives him the strength to resist in the face
of the severe mistreatment to which he is exposed:

I give my back to smiters,
  my cheeks to those who pull out my beard . . .
I set my face like flint,
  and I know I will never be put to shame.

He is confident that his divine helper will soon come to his aid and
see to it that his faithfulness to the community finds expression in an
appropriate destiny (*maṣdīq*). In response to this acknowledgment,
another voice chimes in – probably the prophet's own. The context is
therefore once more a liturgical one:

Everyone among you who fears Yahweh
  will obey the voice of his servant,
  who has to walk in darkness,
  there is no light for him.
He trusts in the name of Yahweh,
  and he is supported by his God (v. 10).

Then God himself turns to the Servant's persecutors: 'Therefore: all
you . . . go into the flames of your own fire! . . . This will be prepared
for you by my (Yahweh's) hand.' Whether this passage belongs to the
cycle about the Servant of God is a not undisputed question, since
nothing is said here about the functions otherwise assigned to the
Servant, the theme being purely personal suffering. (Are vv. 4–9 a
confession by Deutero-Isaiah [similar to Jeremiah's, see 2.6 above]
which has nothing to do with the *'ebed* songs? Verses 10f. are frequently
excluded as a later addition.)

The longest and most famous Servant of God liturgy is to be found

in 52.13 – 53.12. Again the liturgy is preceded by a presentation of
the *'ebed* by his God. It is predicted that the Servant (who now seems
as if he were no longer a human person) will in future be 'exalted and
lifted up and shall be very high'. (These are royal predicates in the
Old Testament.) So kings will not dare to open their mouths in front
of him. Then an apparently new subject is taken up. There is now a
song sung by *a number of people*. They acknowledge that the *'ebed* – who
has just died and been buried – suffered and was slain 'for us'.

> He had no beauty and majesty
> 	[. . .] No appearance that could have filled us with rapture.
> He was despised, forsaken by men,
> 	a man of sorrows and marked by sickness . . .
> Yet our sicknesses – he bore them.
> 	Our sorrows he took upon himself.
> But we esteemed him one stricken,
> 	smitten by God and humiliated.
> But he was pierced through by our rebellions (*peša'*)
> 	crushed by the weight of our guilt (*'āwōn*).
> The punishment required for our salvation came upon him
> 	and through his weals we received healing . . .
> Yahweh allowed to light on him
> 	the weight of all our guilt . . .
> Although he did no violence
> 	and no deception came from his mouth.

The stanza is familiar to Christians from the Good Friday liturgy,
where it impressively summarized the meaning of the Saviour's death.
For centuries, the Christian church assumed as a matter of course
that Isaiah 53 was describing nothing other than the death of *the* Man,
Jesus Christ. But modern historical interpretation has to start from
the assumption that Deutero-Isaiah was thinking of someone in the
very near future, someone whom he probably thought that he himself
would see. But even if he did not have the person of Jesus in mind,
was he nevertheless thinking of something like Jesus' work? Did he
envisage the death of an individual, through which the sins of other
people would be forgiven? Or is the Jewish interpretation right, when
it sees here the path of suffering trodden by the Jewish people?

At all events, the subject is representation or substitution. The
song's meaning emerges from the background of the Israelite view of
atonement. Spheres of action create destiny: this was accepted as a
matter of course by Hebrews. And the view presupposed that everyone
who acted contrary to the interests of the community (*rš'*) or sinned
against God (*ḥṭ'*) was inescapably preparing his own downfall and, in

the long run, had to 'bear' (*nāśā'*) his misdeeds to the bitter end. There
was only one possible way of escaping this bitter fate. Under certain
conditions, Yahweh was in a position to allow the accumulation of
evil acts committed by human beings to be transferred to an animal,
at the sanctuary. This animal then 'bore' the misdeeds, and died
vicariously for the person to whom the deeds belonged (Lev. 16.21f.).
For, as the Hebrew saw it, atonement means that human beings and
the earth are liberated from spheres of misdeeds and consequent
disaster through the help of God. The animal offered dies instead of
the person. This has nothing whatsoever to do with a sacrifice designed
to appease the deity. (It is therefore essentially different from the
mediaeval Christian 'satisfaction' theory!) Elsewhere Deutero-Isaiah
praises Yahweh's continual efforts to turn away the results of sin in
Israelite history. Without these efforts the people would long since have
perished. In one passage he criticizes sacrifices (43.23f.), proclaiming
that God gains nothing by them. On the contrary, rites of atonement
make tremendous demands on him:

> I have not made you labour (*'bd* hiphil) with food offerings,
> 　　have not troubled you with offerings of incense . . .
> But you have made me labour (*'bd* hiphil) with the spheres of your
> 　　sins,
> 　　have troubled me through the burdens of your guilt.

But Israel's continually growing transgressions made the divine
efforts useless, so that Yahweh finally had to 'profane the dignitaries
of the sanctuary' (in the catastrophe of 587/6); and since then it has
no longer been possible for Israel's self-inflicted doom to be turned
aside.
　　Does our passage suggest that the Servant leaps into the breach?
In the face of a situation so bedevilled that no animal suffices for
atonement any more, does the Servant himself become the scapegoat
in his own person? Is it to him that Israel's tremendous sphere of sin
is transferred, so that he may go to his death carrying it (*nāśā*, v. 4)?
The song, which is sung by people professing faith in Yahweh, suggests
something of the kind. But this is by no means certain. For the liturgy
closes with a saying of Yahweh's which perhaps extends the horizon
to take in another group of people who are also involved:

> Cut off from the tribulation of his life he will see [light],
> 　　will be satisfied with knowledge (?).
> He will make (or: has made) many healthful (*ṣdq*),
> 　　he the one faithful to the community (*ṣaddīq*), my servant.
> 　　The burden of their sins [he has taken upon himself].

Therefore I will give him a share of (among?) the many,
   among the mighty he will divide the spoil.
Because he has poured out the strength of his life in death
   and was reckoned among the rebellious.
And he represents an equivalent for sin (*ḥēt'*), he has borne it,
   so that he interceded for the rebellious (or: God let it smite him,
   cf. v. 6).

The divine saying may perhaps be cast in the form of an assurance
that a ritual has been successfully carried out (cf. 'that [represents]
the sin of so and so', Lev. 4.21). God himself confirms the efficacy of
the deliverance from sins achieved by the *'ebed* through his death. At
the same time, it is often 'the many' (*rabbīm*) who are mentioned as
the ones who benefit from the *'ebed*'s death, not Israel. Who are these
people? In Qumran 'the many' was later used as a term for the
members of the community as a whole (cf. Dan. 12.2). Is, analogously,
the mass of the Israelite people meant here? But in the next half-verse
(v. 12), the 'mighty' are mentioned, meaning kings (Ps. 135.10); so it
is sometimes assumed that 'the many' are the heathen for whom the
'ebed has sacrificed his life, even though they do not know it. But is
this interpretation not rather far-fetched? According to the Israelite
view, Yahweh can only use a member of a 'total person' as vicariously
atoning agent: a domestic animal might be used for his master, or a
prominent Israelite could act for the national community. But the life
of the Servant is not (as yet) bound closely together with the life of the
other nations. Moreover, efficacious atonement presupposes that the
person who is to be relieved of his guilt enters into the happening, and
discerns what is meant. How are the nations supposed suddenly to
arrive at this insight? So the most probable explanation is still that it
is Israel's sins which are to be expiated.

   The concluding divine judgment does not merely endorse what the
congregation has previously sung. It also confers a promise. The *'ebed*
will live again, see his descendants, and acquire a considerable
inheritance. To the many, whose sins he has expiated, he will mediate
a salvation that applies to the community as a whole. This sounds like
resurrection, which would make Isa. 53 the earliest passage in the
Old Testament in which such a hope is expressed (apart from Ezek.
34.23? Cf. 4.5.1 above). An interpretation of this kind would certainly
be in accordance with the wording. But a slight doubt remains.
Does the idea of a corporate personality, extending right down the
generations, perhaps play a part here? In other words, is the writer
thinking of a son, who will pick up the father's staff and carry it

forward? (When, later, belief in the resurrection woke to life, the passage was of course instanced as a supporting authority.)

Finally we must look at the fifth passage, 55.3–5. Here the liturgical context is not as clearly evident as it is elsewhere, and most scholars do not number it among the Servant of God passages at all. After a promise to those addressed, the *'ebed* is once more presented by the divine voice:

> Incline your ears and come to me!
> Hear, that the strength of your lives may live!
> I will make with you a covenant for ever,
> (with the) steadfast grace of the covenant for David.
> Therefore: as witness for [peoples] I will install him,
> to be leader and commander of nations.

Here an individual figure is clearly contrasted with the people addressed, who are in the plural. Yahweh then turns to this individual personally:

> Therefore: you shall call upon a people that you know not,
> and a people that knows you not will come running to you.
> For the sake of Yahweh, your God,
> and the Holy One for Israel, for he has glorified you.

Again, there is first of all a reference to the covenant made with Israel, those addressed being members of this people; but then the gaze travels further, to the world-wide mission of the Servant of God. What is new is the mention of the graces of the covenant (*ḥªsādīm*) which were once given to David. Since the Davidic kingdom reached far beyond the frontiers of Israel itself, it can serve as primordial model for the supra-national eschatological task immediately ahead.

5.4.2 A collective or an individual interpretation? Who is the mysterious figure to whom Deutero-Isaiah's God assigns a task which goes beyond anything entrusted to a human being in the whole Old Testament tradition? In the New Testament we are told about an Ethiopian finance minister who, on his way home from Jerusalem, read aloud to himself (as the custom then was) a scroll of the Book of Isaiah. As the Ethiopian arrives at ch. 53, the evangelist Philip suddenly approaches the chariot and asks: 'Do you understand what you are reading?' The Ethiopian answers: 'About whom, pray, does the prophet say this, about himself or about someone else?' (Acts 8.26ff.).

The Ethiopian eunuch's question is still discussed by biblical scholars today, and there are no signs of agreement. All the same, a number of indications incline me with some degree of certainty towards one of the possible solutions. But first of all let me put forward the various possibilities:

(a) *The collective interpretation.* According to this, the Servant of God is Israel itself, either as it actually exists, or in its ideal form; or one important part of it (the exilic community). If one reads Deutero-Isaiah as a connected whole, this view presents itself almost automatically. For in other passages Israel is expressly called *'ebed* (41.8; see above), and moreover it is frequently addressed in the singular, as if it were an individual person. Conversely, the figure celebrated in the liturgies is called 'Israel' in 49.3 (though the text is doubtful at this point). The Septuagint – the pre-Christian Greek translation – already decided in favour of a collective interpretation, and so does almost all Jewish exegesis. But, in spite of its antiquity, there is an objection to this view; for in the Servant of God liturgies the individual features stand out incomparably more sharply than they do elsewhere. More important still, the *'ebed* is entrusted with the task of liberating the exiles and of constituting the association of the twelve tribes anew – and this is clearly an action affecting Israel.

So what about the other possibility – the individual explanation? This is supported by the large majority of scholars. Read consecutively, the liturgies offer a kind of brief biography of a religious personality. What then remains a matter of dispute is, first, the social function entrusted to this individual and, secondly, whether and how far the prophet is modelling the Servant on prototypes belonging to Israel's past.

(b) *The interpretation of the Servant as an individual with a prophetic function.* According to this view, the Servant of God has a pre-eminently prophetic, missionary and pastoral function. This interpretation can be supported by the arguments that, in the very first song, the islands wait for his instruction (*tōrā*, 42.4); that he is given a mouth like a sharp sword (49.2); and that he will make a covenant as Moses did once before. (In the exilic period Moses was undoubtedly seen as a nabi.) 'Preaching and suffering – the basic functions belonging to the picture of the prophet at that time – are the theme of the songs' (von Rad). But what kind of prophet does the writer have in mind? Some people think that a restored Moses is being prophesied. Others see Jeremiah as the model for the eschatological prophet. Supporters can also be found for the possibility already considered by the Ethiopian eunuch – that the prophet meant himself, i.e., that the fragments have to be interpreted autobiographically. If the 'I' of the 'call' vision (40.3ff.) refers to Deutero-Isaiah himself, why should this not also be true of the 'I' in the Servant of God passages? Chapter 53 could then be explained as a lament uttered by the prophet's followers after his death.

What tells against the interpretation of the Servant as prophet is that there is not a single feature which is *solely and specifically* prophetic. The Servant of God does not have to utter a *dābār*. He is quite noticeably *not* entrusted with a proclamation that is specifically prophetic, nor does he act as Yahweh's messenger. The texts emphasize that foreign kings have to pay him high regard. Does this not rather point to a ruler (49.7; 52.13–15)?

(c) The interpretation of the Servant as an individual with a royal function. It is true that the title *melek* is never used, and the *'ebed* displays no warlike features at all in what he does. And yet the very framework, with the courtly form of the presentation (42.1ff.; 52.13–15), suggests a royal position. To this is added the title *'ebed,* which is emphatically used for an individual earthly plenipotentiary of Yahweh's (cf. Nebuchadnezzar in Jeremiah, cf. 2.8.3 above). A number of other themes are also derived from royal ideology: the Servant is called from his mother's womb, he is taken by the hand, and he receives gifts of grace for David (on the mediator of the covenant, cf. II Kings 23). The royal features therefore by far outnumber the prophetic ones. In that respect this interpretation would seem to deserve the preference.

But what kind of king is expected? The Aramaic Targum, or translation (which is probably pre-Christian), as well as Christian interpretation throughout the centuries, applied these statements to the messiah of the end-time, as if this were a matter of course: he is the saving king of the future sent by God (so also Acts 8). But since in all his other prophecies Deutero-Isaiah is thinking of the immediately impending future and since – in spite of all his hymnal exuberance – he always bases his metahistory on actually existing conditions, a man belonging to the dynasty of David could equally well be meant here – someone who shared the prophet's exile at the time. This could either have been the deposed king Jehoiachin himself or one of his sons or grandsons. (Jehoiachin's grandson Zerubbabel was later to restore the second temple, but he himself hardly comes into question, since when Deutero-Isaiah was writing he had not, like the servant, met a violent death.) This Davidic descendant would then be the Servant singled out to be the embodiment of the collective servant, Israel.

The most probable explanation is therefore that Deutero-Isaiah was referring to someone belonging to his own milieu. The liturgies sound as if they had really been performed at some exilic assembly. In this case, the man designated to be the Servant of God would either have been present or could at least conceivably have been so. The objection has been raised that the unique predicates which Deutero-Isaiah uses for the rule of Cyrus exclude the simultaneous activity of another royal figure. The Persian is to rebuild Jerusalem (44.28) and will see to it that all the nations know Yahweh. It is impossible to deny that there is a certain tension between the Cyrus predicates and the functions of the Servant of God, who also has to do with the return to Jerusalem and the 'knowledge' of the nations. Perhaps Deutero-Isaiah initially pinned his hopes on Cyrus and then, at later period, transferred his expectations to the Servant of God (Begrich's view). Or – and this seems to me more probable – Deutero-Isaiah believes that the external military acts of force have to be carried out by Cyrus: he has to defeat Babylon and issue the command permitting the return of the Israelites. But the inward and spiritual functions fall to the Servant of God: the guidance of the homecomers on their way (the Servant himself being in their midst); the setting up of a new Israelite state and cultic centre; and from there the spread of the worship of Yahweh to the ends of the earth. (The first Servant of God liturgy is preceded by a declaration about Cyrus which may perhaps have been part of the liturgy itself; 41.21 is the new beginning, not 42.1.)

(d) Whoever it was whom Deutero-Isaiah divined as being the Servant of God, no one emerged in the next five centuries of Israel's history who can be considered as having fulfilled such high expectations. It was the primitive church which first of all seized enthusiastically on these passages, particularly Isaiah 53, seeing them in the light of Jesus and his cross. Without this Old Testament chapter, the early church would hardly have thought of acknowledging the death of Christ as an atoning event of decisive significance for the whole world. The confession that Christ died 'for us', proclaimed at every Lord's Supper, was originally a cast back to Isaiah 53.

Judaism, on the other hand, now as then, rejects this association. It points to the fact that Jesus did not in any way fulfil what was supposed to be the primary task of the Servant of God – to liberate the deported Israelites and to bring them back to Palestine, and to found a new state and a new cult. If anyone has suffered to an unusual degree in human history, it is the Jewish people. Why should not the century-long brutality of the pogroms, down to our most recent history and the holocaust, conceal the mystery that Israel suffers for the rest of mankind? That Judah vicariously bears the sins of others? Can a Christian really gainsay this with full conviction?

Representation in the framework of Old Testament expiation is generally efficacious in the collective context. It is never thought of exclusively and as happening once, and never again. Have Christians the right to press the 'once-and-for-all' of the death of Jesus to such an extent that, from then on, it has been out of the question for others to 'fill up' or 'complete' the sufferings of Christ (Col. 1.24) – Christians and non-Christians, and certainly the Jews most of all? The sufferings and representation of the Servant of God are certainly not understood in an exclusive sense in Isaiah 53. Perhaps we Christians, too, should learn to understand the representation of Christ we extol in a more comprehensive sense, so that instead of *ex*cluding, it *in*cludes every happening where innocent people die through the violence of others.

5.5 The turn of the ages

5.5.1 The primordial period and the end-time.
More stringently than any prophet before him, Deutero-Isaiah analyses the breach in the history of his people, and of humanity as a whole, reducing it to conceptual form. In one of the rare cases where he uses the genre of prophecy, he writes programmatically (43.16–21):

> So has Yahweh spoken, who (once) making a way (*derek*) in the sea . . .,
> luring forth an (Egyptian) chariot corps . . .
> they languish like a wick which is quenched.
>
> A   Remember no longer the events of the first time (*rīšōnōt*),
> no longer consider the things of primordial days!
>
> B   Behold! I am doing a new thing (*ḥᵃdāšā*).
> It is already springing forth, do you not perceive it?
> This time I am making in the wilderness a way (*derek*) . . .

The contrast between a first or main time, *rīšōnōt* (which is also called fore-time, *qedem*) and a new time (*ḥᵃdāšā*) or after time (*'ᵃḥᵃrōnōt*) – also termed the 'coming' time (*'ōtiyyōt*) – occurs a dozen times (cf. already Isa. 1.26; 9.1; Vol. 1, section 7.6.3). When the first era is mentioned, the prophet points to the exodus from Egypt and the wanderings in the desert, but also to statements about the creation – i.e., to the period of salvation history. As a 'higher' kind of time (primordial time), this is clearly differentiated, according to pre-exilic conviction, from the time succeeding the settlement of the promised land, or after David. The future 'new time', on the other hand, is coupled with the marvellous highway for Yahweh's *kābōd*, and the return home right through the desert, as well as with Cyrus or the Servant of God (42.9). 'The present time' lies between. The modern historian dates this present time as the period of Israel's monarchy; and Deutero-Isaiah's predecessors saw it as eras of increasing disaster. But the present time hardly interests our author any more. His whole stress is on the fact that salvation history is beginning anew, and that a new kind of time, a new *derek*, will be contingently set by Yahweh. Primordial time will return as the end-time. But this end-time is not in any sense a mere copy. On the contrary, the new time will far exceed the analogies of the early time. This becomes evident whenever the coming turn of events is painted as a second exodus (51.9–11; 52.11f.).

What is now proclaimed as promise is not absolutely new and therefore incomprehensible. The span joining first time and end-time is held together and embraced by Yahweh as the First (*rī'šōn*) and the Last (41.4; 46.6f.), so that God actually appears as the primal ground of time, or as the condition which makes it possible for time to come into being at all. He at least already communicated in the primordial period what his final purpose for mankind is going to be. He already anticipated the final history in his *dābār*; even the emergence of a Cyrus is no surprise to anyone who knows Yahweh (46.8–11). Because Israel is so slow of comprehension (48.3–5), her God prepared her long before, through his word, for what was to come. Nothing is further from Deutero-Isaiah's thoughts than a conception of revelation in terms of a particular point in time. Like his people, he knows that he has been absorbed into a history of speech-events which makes possible an understanding of the significance of historical happening and human life. His own visions and auditions are also no more than links in a long chain of knowledge of God in Israel.

Yahweh embraces the times monotheistically, but the different temporal eras are not in themselves homogeneous. This makes recourse to the web of divine active powers necessary, and these influence the superficial course of history to a greater or lesser degree. Unlike Jeremiah or Ezekiel, Deutero-Isaiah hardly ever falls back on the concept of negative forces in his exposition, but he refers all the more emphatically to positive active powers, which move from God to human beings, with the purpose of evoking the eschatological turn of events. For example, 51.4–8 makes it clear how the instruction (*tōrā*, which here means the same as *dābār*) has its origin in Yahweh himself, and prevails among the nations as an order founded on *mišpāṭ*. In this *mišpāṭ*, spheres of salvation based on the community (*ṣedeq*) and marvellous aids towards salvation (*yeša'*) are, together with the strength of Yahweh's arm, bestowed on human beings. In the human community this results in a permanent state of salvation (*yešū'ā* fem.) and behaviour pervaded by faithfulness to the community (*ṣedāqā* fem.) which will never again be broken.

5.5.2 Redemption. Both the primordial era of salvation history and the beginning of the end-time are marked by a redeeming act of Yahweh on behalf of his people. Deutero-Isaiah anchors the idea of redemption in the Israelite religion itself. The language of Israel's cult had already occasionally used the word *gā'al* – which is translated as 'redeem' – to describe the decisive divine intervention through which God set in motion the exodus from Egypt at the beginning of the nation's history (Ps. 74.2; 77.15). *Gā'al* is an expression drawn from family law. The word originally meant the restoration of a clan's integrity through an act of redemption, when a part of the clan had been lost; perhaps one of its members had sunk into slavery, or perhaps a piece of inherited land had had to be sold, etc. The expression was then adopted to express the Jerusalem view of the king. According to this, the Davidic king acted as the patron and redeemer of any of his subjects who could not draw on the support of an actively functioning clan organization (Ps. 72.14). In line with this, Deutero-Isaiah sees Yahweh as the king of Israel, who from time immemorial had pledged himself to redeem his people. This redemption was to be carried out anew in the liberation from Babylonian slavery, as it was once before, when Pharaoh's army was destroyed. In this Yahweh shows himself to be the power of the holy which hovers over Israel in a particular way. Isaiah uses the expression 'the Holy One of Israel' to stress the distance between God and man (cf. Vol. 1, section 7.8.5). Deutero-Isaiah employs the phrase in the opposite sense, as a reminder of the nearness of the Redeemer to the oppressed (41.14; 43.14; 47.4; and frequently elsewhere). Redemption is a unique, contingent historical act. It cannot be viewed as an active force. As an expression of the divine will it can only be expressed verbally, and emphasizes the personal character of the word basis of all positive reality, which is inclined towards Israel in a special way. The use of the term *gā'al* also brings out the fact that the eschatological turn of events will not bring about anything abruptly new. It will not mean a rupture, the discontinuance of history. It will spring out of a continuity, from the abiding faithfulness of God as the fundamental force of Israel's history.

5.5.3 Conversion to the eschatological hour. I called the prophets of the Babylonian era prophets of conversion. The description applies especially to Jeremiah and even more to Ezekiel. It is true that the prophets of this third period also put forward a *dābār* pregnant with impending doom, and that they see the trend towards this disaster as irreversible. But the *dābār's* compulsive power no longer touches the individual as directly as once it did, with Amos or Micah. Can Deutero-Isaiah also be described as a prophet of conversion? His whole message is a solicitous appeal for trust in Yahweh, in spite of all appearances to the contrary in the present constellations of history. That is why he exhorts the people to wait (40.3), and occasionally

expressly urges them to be converted (44.22). We find the most urgent
of these appeals in the final chapter, 55.6–9:

> Seek Yahweh, since he may (now) be found!
>   Call upon him, now, when he approaches!
> Let a wicked man forsake his way,
>   an evil man his thoughts.
> Let him return (*šūb*) to Yahweh, that he may have mercy upon him,
>   to our God, for he makes great (atoning) forgiveness.
> For my thoughts are not your thoughts,
>   and not your ways my ways . . .
> But as high as the heaven is above the earth,
>   so high are my ways above your ways
>   and my thoughts above your thoughts.

The last sentences are usually interpreted as a metaphorical way of
stressing God's incomprehensibility and the inability of men and
women to know him. This is probably a crass misunderstanding of
what the Hebrew intends to express. 'Height' is the quintessence of
power and the ability to prevail, and is hence a royal predicate (Isa.
6.1; 53.13). It is not an indication of infinity. Heaven is not a static
entity; it is a field of force. So what the prophet means is that human
thoughts (*maḥ°šābōt*, in the sense of purposeful designs) are powerless,
and that human ways (which are governed by the correlation between
act and destiny) frequently go astray. But Yahweh's thoughts and
ways remain purposeful and always attain their goal. They can neither
be distorted nor turned aside. So conversion means turning from one's
own questionable way to the steadfast way of God. It means relying
on God's thoughts, which can be discerned in the prophetic *dābār*. So
Deutero-Isaiah's conclusion brings him back to his beginning, where
the word which finds so mighty a consummation is also held up as
hope to transitory human beings (40.8).

Deutero-Isaiah therefore certainly belongs among the prophets of
the Babylonian era who call the individual to repentance in the face
of a mighty, divinely effected revolution. But at the same time *šūb* for
him has a different position and importance. For nothing is said about
what happens to the people who refuse to be converted, and who resist
belief in the prophetic word. There is not the slightest indication that
there are men and women in the nation who are not going to experience
the impending turn to salvation, but who will have to die first, because
of their wickedness or lack of faith. On the contrary, everyone is
included, even the people who are, in the religious sense, the blind
and the halt, whether they are in exile or in the homeland. Yahweh's
will towards salvation, and the positive forces of activity which well

up from that, are so much in the forefront of attention for this prophet in exile, that it is only in the context of the past that he feels able to talk about the completion of the correlation between evil acts and destiny; or he may at most apply it to the Babylonian oppressors (47.11). According to Deutero-Isaiah's conviction, Yahweh is a God friendly to human beings, whose will is directed towards redemption for Israel, and who desires to help all his created beings towards salvation. His *ṣedeq* will soon prevail victoriously against all evil on earth, and will call into being a better human society for the future. Here a changed understanding of God is heralded. It finds no correspondence among the other literary prophets. Deutero-Isaiah has not unjustly been called 'the evangelist of the old covenant'. But he was far in advance of his time, and pierced far beyond the knowledge of God shared by his people. And since his prophecies were not granted early fulfilment, his own followers saw themselves forced to make corrections, and to return to a more customary understanding of God.

II

The Zenith and the Decline of Prophetic Activity in the Persian Period

6. Trito-Isaiah

6.1 The turn to salvation

With Cyrus' victory the situation changed abruptly. From that time on the Israelites ceased to be second-class citizens. Even a career at court was open to them. It was not long before one of them, Nehemiah, advanced to the position of the great king's cup-bearer. Moreover the new rulers encouraged the cult of the God of heaven in Jerusalem, who had certain things in common with their own supreme God. In 538 BC, Cyrus already gave permission for the ruined temple on Zion to be rebuilt, and allowed the temple vessels which had been carried off to Babylon to be taken back to Jerusalem. A prince belonging to the dynasty of David, Sheshbazzar, was sent to Palestine from exile as special Persian commissioner for the restoration. So only a few years after Deutero-Isaiah's proclamation, the doors really did open for the prisoners, and Cyrus cleared the way for Israel's revival.

But did not the exilic prophet promise far more? Was the glory of Yahweh not to shine out over the earth, going before the exiles on the marvellous highway through the desert? The theophany which Deutero-Isaiah had painted in such glowing colours failed to materialize. Cyrus was not converted. And in Jerusalem restoration measures soon came to a halt because of an extremely uncertain political and economic situation. Israel's fate had taken a new turn; but it certainly did not mean an eschatological revolution. Deutero-Isaiah had overcome the discouragement of the people for a time, but it can be no surprise to discover that this discouragement now made itself felt once more.

The last ten chapters of the Book of Isaiah (56–66) tell us about this. The language is so closely reminiscent of Deutero-Isaiah that he has continually been taken to be their author (e.g., Smart, *History and*

Theology in Second Isaiah, 1967). But the conditions underlying these writings are completely different, pointing to the Palestinian homeland and not to the *gōlā*. Moreover the linguistic genres have hardly anything in common with those used by Deutero-Isaiah. Since the different sections lean on Deutero-Isaiah to a varying degree, scholars generally assume that they are the work of a number of different authors. The central section, 60–62, is generally attributed to one of Deutero-Isaiah's pupils. In my view there are hardly any cogent reasons for denying the same authorship to chs. 56–59 and 65.16–66.14, though an older popular lament has been incorporated in 63.7–64.12.

The texts give us no chronological information, but the period of Trito-Isaiah's activity can be narrowed down fairly exactly. The close links with Deutero-Isaiah suggest that the author was the latter's pupil, and that after Cyrus' edict he returned to the homeland (perhaps with Sheshbazzar?). There he entered into a dispute with people who had listened attentively to the strains of Deutero-Isaiah's proclamations, but were now turning away in disappointment. 60.1ff. opposes the building of the temple (which was apparently under discussion but not yet under way). So we can best assign the prophet to the years before 520; for it was after that that the new building began to be tackled in earnest.

6.2 The delay of the eschatological turn of events. Social and religious criticism

In 59.9 a popular lament (vv. 11, 14) gives vivid expression to the mood of the people:

> Still far off is for us is a healthful order of existence (*mišpāṭ*),
>> salvation founded on faithfulness to the community (*ṣᵉdāqā*) has not reached us.
> We hoped for light – behold darkness!
>> Instead of rays of brightness – we walk in gloom.

Deutero-Isaiah, full of enthusiasm for the future immediately ahead, had prophesied that unfading and imperishable *ṣᵉdāqā* was going to break in. But nothing whatsoever of this could be seen, even though Cyrus was in power and the first homecomers from Babylon were arriving. Trito-Isaiah has a clear explanation for the delay:

> The hand of Yahweh has not become too short for saving help, nor his ear deaf.
> But rather the weight of your guilt (*'āwōn*) has become a wall dividing you from your God (59.1).

Resolutely the prophet reaches back to earlier prophets – before

Deutero-Isaiah's almost unconditional promise of salvation – and demands, in the first instance, different ethical behaviour. There will be no eschatological theophany without people who show more signs of an increased faithfulness to the community than the prophet's contemporaries. A Yahweh *tōrāh* is put at the beginning, as if it were a motto (56.1), and this is both modelled on the writer's master (cf. 51.5) and deviates from him:

> Thus has Yahweh spoken:
> Keep *mišpāṭ* and perform faithfulness to the community (*ṣᵉdāqā*).
> For my saving help is ready waiting (*qᵉrōbā*) to come,
>   my *ṣᵉdāqā* to be revealed.

Although the word 'repentance' is hardly used, the behaviour of the individual takes on more importance in these chapters than in any other prophet. The writer does not stop short at general exhortations. His social criticism does not fall behind Amos in ferocity, and it is linked with an unusually radical criticism of the cult. And yet the post-exilic community is anything but indifferent to religion. Cheated of their hope for an immediate break-in of paradisal conditions, it gathers together for special fast rites and fast days (*ṣōm*) and prays fervently for salvation (probably at the site of the ruined sanctuary on Zion).

> Like a nation that has done *ṣᵉdāqā*,
>   and has not forsaken the *mišpāṭ* of their God,
> they implore of me the (eschatological) *mišpᵉṭē-ṣedeq*,
>   they desire the drawing near of God (58.2).

But the God of the prophets thunders into the midst of the rites (vv. 5–9):

> Is this what the fasting should look like which I choose:
>   a day in which a man mortifies the strength of his life?
> Is the aim to bow the head like a reed,
>   to lie down on sackcloth and ashes?
> Will you really call this fasting
>   and a day acceptable to Yahweh?
> Is not rather this the fast which I choose,
>   [murmurs Yahweh, the Almighty Lord]:
> to loose the bonds of wickedness,
>   undo the thongs of the yoke,
>   to let the ill-treated go free,
>   every yoke you should break!
> Does it not mean breaking bread for the hungry?
>   You should help the homeless to prosperity . . .

Then shall your light break forth like the morning,
    and your healing shall spring up speedily.
Before you will go your *ṣedeq*,
    the radiance of Yahweh's glory (*kābōd*) will be your rearguard.
Then you will call, and Yahweh will answer you,
    you will implore and he will respond: here I am.

Although the upper classes had been deported, conditions of subservience had developed in occupied Judah which allowed a select few to become relatively wealthy, while the mass of the people were exploited and reduced to economic dependency. The leading representatives of the national group, who were also responsible for lamentation ceremonies and fast days, are depicted by Trito-Isaiah as greedy dogs, bent only on profit (56.9–12). Critical prophecy was characterized throughout the centuries by a highly sensitive moral conscience. Social criticism was inherent in it, as it were. As soon as external conditions changed to the detriment of the lower classes, the protest broke out – with Amos and Micah in the Assyrian period, with Habukkuk under the Babylonians, and with Trito-Isaiah in the Persian era. And where social criticism was vocal, criticism of the cult was not far off. For the prophets were confronted with a society which believed that the cult provided an indispensable foundation for healthful life. It seems to be an ineradicable delusion of the human mind that it is possible to acquire a positive relationship to the numinous powers through devotional practices and sacrifices, even if this piety finds no correspondence in a parallel concern for other people and the general good. But the absolute indispensability of this link is precisely the point on which the prophets insist. To this extent their monotheism really *is* an ethical monotheism, which is coupled with a monanthropology that makes this God the centre towards which all human beings are orientated. Mere religious asceticism, a renunciation of food and pleasant clothing, in order to 'make an impression' on God, is a waste of time. Renunciation of one's own well-being – certainly! But it must be for the sake of one's neighbour in need.

Trito-Isaiah is not only permeated through and through by the conviction that a healthful relationship to Yahweh depends on continuous *ṣᵉdāqā* towards one's fellow countrymen. His actual understanding of God is an enlightened one. God does not require human gifts at all. For this reason the prophet rejects plans to rebuild the Jerusalem temple in grandiose form. Deutero-Isaiah's polemic against the images of the gods as human inventions is now taken even further, and extends to the building used for religious purposes (66.1ff.):

Heaven is my throne,
   the earth is my footstool.
Where then is a house which you could build for me? . . .
All these things my hand has made.

The objection that a temple is necessary for sacrificial ceremonies is
not convincing. In the dispute about the project to rebuild the temple,
the late Trito-Isaiah (56.7 still reflects an earlier view) dissociates
himself from the foundations of Israelite cultic religion as does no
other prophet. The God whom he hears speaking within himself
loathes blood and incense. What takes place in the temple is a crime
against animal (and plant) life:

He who slaughters the ox – a killer of men!
   He who sacrifices the sheep – a strangler of dogs!
He who present food offerings – (that is like) swines' blood!
   He who lights incense – a worshipper of evil things! (66.3).

At the same time, it would be a modern misunderstanding to deduce
from statements like this that Trito-Isaiah totally rejected the general
conviction about the sacred place, and about a particular presence of
Yahweh on Zion, as the cultic centre of the world. Of course for him
Zion was still the holy mountain, even though no grandiose temple
stood there. It was a privilege for anyone to be allowed to set up a
stele there, bearing his own name (56.5). Yet Trito-Isaiah turns this
holiness against the priests. He tears down the barriers between what
was ritually clean and unclean. According to the traditional view, a
eunuch or a non-Israelite was unable to participate in the Yahweh
cult (Deut. 23.1–8). From the very beginning, Trito-Isaiah's God
does away with this conception. Deutero-Isaiah had dreamt about
Yahweh's salvation, which was to reach out from Jerusalem to the
ends of the earth. According to Trito-Isaiah, this presupposes a
corresponding openness towards all human beings on the part of
the Judaeans. Seeing themselves as a holy people, the post-exilic
community was showing an increasing tendency to close themselves
to the outside world. Trito-Isaiah proclaims that God's will is the
exact opposite of this: 'My house shall be called a house of prayer for
all peoples' (56.7). Anyone who adheres to this God is welcome.
   There is only one sphere of holiness which has to be preserved
absolutely: the sabbath. Keeping the seventh day of the week free of
work, and using it for worship, means acknowledging Yahweh's
covenant with Israel (56.2–8). One day 'all flesh' will recognize the
sabbath as a healthful institution, and will make pilgrimages to Zion
on the appropriate days (66.23, a later interpolation). Some scholars

are distrustful here, suspecting that a post-exilic religion of the law is invading prophetic preaching. But although Trito-Isaiah may have been influenced by Ezekiel at this point (Ezek. 20.12 and frequently elsewhere), he never takes over Ezekiel's teaching about the law. It is more probable that what is being expounded here is a prophetic conviction common to the whole Babylonian period – the conviction that Yahweh has created the rhythms of time for both history and the eschaton; and that he has assigned a decisive role to the number seven (for Jeremiah's view cf. 2.9.3. above).

This interpretation of time may explain why Trito-Isaiah waits for a sabbatical year, as a year of God's good pleasure, which will usher in the eschatological turn of events. Deutero-Isaiah had linked the dawn of this new era with the activity of the Servant of God (49.8). Trito-Isaiah also makes an anonymous spokesman come forward in this context. He presents himself as Yahweh's plenipotentiary (though without the title *'ebed*; cf. 61.1–6):

> The wind of the spirit (*rū*ᵃ*ḥ*) of the Almighty Lord Yahweh is upon me,
>> because Yahweh has anointed me . . .
> to proclaim to captives a year of release (*d*ᵉ*rōr*),
>> an opening to those in bonds . . .
> that they may be called trees of the salvation of the community (*ṣedeq*),
>> a planting of Yahweh's for his glory.
> And they shall build up the devastations of primordial times . . .
> They shall employ strangers to feed your flocks,
>> foreigners shall be your ploughmen and vine dressers.
> But you shall be called priests of Yahweh . . .
>> You shall eat the wealth of nations.

The song is generally interpreted as a statement made by the prophet about himself. But the liberating act which is described goes beyond any prophetic authorization, and is reminiscent of the royal power of disposal. (The same impression is given by the power conferred over members of a foreign tribe.) Is some person, who is designated to be ruler (perhaps Sheshbazzar?), appearing in front of the congregation here, in a liturgical setting? (When Luke's Jesus – Luke 4.14–22 – relates the saying to his own authority, he is certainly not thinking merely of a prophetic office.)

6.3 The eschatological theophany and a renewed society

In spite of all his criticism of his fellow countrymen, Trito-Isaiah still hopes that God's glory will appear in the imminent future and will

transform the earth. But he detaches the eschatological turn of events
from any movements which are apparently taking place on the world
stage. Neither a Nebuchadnezzar (as in Jeremiah) nor a Cyrus (as in
Deutero-Isaiah) are presented as signs of the impending world-wide
transformation. The break-in of Yahweh's *kābōd* into this world, and
the far-reaching results for mankind which will follow, now turns into
a far-off expectation (like, later, the early Christian hope for the
coming of the kingdom of God). This is the real meaning of the cry
which is familiar from the Advent liturgy of the Christian church:

> Arise, become light, for your light is coming,
>   and the glory (*kābōd*) of Yahweh is rising above you.
> For behold, gloom covers the earth
>   and deep darkness the people.
> But above you Yahweh will arise,
>   and his glory will appear above you.
> And nations will come to your light,
>   kings to the brightness that radiates over you (60.1f.).

The active forces which Yahweh uses to evoke the new turn given to
the world are presented in notably material and spatial terms. But at
the same time Trito-Isaiah links them so closely with Yahweh himself
that it is God's own spatial dimension that is stressed. It seems as if
the lack of political ties is compensated for by the material character
of the theophany:

> Yahweh saw . . .
>   that (there was) no *mišpāṭ* . . .
> Then his own arm helped him,
>   his *ṣ⁴dāqā* upheld him.
> He put on *ṣ⁴dāqā* as corslet,
>   the helmet of saving help on his head.
> He put on garments of vengeance,
>   wrapped himself in zeal as a mantle . . .
> From sunset they see the name of Yahweh,
>   from sunrise his *kābōd*.
> To Zion will come a redeemer
>   for those of Jacob's rebellion who are converted (59.15–20).

Once arrived at Zion, Yahweh concludes the new covenant. In the
new Jerusalem, forces such as the state of salvation (*y⁴šū'ā*) become a
wall, faithfulness to the community becomes an authority, and well-
being (*šālōm*) a commander (60.17f.). Here these active forces resemble
angelic powers (cf. 61.10f.; 62.1; 63.1–6. a later interpolation), and
they make a political organization seem superfluous for the Israel of

the future. Something like a society free of domination will at last become an earthly reality.

Although the dawn of eschatological salvation is not anchored in contemporary history, Trito-Isaiah nevertheless describes its economic conditions and their results with a detail we do not find in any other of the prophets. Not only will the nations be at the disposal of the Israelites for menial work. Israel's former oppressors will even have to hand over their silver and gold in Jerusalem. In the new nation a just correspondence between work and enjoyment will be ensured: 'I will not again give your grain . . . to be food for your enemies . . . but those who harvest it shall eat it and praise Yahweh' (62.8f.). Human labour will cease to be a toil, women will bear children without pain, people will live to be at least a hundred years old, and peace will reign in the animal world (65.15.25; cf. 11.6–8). But the premise is still that the Israelites change their way of living. They *themselves* must prepare the way for Yahweh's coming – while Deutero-Isaiah had still envisaged that this way would be prepared by heavenly beings (40.3–6, like 57.14–21 and 62.10ff., is reinterpreted, in a similar way to Mark 1.3f. later; just as Deutero-Isaiah himself reinterpreted traditional cultic hymns).

With Trito-Isaiah a prophet appears on the scene who, in the wretched conditions of post-exilic Jerusalem, tried to change the golden sovereigns offered by Deutero-Isaiah into smaller coin. He did so by rectifying Deutero-Isaiah's ideas about the unconditional grace of God, excluding the notion of cheap grace without human repentance. But at the same time he raised God's true being from the level of cultic pursuits in a way that was truly revolutionary. This last idea found no echo among the people by whom he was surrounded. Haggai and Zechariah (who appear as prophets on the Jerusalem stage soon after Trito-Isaiah) were to proclaim the contrary: in their opinion there is no healthful relationship between man and God without a properly ordered cult. And it was they, not Trito-Isaiah, who from then on were to determine the course of Israel's religious history.

7.   Haggai and Zechariah ben Berechiah

7.1 Propaganda for a new temple

7.1.1 The political success of prophecy. The Persian kings exerted themselves to win the support of the Israelites. In 538, soon after the conquest of Babylon, Cyrus issued an edict officially permitting the temple in Jerusalem to be rebuilt (Ezra 6.3–5; 1.2–4). Sheshbazzar, the first provincial governor nominated by the Persians, tried to take up the work, but failed, probably because of political unrest coupled with the poor economic circumstances of the time. It was only in 520 that a second governor, Zerubbabel, a descendant of Jerusalem's ancient royal house, took up the attempt once more. This time he was supported by Jeshua, a high priest (it is the first time the title is used). The building of the temple got under way. Zerubbabel was supported, if not actually urged on, by two nabis, Haggai and Zechariah. The success of these 'twin prophets' was enormous, although they were only active for a short time. Their sayings are precisely dated. Haggai made his first fiery speech on 29 August 520 BC. Clearing-up work began twenty-four days later, and on 18 December 520 the foundation stone was ceremonially laid. On this occasion Haggai again addressed the people. We hear nothing more about him after that. His fellow-nabi, Zechariah, took up his proclamation a little later, in October/November 520. In February 519 he experienced his Night Visions. (We shall be looking at these more closely in a moment.) His final word was spoken in December 518. His appeal to the people and their leaders bore fruit, for the rebuilt temple was consecrated in 515 BC. But he does not seem to have experienced the success of his efforts, and neither do Zerubbabel and Jeshua, the two non-prophetic figures who played so important a part in the temple's rebuilding. None the less, the achievement of these men cannot be estimated too highly. According to all historical criteria, Israel's continued existence in the centuries that followed would have been unthinkable without the renewal of a cultic centre. For five hundred years the temple was to be the backbone of Israel; and for Jesus of Nazareth it was still 'that which is my Father's' (Luke 2.49). The high priest who was in office there really united the whole of the nation in himself, and possessed the highest authority. For this Haggai and Zechariah laid the theoretical foundations. If historically palpable success is to be the yardstick, none of Israel's prophets were as successful as these. Never before and never afterwards did prophecy find so general an echo in the public awareness. Never was prophetic theory translated so directly into general political practice. Never otherwise did it evoke institutions that were to last for centuries. Consequently it is worth going into this last climax of prophecy in more detail, even if the prophecies which were *associated* with the building of the temple, but went beyond it, were anything but fulfilled.

7.1.2 Judaism as it is alleged to be. The twin prophets usher in the post-exilic age. For a good hundred years, Old Testament scholars have made a practice of pointing to this historical turning point as marking the transition from Israelite religion to Judaism. They see it as a change in the *form* taken by Israel's religion, at least, if not actually a change in the religion itself. And this new form is bound up with the notion of narrow-mindedness, exclusiveness, the absolutism of the law, and a righteousness of works. Consequently these two men – but Haggai especially – are often called 'the fathers of Judaism'. Even so careful an interpreter as Rudolph (*Commentary*, p. 57) writes about the 'heavy mortgage' which has 'burdened Judaism ever since the time of Haggai', attributing to him a 'doctrine of retaliation' as the mainspring of his message.

Now, there is no doubt that the exile was a caesura that cut deep. At the same time, from 732 BC at the latest, Israel/Judah had been a non-independent part of a foreign empire, governed by dependent native rulers. In the post-exilic period this dependency grew, but the change was only a partial one. In addition, with the second temple a great deal of the Deutero-nomically influenced religion of pre-exilic times was taken up once more – so much so that it is hardly justifiable to talk here about a historical watershed. Is the law ever really made totally absolute in any of the texts available to us? Down to the Maccabean period, nothing of the kind can definitely be demonstrated. It therefore seems to me inappropriate and anachronistic to introduce the name Judaism to describe the Persian (mid-Israelite) period; the word Judaism belongs to a totally different epoch.

There is not a word at this point about the fixed and established law as the norm for human behaviour (this conviction being character-istic of Judaism). Fasting, one of the most important religious observ-ances among ancient oriental cults, is treated ironically as superfluous, even when the occasion is a ceremony of lamentation recalling the destruction of the temple: 'These seventy years, was it for me that you fasted?' (Zech. 7.5). It is true that the *derek* way (as Haggai calls the act-destiny correlation) is in such a miserable state in Israel that heaven and earth are closing themselves up and withholding their blessing, because the people are putting their own luxurious way of living first. They are self-centred and are therefore taking no part in building the temple (Haggai 1.4–8, 10). Because the house of God is left desolate (*ḥārēb*), Yahweh is calling forth devastation (*ḥōreb*) over fields and cattle and human beings, and all the products of human hands (Hag. 1.9; cf. 2.17). But no laws are infringed in this case; and Yahweh only *intensifies* with his own actions what human beings have already begun. The strict correspondence here between the acts of God and the acts of man suggests that we should avoid talking about retaliation as a pre-eminently motivating force. According to the prophetic view, it is stupid and unwise to keep one's eyes fixed merely on results in the superficial sense, without being aware of the ties between human fate and the house in which God himself comes close to the earth, and where he makes beneficial supernatural forces available to men and women.

7.1.3 Holiness as the factor that evokes the fertility of the earth. Haggai and Zechariah are given the title nabi. Does this mean that they are identified as cultic prophets officiating at Zion, where priests and nabis continued to hold office in spite of the destruction of the temple (Zech. 7.3)? Whatever their social position may have been, in their thinking at least they were prophets within the context of the cult, Haggai even more so than Zechariah.

Haggai's intellectual world depends entirely on the priestly dichotomy between a holy and an unclean world. We find similar ideas in the Priestly Writing and in Ezekiel. As soon as holiness once more rests on Zion, and the *kābōd*, the radiance of the divine glory, has again its extended presence on earth, *šālōm* will spread over the earth by way of the cultic place, of course rippling out in concentric circles in accordance with prophetic monanthropology (Hag. 2.3–9; cf. 1.8; Zech. 2.9; 8.13). But until then 'this people here' will necessarily remain in a state of impurity, 'unclean in the power of its life' (*ṭᵉmē'-nepeš*); and everything which is the work of its hands will inevitably be infected by this disastrous sphere. Haggai stresses this in the speech he makes on the day when the foundation of the temple is laid (Hag. 2.10–19). Only the holy presence of God makes it possible for people to be liberated from the correlation between misdeed and calamity, which paralyses the doer of the deed, and entangles sinners more and more as time goes on; for it is the curse of the evil act that from the moment when it is committed, evil is forced to go on bringing forth evil. But the foundation stone of the temple represents the first efficacious token of the divine presence; so it can be the place of an atonement which liberates the cultic community from the guilt which clings to it, and which has been imposed in the course of history (Zech. 3.9). So the feast day brings an abrupt change in the situation. From now on blessing and fertility will stream from the temple with positively magic efficacy:

But now! Turn your mind to this day and what will come after it.
Before a stone was placed upon a stone in Yahweh's temple, before they were there, one came to a heap of corn of (what had been) twenty measures, and they had become but ten . . .
Turn your mind to this day and what will come after it . . .
Will the seed still remain (dead) in the furrow(?)?

Will the vine, the fig tree, the pomegranate and the olive tree still
yield no fruit?
From this day on I will bless! (Hag. 2.15–19; cf. Zech. 3.8–10).

The modern reader finds it difficult to follow such flights of fancy, and
to assent to such a one-track kind of causality. Today it seems to
us inconceivable that the vegetation of a country should change
completely because a particular foundation stone has been laid. But
the saying is a striking example of monanthropological thought.
According to this way of thinking, there is no such thing as nature as
a self-acting force, suspended between the two poles of reality, between
God and his holiness on the one side, and man with the work of his
hands on the other. But one wonders whether, at the time, people –
clinging in faith to the prophetic saying – were not really convinced
in succeeding years that they actually had gathered in exceptionally
large harvests, even if modern statistics were to arrive at different
findings?

7.2 The double rule of prince and priest. Actualizing eschatology

The words which Haggai proclaims to Zerubbabel, the ruling
governor, are just as high-flown as the expectation of the period of
blessing which is to ensue immediately after the reopening of the
temple. He designates him as nothing less than the ruler over the
whole world. Yahweh will soon shake the universe so that the thrones
of the ruling princes will topple and a struggle of each against all will
break out on earth. Then Zerubbabel will be the signet ring on the
hand of God, the ring which God will use to stamp his will to peace
into the very earth itself (Hag. 2.20–23). However, Haggai does not
usually confine what he says solely to the governor. He also addresses
the high priest, Jeshua (1.1; 2.2). Zechariah goes a step further in the
same direction. It is true that he also sees the Davidic prince, with his
provocative Babylonian name, 'branch of Babylon', as the future ruler
of the world. He is going to defeat the great mountain (the great
power of the moment?) without weapons, solely through the wind of
Yahweh's spirit (4.7). But Zechariah moves the high priest into a
position of equal rank. In a symbolic action (6.9–15), the prophet
causes (two) crowns to be made, which are first of all placed on the
high priest's head but are then deposited in the temple as votive
offerings (until the new eschatological beginning). At the crowning,
Zechariah utters the promise:

Behold a man, a branch (*ṣemaḥ*) is his name, . . . will shoot up.
He shall build Yahweh's temple,
    and he shall bear splendour.

He shall set himself on his throne and rule,
   and there shall be a priest on (beside?) his throne.
Planning of *šālōm* shall spring up
   between the two.

The text has often been made worse by attempted emendation. Some scholars think that what was originally meant was a crown which had been set on Zerubbabel's head – as if any such coronation would have been possible during the presence of Persian troops of occupation! Other interpreters conjecture that after the disappearance of Zerubbabel, the high priest alone was to be crowned. If the text is left as it stands, it predicts that in the future state of salvation there will be two people at the head of Israel (cf. 4.14). It is only the high priest who can be crowned without danger. So he embodies in his person both aspirants to the throne. Earlier prophecies had already prepared the ground for a coupling of the two offices (I Sam. 2.35; Jer. 33.20–22; Ezek. 44.15ff., as well as 45.7ff.); but it is here that it is formulated for the first time as a dyarchical principle. The view that Israel will be represented in the End-time, not through a single 'embodiment' of its corporate personality, but through a double head, later had its influence in the expectation of two messiahs, one of them a priest and one a king. We find this version of the messianic hope five hundred years later, in the Qumran texts. This suggests that the division of offices and separation of powers reflected a need that was more than merely pragmatic. (The same may be said of the still later mediaeval parallelism of papacy and Empire.) It may well be that the inevitable pollution of the king's 'hands' through violence and blood was one reason. But in addition there is probably the fear that power could be abused if it were in the possession of one person only.

The expression *ṣemaḥ* for the messianic saviour king (also Zech. 3.8) is taken from the Book of Jeremiah (Jer. 23.5; 33.15). It seems to have been intentionally chosen as a word-play on the name Zerubbabel, 'branch of Babylon'. But is it intended to indicate the *identity* of the two, or their antithesis (at a time when Zerubbabel had already dropped out as claimant)?

When the two prophets view as the essential eschatological saving figures men personally known to them, in their own immediate circle, they are going a step beyond all previous critical prophecy. Of course Amos and Isaiah already believed that the hands on the clock of world history were pointing to five minutes to twelve. But for them the decisive hour had simply not yet dawned; whereas Haggai and Zechariah believe that it has actually arrived. They are convinced that the temple which is in the course of being built will become the centre of a renewed humanity. The governor already in office, Zerubbabel, together with the now officiating high priest, are the men to whom Yahweh entrusts the future world-wide peaceful order. This view has been termed *actualizing eschatology*, meaning the realization of end-time expectations in the present. In some sense this eschatology can already be detected in Deutero-Isaiah, when the eschatological Servant of God is presented, and the military hero Cyrus is celebrated as messiah. But Deutero-Isaiah had not seen the Persian king with his own eyes (or perhaps the Servant of God either?). This means that there was still a gap between the present and eschatological vehicles of salvation, which after 520 no longer seemed to exist.

There would seem to have been two reasons for the transition to actualizing eschatology. One is the deliberate reversion to the literary prophecy that was already in existence. Jeremiah had talked about seventy years of desolation for Jerusalem (25.11; 29.10). This period of wrath (which must be dated as beginning in 587/6, according to our reckoning) had almost been completed. So the new beginning was immediately imminent! Again we see how eagerly the prophets of the Babylonian and Persian eras were on the look-out for numbers in history. The second reason is to be found in actual political events. In Persia, orderly succession to the throne came to an end in 522, with Cambyses. A civil war broke out between Darius, who came from a subsidiary Achaemenid line, and the Magian Gaumata. Darius prevailed, and defeated a series of other rebels as well, as he proudly announces in his inscription in Behistun.[31] Soon after peace has once more been established in the empire, Zechariah begins to complain about the deceptive peace reigning in world politics. Like Haggai, he distrusts it. He earnestly hopes that Yahweh will soon remove Darius from his throne by means of a marvellous cosmic war. So Trito-Isaiah's prophetic successors in Jerusalem, unlike him, are concerned to link their prophecies with actual political conditions.

But Darius was not overthrown. Nor did Zerubbabel become universal ruler nor Jeshua become eschatological high priest. Successful though the twin prophets were when they urged on the building of the temple, they were obviously mistaken when they promised that a new order of salvation would immediately follow all over the world. Christian interpreters see actualizing eschatology of this kind as a regrettable prophetic *faux pas*. But does this view not fail to grasp the prophets' understanding of the *dābār*, the effective word which has its origin in God? Their interpretation is fundamentally different from our modern view. Neither information nor communication are the decisive factors in the use of this speech sign; the essential element is dynamic, not noetic. The *dābār* is an active force, which 'lives on' until it reaches the recipient and is materialized in him (Zech. 1.5f.). So the *dābār* is like a remote-control weapon, whose direction can be altered without its losing impact. How else can we explain the fact that the supporters of Haggai and Zechariah retain the sayings about Zerubbabel, and do not expunge the names? According to the Hebrew understanding, even when proper names are used in a prophecy, this indicates no more than a trend, not an unalterable point. For the most part the prophecies of disaster uttered by the literary prophets were fulfilled; but from the very beginning this was not true of the prophecies of salvation. The calamity that is fulfilled and the salvation that fails to materialize diverge materially. This is true even in Isaiah's expectation of the messiah; and it applies even more to Deutero-Isaiah's proclamation of God's eschatological return home to Zion. The fact that the hope continued to be passed on is only explicable if later readers reckoned as a matter of course with the possibility that, in the prophets' expectation of salvation, the temporal perspective is foreshortened. That is to say, later readers were still convinced that the *dābār* of salvation which had once been proclaimed would yet be fulfilled. For this *dābār* gave expression to a future which subsequent insight grasped as being the logical development of the metahistory hitherto determined by God. It is possible to talk about an 'erroneous belief'[32] in connection with these prophecies only if the prophetic understanding of the Word is ignored.

Of course there is a surplus of hope in the prophecies of salvation, since at the expected time they are only fulfilled in part, or are not fulfilled at all. This led to temptation and disappointment among the prophets' listeners. But the prophets' own followers felt the delay in fulfilment to be an incentive to adaptation and new interpretation. It was not in any way seen as a refutation (see the relation between Trito-Isaiah and Deutero-Isaiah). Nevertheless it was another five hundred years before an Israelite again dared to present an actualizing eschatology in the language of prophecy; and that was Jesus of Nazareth.

7.3 A night in February

A cycle of seven Night Visions (with an eighth as coda) provides the basis for Zechariah 1.7 – 6.8. Here the genre of prophetic visionary accounts is fashioned into its most splendid form. A large number of actors are introduced, all of whom play an imporant part in Zechariah's metahistory. The wealth of images in the fascinatingly taut succession of scenes finds no parallel in the literature of the ancient East. Yet the language is economical and allusive; not a detail is superfluous or introduced merely for the sake of ornament. Nowhere else in the Old Testament does the Hebrew world picture emerge as clearly as it does here. But it remains questionable how far these are all genuine, ancient *Israelite* conceptions. Zechariah belonged to the priestly family of Iddo, which had been deported to Babylon. Was he one of the people who had returned home (Neh. 12.2)? And is the web of his ideas shot through with Babylonian conceptions? At all events he becomes an important point of transition for the mental development of post-exilic Israel. His metahistory was based on his subsequent insight into what the Night Visions had revealed to him; and his method here had a greater influence than any other kind of prophetic theory of history.

In the first Night Vision (1.8ff.), the prophet's inner eye moves to the western edge of the disc of the world. There he sees two myrtle trees, rising out of the depths of the sea and marking the entrance to heaven. It is evening. The prophet sees supernatural riders gathering together, mounted on mysterious brown, light-red (?) and white horses. They have traversed the earth – presumably the three continents known to the geography of the time (Asia, Europe and 'Libya'). Their leader comes to a halt between the myrtles, and makes his report to the *mal'ak yahweh*, Yahweh's (chief) angel or (chief) messenger, who is also standing there. The earth is quiet, he says. But the *mal'ak yahweh* finds this anything but reassuring. He immediately ejaculates a petition (in the same way as earlier prophets; cf. Amos 7.1ff.): 'Yahweh Sabaoth! How long wilt thou deny thy mercy to Jerusalem and the cities of Judah, which thou hast treated as cursed these seventy years?' The presumption underlying the scene is that there will be a turn in Israel's fate and a way out of her oppression only if the world of the nations as a whole begins to move. Then Zechariah perceives how Yahweh conveys consoling words to the *angelus interpres*, the interpreting angel, a second *mal'āk*, who accompanies him (as, later, Virgil accompanies the poet in Dante's *Divine Comedy*). Unlike the earlier prophets, Zechariah is no longer able to understand what God is saying directly. But the *mal'āk* who 'speaks in him' – i.e., stands ready to interpret for the prophet – translates the divine message for him. God's wave of wrath, *qeṣep*, hung over Jerusalem for a short time and used the foreign nations as agents of doom. But it is now swinging round against the nations, while Yahweh himself is returning to Jerusalem and allowing his house to be built there.

Before God returns home, earthly impediments will be set aside. So the second vision opens up a vista over the whole world. Four mighty horns tower up threateningly from it. The interpreting angel explains that these are the great nations (Egypt, Assyria, Babylon and Persia?) who have scattered Judah over the lands. Afterwards huge smiths

appear, supernatural beings, apparently armed with hammers with
which to strike off the horns (1.18–21).

The vision moves further on, to Jerusalem, which for the Israelites
is the earth's centre, its navel. Zechariah becomes aware of a man
who wants to measure the length and breadth of the city's future
layout with a measuring rod. But he is ordered back by a special
messenger (*mal'āk*). Jerusalem is to rise again as an open city, a
settlement without walls, overflowing with people and cattle. Yahweh
himself, returning to the city, will become a wall of fire surrounding
it, and he will be the *kābōd* – the radiant glory – within it (2.1–5).

The central vision moves from the holy city to the temple mount.
There a lamp towers up, crowned with a great bowl full of oil. At its
edge the bowl opens into seven smaller bowls, each of them with seven
lips, so that forty-nine wicks are burning. The lamp symbolizes the
seven eyes of Yahweh, which survey the earth. According to the
context, the lamp even now hovers invisibly over Zion or will in the
near future become the main feature of the newly consecrated temple
there. Scholars are divided as to whether the lamp symbolizes merely
the temple, or God himself. Probably the question is wrongly formulated; for the temple is going to become Yahweh's dwelling (2.10) and
the light which streams out from it is nothing other than the *kābōd*
which dwells in the midst of Jerusalem (2.5).

Significantly enough, for Zechariah the main feature of the
sanctuary is not the sacrificial altar, or the ark, as was the case before
the exile. It is the lamp with its extraordinary light. Is this the influence
of a religion which took its bearings from the stars? Are the seven eyes
perhaps actually identical with the seven planets? At all events, for
men and women they represent a vitalizing power. (That the eyes
survey the earth will hardly be intended to suggest close supervision.
That was a task entrusted to the riders in ch. 1. It is therefore
inappropriate to assume that 'the eyes of the king' – the Persian secret
police – provided the model.) Right and left of the lamp stands an
olive tree, connected with the lamp by pipes (perhaps funnels?).
Unfortunately it is not clear whether the trees keep the lamp filled
with oil, or vice versa. Zechariah asks the meaning of two tufted olive
branches. (Are they part of the trees, or identical with them?) He is
told: 'These are the two sons of oil who stand above the (enthroned)
Almighty Lord of the whole earth, ready to do him service.' The 'sons
of oil' are generally taken to be the high priest, Jeshua, and the
prince, Zerubbabel (the two pillars sustaining the double sovereignty)
because their offices have been – or will be – conferred on them
through anointing with holy oil. But this interpretation is not certain.
The fact that the two are standing above the Almighty seems to

presuppose that they are in heaven. Are they perhaps meant to be the heavenly representatives of monarchy and priesthood? On the other hand, it is astonishing that there should be talk about 'sons of the juice of the olive'. Do Jeshua and Zerubbabel only represent the olive bushels on the tree, as distinct from the tree itself? However they are to be explained, the two 'sons of oil' certainly have to do with the eyes of Yahweh, which means that, like these eyes, they exercise a global function, and do so from the temple in Jerusalem, the centre of the world.

Further visions overcome the prophet. In 5.1–4 he becomes aware of *a book scroll* 10 metres by 5, which is flying over the earth. This is interpreted as a curse, a destructive power hovering over every dwelling place. Wherever anyone commits theft or perjury, this power penetrates his house and eats away the walls. So spheres of misdeeds and consequent doom are not merely consummated in human beings themselves; they also find completion in the places which have been infected by them.

In the scroll vision, the point is the elimination of the consequences of sin. The following vision is concerned with the actual roots of the evil act (5.5ff.). A huge cask comes into view, in the midst of the landscape. Its leaden cover is raised and an ugly woman can be seen. The interpreting angel identifies her as the personification of wickedness (*riš'ā*). The angel otherwise confines himself to words, but here he becomes violent, pushing the woman back into the cask and closing the lid. Two other supernatural women with storks' wings suddenly appear on the scene and carry off the perilous freight to Mesopotamia, where a pedestal is already waiting for it, and a temple is being built to receive it. The text does not expressly say so, but the trend of the eschatological events suggests that the woman will only stay there temporarily. (Comparable with the incident is the elimination of wickedness from the cultivated lands by means of expiatory rites; cf. Lev. 16.21; 14.4–7.) The wickedness is concentrated on that particular spot of earth first of all, so that it may be got rid of completely. Up to now human wickedness has had its 'official residence' near Jerusalem. If it were to be destroyed there, the Judaean people would again be affected. That is why the threatening power is carried off to a faraway place.

The last vision (6.1–8) transports Zechariah to the eastern ends of the earth, where the two bronze mountains of the sunrise stand. Four chariots drive out of the mountain, drawn by four horses of different kinds, each of them intended for a different direction. The horses represent the winds of heaven (*rūᵃḥ* plur.). The chariot drawn by black horses brings the wind of the spirit (*rūᵃḥ* sing.) to the north. With this the account of the Night Visions comes to an abrupt end. The north country means Mesopotamia (in accordance with the way the points of the compass were defined at that time). Commentators discuss whether it is to the exiled Israelites that a wind of the spirit blowing in that direction is given, so that they may be converted, and capable of returning home; or whether the conversion of men and women is beginning in Babylon (cf. the conversion of the nations, 2.15; 8.20–23); or whether this time the wind of the spirit is a negative force, a gust blowing to destroy the foreign nations, so that Israel may be helped to achieve greater glory. If we take the visions as a whole, a destructive action seems the most likely explanation. According to 5.11, wickedness found its home in the north. It is here that it must be encountered, before the world can really be better. That is why in another passage Zechariah calls to his contemporaries to flee from the northern country (2.6f.).

However, this by no means signifies that Zechariah sees God's history with human beings as foundering in a fathomless end-of-the-world. What he says about future salvation is far too unequivocal for any such view to be possible. But the cycle of Night Visions does not purport to be the outline of a complete eschatological drama. The visions are concerned solely with the most immediate future: the break-through to the End-time with its blessedness – a break-through which on the evidence of metahistory was sure to come. Other prophets had already written about this End-time more precisely. Zechariah merely intends to provide notes to what had been said long before by 'the former prophets' (a phrase he uses frequently). His series of Night Visions describes no more than the prelude. What is going to happen after the great upheaval (*rā'aš*) is another matter altogether. The Night Visions show how variously sin and the misuse of rule weigh on human history, working themselves out in doom, in accordance with the correlation between act and destiny.

If we survey the whole cycle, we can see that there is a logical progression from the first vision to the last. Geographically, events begin in the west and move over the centre of the earth to the east. This progression in space may perhaps correspond to a temporal sequence: evening (sunset, the west), midnight (the north), morning (sunrise, the east). The horizontal movement is part of an elaborately wrought symmetry, in which the middle vision is the zenith. The two 'outermost' visions – the first and the last – have their setting beyond the human sphere. The second and third – representing the elimination of external political hindrances – correspond to the fifth and sixth, where sin as inner hindrance is eradicated. But the dramatic tension increases steadily, from the first vision to the last, from the complete quiescence of the worlds to the movement of their end.

The prophet himself has interpolated a later vision into ch. 3. This stands out from the rest because it has a different structure; but in content its position is appropriate enough, since it centres on the purification of the high priest, Jeshua. This has to take place before the temple with the lamp (4.1ff.) can take up its function. Here Zechariah sees Jeshua standing before Yahweh's chief angel. Satan has just arrived there, with an accusation against the high priest. Satan is by no means God's adversary (as he was later to be in apocalyptic and the New Testament). He is more like a prosecuting counsel, the heavenly attorney general. But Yahweh's angel rejects Satan's indictment, commanding that Jeshua's filthy clothes should be taken away and that he should be dressed in festive garments. The incident brings out the 'enveloping' character of the act-destiny correlation. Then Jeshua is installed in office. He has to administer the temple, and is therefore given the right of immediate access to the angelic beings. The high priest seems thereby to have been assigned a task which had previously been thought to belong to Zerubbabel (4.9). It therefore seems as though there had been complications with Zerubbabel during the building of the temple, and that these made the prophet surrender the hopes placed in the governor. In the coda to the vision, therefore, it is Jeshua who is installed as 'omen' or foretoken of the future messiah (3.8), not the governor in office. But a dubious light has evidently been thrown on the high priest as well. However, according to the vision his faults seem to be forgivable; and they have in fact already been forgiven in the reality underlying human events.

Quite apart from their specific announcement of a sudden turn of events all over the world, the Night Visions are illuminating in what they reveal about a new dimension in prophetic metahistory. I shall look at this next.

7.4 Metahistory and angelology

Outside the Night Visions, Haggai and Zechariah adopt the usual prophetic practice of pointing to a whole complex of divine active powers which are at work in the world. These open up new possibilities contingent in human history; or they may influence history, so that human acts can find their completion in a corresponding destiny as soon as possible. For both Haggai and Zechariah, the wind of the spirit (*rū^{a}ḥ*) is of pre-eminent importance here. The *rū^{a}ḥ* proceeds from Yahweh and sweeps over the earth, being connected with the winds that blow from the different points of the compass (Zech. 6.1–8). The wind of the spirit inspires prophets (Zech. 7.12); it makes a human leader like Zerubbabel unconquerable by armies and the forces of power (Zech. 4.6); and it brings about the almost superhuman achievement of the temple, built by a wretched and poverty-stricken national group (Hag. 1.14; 2.5). Hardly less important is the radiance of glory, the *kābōd*, which descends upon the new temple. As well as influencing the country's fertility, the *kābōd* also has a mysterious relationship to all the gold and silver on earth (Hag. 1.8; 2.7–9). It will be the protective blaze surrounding the new Jerusalem to protect it (Zech. 2.5). A cloud of wrath, called *qeṣep*, is often mentioned. This is a foreboding power proceeding from Yahweh. In the long term it has an effect on human wickedness. For seventy years it had hovered over Jerusalem, but now it was moving away to the other nations (Zech 1.2f., 15; 7.12; 8.14).

Zechariah counts as a minor prophet because the writing he has left behind him is a short one. But he nevertheless stands out among all the literary prophets because in his Night Visions he develops a world-wide cosmic panorama unparalleled in the Old Testament. Israel, although she is Yahweh's own people, is not intended to isolate herself. It is true that the whole pageant, from the second to the penultimate vision, is centred on Israel's fate. But what happens seems to be 'pervious', so to speak – accessible to humanity in general; for it is with the pilgrimage of all mankind to Jerusalem that the Book of Zechariah closes (8.20–23). The God whom Zechariah worships is for him the lord ('*ādōn*) of the whole earth. In order to make this comprehensible to men and women, a multiplicity of other beings play a part in the Night Visions. These are active in the field of force existing between Yahweh and the human history that is exposed to view. The theologian generally classifies these beings as *angels*, although it is to only a few of them that Zechariah gives the equivalent Hebrew title, *mal'āk*, messenger. Figures of this kind are foreign to earlier prophecy. The first hints can be found in Ezekiel (ch. 9) and Deutero-Isaiah (40.1–11); but there is nothing as systematic as what we find in Zechariah. Here numinous riders are in action. They travel over the earth every day, and in the evening give a report to the Almighty through their commander. Smiths emerge from an imaginary room and knock off the horns which reach into invisible, supernatural space from the visible powers who rule the earth. A man, imperceptible to the normal eye, measures out the future ground-plan of the city of Jerusalem. A woman sits in the midst of the open country, and concentrates in her own person all existing (and potential?) human wickedness. Female figures with storks' wings fly from Palestine to Babylon. And above it all Satan appears as heavenly prosecuting counsel. Especially noteworthy is the fact that, in addition to the *rū^aḥ*, the prophet is given a supernatural companion, the interpreting angel.

Like all Hebrew active forces, the beings we have mentioned are substantial, three-dimensional, and yet invisible. But they do not descend upon people from above, as auras (as they do in Zechariah's prophetic forerunners). They have an actual form, and are so much like persons that they are capable of speech. They do not belong to a transcendent world, and they are not heavenly archetypes of earthly phenomena. They live and work within the created world. Their sphere of operations reaches from the mountain of the sun in the east to the myrtles in the extreme west. They are connected with the winds, the horns of the mighty nations, and the cornerstone of the whole world – the holy rock on Zion, where the mysterious lamp towers up, representing the eyes of Yahweh. In fact, what the prophet sees in his vision into the depths lays bare the foundations of existence. For him, these 'angels' are not irrational forces. They are powers whose existence subsequent perception knows to be necessary. It is only Yahweh himself who dwells in eternity. It is only his voice that comes from that other world; and though the prophet can hear its sound, he cannot understand what it says.

It is difficult for a modern reader to see the angels as anything more than the fantasies of an unenlightened, child-like age. How does an Israelite prophet in the post-exilic period come to extend the traditional metahistorical categories by a doctrine of angels? Occasionally scholars have assumed that this reflects a remythologization of the Israelite religion, after the exile. They suspect the re-emergence of polytheistic notions which had long since been outlawed by the Yahweh religion. The reason for the return of mythology is sought for in the increasing contact with the great religions of the ancient East, by which Israel was surrounded. For the images of the Night Visions show surprising similarities with Babylonian conceptions. 'Light' as the characteristic of Yahweh's earthly hypostases is reminiscent of the aspiring astral religions of the time. The seven eyes of God can hardly be separated from the seven planets. The colours of the teams of horses which chase across the earth remind us of the colours of the planets; and the horses themselves are like deities – for example, the chariot-driver God, Rakib-El, in North Syrian Senjirli.

And yet for Zechariah the world of symbols fits effortlessly into his monotheism, in the graduated form in which he understood it. He and others like himself had never taken over the ideas of his religious neighbours, not being prompted to do so by any need to bolster up their own religious self-confidence. Generally speaking, the concept of personified beings who mediate between the deity and human beings results from an increasing sense of the remoteness of God, and a growing transcendentalization. Now, the terms in which Zechariah thinks of God are certainly less material than those of Isaiah (cf. Isa. 6); but this transcendentalization applies only to a transitional, present phase. As soon as the temple has risen again, Yahweh will return to Jerusalem once more, at least in the form of his *kābōd* (cf. Isa. 6.3). And we sense far less disquiet about the remoteness of God in Zechariah than for example in Jeremiah's Confessions.

We might perhaps rather ask whether we should not seek for the reason in an increasing and more subtle differentiation in the experience of God. Once human beings cease to draw their understanding of God solely from the enthusiasm generated by cultic ceremonies, they experience the numinous in many different ways; and these are by no means homogeneous. Zechariah makes the religion of the cult the main goal of his efforts; but in the same degree, the pansacrality of pre-exilic times has slipped from his grasp. For if all sensory phenomena, as well as everything that is mysterious in everyday experience, is associated with God, then God is not experienced as a self-contained personality, like another man or woman. He is at most believed in as a unified will underlying a multiplicity of intertwining strivings and tendencies. Is this the reason for the introduction of angelic powers into metahistory? Where a person traces back his own life and the lives of his group to an invisible foundation which provides their significance, he may continually and gratefully experience his existence as a gift from God. But what about suffering and failure? What about the injustice which so often gains the upper hand among men and women? Earlier prophets had chosen a monanthropological approach, which traced all unfavourable experiences back to man, and all favourable ones, ultimately speaking, to God. Someone like Zechariah is not content with this simple either-or. He does not find it sufficient explanation to assume that the wind of the spirit comes to people, sometimes quickening and inspiring, sometimes threatening and overthrowing them. For Zechariah, the forces which find out evil, impeach or eliminate it, are separate from the personal centre of God himself. But the same is true of powers which – as he believes he can sense – intercede for him and his people, relieving his conscience and the conscience of others.

A significant feature of this new kind of metahistory is that the course of political and military history becomes no more than an echo of a supernatural underlying event which has already run its course. It is true that from time immemorial the prophets had employed symbolic acts in order to anticipate future events (cf. Isa 8.1–4; Jer. 13). But now a 'prototypical' history is systematically made to precede the history of human affairs. An angel brings to God in supplication the same grief that echoes in the Israelites' lament (Zech. 1.12). The kingdoms of this world are conquered beforehand in the invisible world; there, the future representative of salvation is installed; there, the evil which is normally imperceptible is already removed from the land; and so forth.

In view of this, it is a subject for discussion among Old Testament scholars whether Zechariah can already be considered to fall under the heading of *apocalyptic*. The name apocalyptic is used to designate an eschatological movement round about the turn of the era. Its most important document is the Book of Revelation (which is called *apokalypsis* in Greek). Apocalyptic writers love visionary, enigmatic language, laden with symbols. Drawing on the prophetic writings of the past, their aim is to reduce the expected events of the End-time to a systematic pattern, and to present the fermenting forces of human history through the medium of metaphors and images. The underlying supposition is that all the conditions of earthly rule at present are evil, and the product of demons. But in the imminent future the world will come to an end, the Last Judgment will take place, and after that the kingdom of God will prevail. Zechariah's metahistory certainly does anticipate apocalyptic ideas, in its visionary framework, its angelology, and its reference to a history-above-history, parallel to earthly events. But his ideas are too firmly rooted in prophetic monanthropology for him to suggest that the present state of the world is the work of evil superhuman powers. So it would seem hardly appropriate to view him as being already an apocalyptist.

8. From Malachi to Jonah: The Final Cadence

8.1 Malachi

The series of Old Testament prophetic books ends with Malachi. Here, as in Haggai and Zechariah, God is often referred to as 'Yahweh of hosts' (*ṣᵉbāʾōt*). Malachi also shares the monanthropology of Haggai and Zechariah, which is centred on the temple community. But he presupposes that the cult and the temple are already in existence; so his activity must have been after the consecration of the temple in 515 BC. He criticizes the way in which the cult is being practised. The worst animals, which the Persian governor would never accept, are being sacrificed, not the best (1.8). The priests themselves attach no importance to ritual purity, and they are responsible for the deplorable conditions. Tithes are not being paid (3.6–12). Abuses of this kind are more easily conceivable before Ezra's cultic reforms (458 BC) than afterwards. This lax ceremonial practice suggests that those participating in the Yahweh observances doubt the efficacy of the cult. After the tremendous enthusiasm that had accompanied the building and consecration of the second temple, a slackening of religious fervour in succeeding years is quite understandable. Haggi and Zechariah had promised that this point in time would see the beginning of the eschatological turning point, and that the soil too would take on a new, superabundant fertility. Believing them, most Israelites had made a superhuman effort and had gathered together the means to erect a handsome building for the cult. But there were still no signs of the blessing that was supposed to follow immediately on the day of the temple's consecration. External circumstances were as depressing as ever. Zerubbabel had disappeared from the scene without having elevated Jerusalem to be the centre of the world. The Persians were still occupying the country. All this means that Malachi must have been active round about 500 BC. The delay of the eschaton (the coming of which had been expected to coincide with the consecration of the temple) was a mortgage that weighed heavily on the people (2.17ff.; 3.13ff.). The disappointment was keener than that caused by the non-fulfilment of Deutero-Isaiah's promise, about forty years earlier. For Deutero-Isaiah's predictions had been no more than a rough outline, and were therefore open to reinterpretation – more so than the highly concrete actualizing eschatology of Haggai and Zechariah.

The Book of Malachi comprises six discourses. Each of them begins with an impeachment of untenable conditions and ends with a prediction. The genre of prophecy is taken up, but here it is remodelled into discourse form. In each case, Malachi begins by rebuking the people he is addressing. He incites them to contradict, and then counters with a rejoinder in the name of his God.

> You weary Yahweh with your talk.
>   And you say: 'How have we wearied him?'
> By saying: 'Everyone who does evil
>   is good in Yahweh's judgement.
> For in such he delights.'
>   Or: 'Where is the God of *the healthful order of existence* (*mišpāṭ*)?
>   (2.17).

More than any prophet before him, Malachi seeks for points of reference which will be relevant to the spiritual needs of his people. Doubt is being publicly cast on the conviction, hallowed of old, that the man who does evil will of course be judged as evil by Yahweh; and that he is doomed to destruction, because of the correlation between act and destiny. A religious formula to this effect has been ironically 'rewritten' by the people, and turned into an 'anti-dogma'. The divine *mišpāṭ* ought to guarantee the healthful destiny which is the outcome of faithfulness to the community. But everyday experience shows that this is simply not true. Earlier, the prophets had been reproached because the fulfilment of their prophecy was delayed; and this was thought to show that God was not as powerful as they alleged (Isa. 5.19; 40.27). Now these complaints break out with renewed violence under the miserable conditions of the post-exilic period. The sceptics do not deny God's existence, but they do contest Yahweh's power to intervene effectively in world events. Yet the God of the prophets abides unwaveringly by the predictions:

> Behold, I send my messenger (*mal'āk*),
>> and he will prepare a way before me.
> So that the Almighty Lord for whom you long
>> will suddenly come to his palace.
> But the messenger (*mal'āk*) of the covenant,
>> [. . .] behold, he comes (came earlier?) . . .
> But which of you can endure the day of his coming?
>> Who can stand when he appears?
> For it/he (the day? the messenger?) is like the refiner's fire
>> and the fuller's lye.
> As refiner and purifier of silver he will tarry
>> and will purify the sons of Levi.
> And he will refine them like gold and silver,
>> and they will become [. . .] presenters of offerings in *ṣᵉdāqā*.
> Well pleasing to Yahweh will be the offerings of Judah [. . .]
>> as in primordial days and the years of the fore-time.
> I will draw near to you with *a healthful order of existence* (*mišpāṭ*),
>> and I will be a swift witness against the sorcerers, adulterers
>>> and those who swear falsely.
> Against those who force down the wage of the day labourer,
>> widows and orphans.
> And who oppress the sojourner,
>> but do not fear me,
>>> says Yahweh *ṣᵉbā'ōt*.

So Malachi still upholds Deutero-Isaiah's prophecy about the preparation of an eschatological divine highway (Isa. 40.3–6; 57.14ff.; 62.10ff.). God's *mišpāṭ* will quite certainly prevail one day. When the new eschatological beginning comes, the correlation between act and destiny will function once more (3.18).

But according to Malachi this turn of events will not take place by way of a highly personal manifestation of the deity, as the prophets had previously expected. It will not come about in the form of a visitation, as a theophany in visible form. This will only happen afterwards. First of all the way will be prepared by a forerunner, a mysterious messenger. Whom does Malachi mean? Is he thinking of a human messenger, or a heavenly one? The statement is complicated by the fact that the theophany is not preceded by only *one* messenger. This first messenger is evidently followed by another, a messenger 'of the covenant'. Are these two different figures? The functions of the 'second of them are more easily discernible. The messenger of the covenant has to purify and 'refine' the priests, the sons of Levi. But this means eradicating evil-doers from the priestly class, and freeing the other priests from their sins. This will make sacramental or sacrificially efficacious offerings possible once more. So it is then that the saving effects of the temple cult will begin – the effects of which Haggai and Zechariah had been so sure. Trito-Isaiah had relativized Deutero-Isaiah's expectations of the future by declaring that the moral and religious behaviour of human beings was the presupposition for the eschatological theophany. In a similar way, Malachi relativizes the oracles about the beginning of the era of salvation which had been proclaimed by Haggai and Zechariah.

Deutero-Isaiah had promised that the way was about to be prepared for the eschatological era (Isa. 40). Here, for the first time, this preparation is interpreted as the elimination of human guilt (similarly Mark 1.2–4). Seen from this aspect, it would appear obvious to relate the twice-mentioned messenger to the same figure. As the messenger of the covenant, he is reminiscent of Deutero-Isaiah's Servant of God, who was promised as 'covenant of a people'. Is Malachi, like Deutero-Isaiah, thinking of a human forerunner to God's eschatological coming? Perhaps a priest (possibly Ezra, who really did purify the Jerusalem priesthood, cf. 2.7)? Or a prophet (Mark 1 was to apply the passage to John the Baptist)? Later readers may perhaps have related the saying to the prophet himself, and therefore gave his presumably anonymous book the title Malachi ('my messenger' – not, probably, a proper name). However, since *mal'āk* often means a supernatural messenger sent by God, other scholars have thought in terms of an angel, like the heavenly beings who were supposed to have been responsible for the covenant on Sinai (Acts 7.53; Gal. 3.19) – though evidence for the view that angels were involved there only dates from a much later period.

That in the future, sacrifices will again be made 'in *ṣᵉdāqā*', does not only mean that then the priests will once more act in faithfulness to the community and will cease to pollute the sphere of the holy as they are doing at present (1.6ff.). The idea is also that, through sacrifice,

Yahweh will again accept the cultic community into his *ṣᵉdāqā* (cf. Vol. I, section 4.5). After the new beginning, 'the sun of *ṣᵉdāqā*' will rise again on those who worship Yahweh (4.2). The conditions of the primordial period and the fore-time of salvation history will in this way return again – the time when, on the settlement of the promised land, the people were also endowed with the capacity to do what was good by means of the active powers of *mišpāṭ* and *ṣedeq* (cf. Vol. I, section 4.5.3). From now on, *mišpāṭ* will again reign as the order of salvation on earth.

With Malachi, the horizon of Israelite prophecy contracts quite noticeably. The subject is now the everyday world of a little cultic community, standing on the fringe of the movements of world politics. Once more the task was to come to terms, mentally, spiritually and ethically, with the non-appearance of the new eschatological beginning. This had already been the problem when the people were faced with the imminent expectation which had been kindled by Ezekiel and Deutero-Isaiah. Again a disciple of an earlier prophet arose to keep the hope alive. But, like Trito-Isaiah, he postponed the entry of eschatological salvation to an indefinite point in time, without being able to tie it down to any political movements which the onlooker could discern. Again like Trito-Isaiah, however, this prophet assumes an astonishing universalism on Yahweh's part:

> From the rising of the sun to its setting
>   my name is great among the nations.
> In every place incense is offered to my name
>   and a pure offering (1.11; or should the passage be translated in
>   the future tense?).

Unlike Trito-Isaiah, Malachi makes cultic practice the decisive criterion of behaviour that is faithful to the community. Protestant scholars have censured this, on the grounds that he was departing from true morality and 'from an Amos, who demanded judgment, but not cultus'.[32] But had it not been for men like Malachi, and had piety not found a focus in the temple, Israel would never have survived the following turbulent five centuries of world history.

An admonitory coda was added to the little book at a later point (3.22–24). This promises that the prophet Elijah will return and will turn the hearts of fathers to their sons and sons to their fathers before 'the great Day of Yahweh' (a quotation from Zephaniah). This is an interpretation of Mal. 3.1, made at a time when people were already assured that there was an established chain of prophecy in Israel's history, Elijah being viewed as the highwater mark. Since Elijah was supposed not to have died, but to have been translated into heaven

(II Kings 2), it was easy to imagine that he might return. The prophecy had a considerable aftermath in the New Testament (Matt. 11.14; 17.10–13; John 1.21, 25). Where the religion of the Old Testament and its history is concerned, the idea shows how Jewish circles continued to ponder over the interpretation of prophetic utterances, even after literary prophecy had come to an end.

8.2 Deutero and Trito-Zechariah

Two anonymous collections of sayings have been added to the little book of Zechariah. We find these in chs. 9–11 and 12–14. They have the same heading as Malachi: 'Charge (*maśśā'*): the word of Yahweh to/in . . .' Nowhere do the opinions of scholars diverge so widely about prophetic writings as here, and nowhere are the findings of research so uncertain. The first part of the additional material is given the name Deutero-Zechariah, and the second part Trito-Zechariah; but this is merely an expedient. We have seen that it is impossible to be sure that Trito-Isaiah was the work of a single hand; but it is even less probable that Trito-Zechariah derives from any one single author.

Some of the fragments describe the eschatological war of liberation to which Yahweh incites the Israelites, in which, filled with hate, they will fall upon their enemies and 'drink their blood like wine' (9.11–17; 10.3–12; 12.3–8). However, according to other passages Yahweh alone will crush the nations, by means of a miraculous divine intervention (9.1–8; 14). The warlike mood of statements like this lends a nationalistic tone to these passages which we do not find anywhere else in literary prophecy. The prophecy about the messianic king is in curious contrast to this, for he will come to Jerusalem 'faithful to the community and endowed (? *nōša'*) with saving help, poor and riding on an ass'. Once in Jerusalem, he will have all weapons of war destroyed and will reign as the king of peace from that time on until the end of the world. Has some anonymous, pre-exilic prophecy been picked up here, and incorporated into a later context?

Some of the texts are concerned with internal political conditions. For us they are obscure, because we have no information from other sources which would throw light on them. This is true of the 'shepherd's discourse' (11.4–7), where the unnamed prophet is charged to pasture the herd (apparently the Israelites) and to protect it against a group of buyers, sellers and other shepherds. Within a month the prophet succeeds in getting rid of three shepherds. He lets himself be paid thirty silver pieces by them (the shepherds) as payment for his work. He then 'casts' the silver into the temple. Finally he breaks his shepherd's crook as a sign that Israel and Judah are no longer brothers. Complicated political affairs must be behind all this. (Some scholars connect the breach between Judah and Israel with the

Samaritan schism, since the Samaritans – the remaining population of the Northern Kingdom – broke away from the religious community in Jerusalem, probably towards the end of the fourth century BC. But it is surely more or less out of the question that a Judaean could at that time have applied the honorific name 'Israel' to Judah's rivals in the north.)

According to 12.9–13.1, Israel will one day lament the one whom it has itself pierced through. 'The whole land shall mourn, each family by itself' – the house of David, the house of Nathan, the house of Levi, and the family of the Shimeites. Nathan was probably a family of Jerusalem prophets (cf. Vol. I, section 3.3). Since it is mentioned before the priests (Levi), we can assume that the passage dates from the time before Ezra. For after that the priesthood took undisputed precedence over every other 'estate' in the nation. But in this case 12.9ff. must either be a pre-exilic saying, or a reference to some event during the period of the exile which is unknown to us. Is it a glance back to the suffering and dying Servant of God in Isaiah 53 (Rudolph's view)?

Ever since the nineteenth century it has been the fashion among Old Testament scholars to push the date of Zechariah 9–14 forward to the Hellenistic period, after 333 BC – even though the Greeks (Yavan) are only mentioned in one gloss (9.13). The reason for assigning this date to the passage is that, as far as we know, Israel was not involved in any warlike entanglements between 587/6 and the Maccabean rising of 168/7 BC; whereas acts of war are evidently the presupposition behind these chapters. But very little historical material is available to us for the Persian period; and in view of the general unrest of the time, we can hardly assume that Judah enjoyed undisturbed peace. It is therefore by no means impossible that the chapters date from this period (fifth to fourth century BC). It is even probable, since the heading is evidence that the same editorial hand was at work both here and in Malachi. Moreover the eschatological literature of the Hellenistic period (e.g., Enoch and Daniel) is entirely different in character. Nor is there a clear reference to any event which took place after 350.

Like Deutero-Isaiah, Trito-Isaiah and Malachi, Deutero- and Trito-Zechariah show that, from the Persian period onwards, the prophets liked to remain anonymous. In fact, it was in any case unusual in the ancient East to name the author of a book. It is a surprising exception when the names of the earlier literary prophets appear in the heading (cf. Vol. I, section 9.3). So the later change to anonymity means only that normal literary usage now prevailed in the case of the prophetic books as well. Can we go further, and deduce that the change also suggests a decline in prophetic self-confidence?

Or that the prediction of the future was now separated from the particular moment of history, which appeared to the first literary prophets to be of such essential importance in their inspiration? A few centuries later, when the apocalyptic writers began to be interested in predictions of the future, they started to adopt pseudonyms, choosing as patrons men of God belonging to earlier times when they composed a book (e.g., Enoch, Ezra or Baruch). Is this already true of Deutero-Isaiah? Did he already deliberately incorporate what he had to say in the Book of Isaiah? And can the same thing have been true here? Did younger prophets deliberately go under the name of Zechariah?

8.3 The story of Jonah

If by a miracle we mean an infringement of the laws of nature, then the greatest miracle reported in the Old Testament is the description of how, at his God's command, a prophet spent three days in the belly of a great fish, and was then vomited up on to land again. In earlier centuries this event served as an important proof of God's almighty power. But at the beginning of modern times it became suspect. Calvin already confessed that he would not have believed the story had it not been in the Bible. But it was in the nineteenth century especially that many people found themselves unable to believe the Bible at all because it contained so improbable a narrative. Yet in the context of the Book of Jonah itself, the sojourn in the fish's belly is no more than an intermezzo. The main theme is entirely different. The story is really about God's relationship to a mulishly obstinate prophet. That is to say, what we are reading is a didactic writing, an extended prophetic legend. It really belongs among the stories told about the prophets in the Books of Kings, rather than to the collection of the twelve prophets. For the prophetic books are really compilations of sayings: whereas the Book of Jonah does not contain one single complete prophetic utterance.

Events are triggered off because Nineveh, the capital of the Assyrian empire (today a mound of ruins called Kuyunjik, near the city of Mosul), has committed evil ($r\bar{a}'\bar{a}$) which has risen up as far as the face of God himself. Yahweh, being responsible for the moral order on earth, feels compelled to intervene. He looks for a prophetic messenger in Israel, the people whom he knows, and picks out a man called Jonah. (According to II Kings 14.25, Jonah was a North Israelite nabi who lived in the Assyrian period.) God commands Jonah to go on foot to Nineveh. Jonah evades the command, and instead starts off for the extreme west, on a ship that was sailing to Tarshish. But once they have put out to sea, Yahweh sends a storm. In their extremity, the sailors throw dice in order to find out which of them has brought about the storm through his evil-doing, and so has to be thrown overboard. The dice reveal that Jonah is the man responsible. He is then swallowed by the fish, and cast up on land again. Now there is nothing left for him to do but to go to Nineveh, and to proclaim its downfall. The citizens of Nineveh immediately believe 'in God', and trust what Jonah says. The king himself throws off his tokens of sovereignty and clothes himself in sackcloth and ashes. In addition, he commands the people to follow his example and they obey. 'And they turned from their evil way.' God thereupon repents (*šūb*) of the white heat of his anger, and withdraws the threat (*niḥḥam*).

Jonah, on the other hand, becomes furiously angry, and commits 'great evil'. He is angry with God because he is so forbearing and because he 'had repented of the evil' he was going to do, and he begs to die. The God to whom he addresses his imploring prayer answers merely with a counter-question: Is Jonah's anger justified? Jonah goes out into the fields and sits down to watch what is going to happen to the city. Although he has deserved that some disaster should fall on him, God first of all saves him from the 'evil' of a sunstroke, and lets a castor-oil plant spring up to give him shade. But then a worm is commanded to perforate the plant, so that it withers away. Jonah is again asked by his God whether his anger – this time over the castor-oil plant – is justified. The prophet obstinately maintains that it is. God then addresses him for the last time: 'You pity the castor-oil plant, for which you did not labour and which you did not make grow . . . And should I not pity Nineveh, that great city, in which there are more than a hundred and twenty thousand persons?' Here the text breaks off – abruptly, we feel. We are not told what happened to Jonah after that, or to Nineveh either (although according to the Books of Kings the city's repentance cannot have lasted long).

The book is not concerned to produce evidence for miracles. Its purpose is didactic. About this scholars today are unanimous. But what is still not clear is how far the narrator was deliberately telling a 'fairy tale', and how far he thought that the whole story really happened. Another disputed point is the kind of teaching at which he was aiming.

(a) The little book is most generally viewed as a story with a purpose, *directed against 'Jewish' intolerance*, which was threatening to spread in the post-exilic community, This is Rudolph's view. The reasons put forward are that the heathen sailors behave in an exemplary fashion, both in their attempt to save their foreign passanger, Jonah, and in their prayer and sacrifice to Yahweh, as the God of heaven; and that Nineveh repents immediately, at the first prophetic call. On the other hand, the only Israelite in the story, Jonah, shows himself to be hard-hearted and merciless towards both man and God.

(b) When a fish vomits up a man, or when Jonah flies into a rage because a castor-oil tree withers away, the reader can only find the episodes absurd. Is the whole story *a satire?* Is Jonah a caricature throughout, intended to make the reader smile (Wolff's view)?

(c) Or is the book's purpose a devastating *self-criticism* on the part of prophecy, which was gradually disappearing from Israelite society? Was the writing 'the last and strangest blossom on the ancient literary stem, which had almost withered away? . . . But in its capacity for calling itself in question before God to the very uttermost, something of prophecy's finest spirit . . . has risen again' (von Rad).

(d) What I have put forward is no more than a selection from a multiplicity of current interpretations. I should also mention an *allegorical* explanation, according to which the fish's belly symbolizes Israel's fate in Babylonian exile.[34] Nor, needless to say, are *psychoanalytical* speculations lacking: in this view the man inside the fish is an expression of longing for the mother's womb.[35]

In a search for firmer ground I would give preference to an approach based on the language of the text. It is generally agreed that God's final address stands out from the rest of the narrative. It is not only God's sympathy with sinful humanity which is stressed here. Equally significant is the withdrawal (*niḥḥam*) of a divine intention, which is talked about at the key points in the story (3.9f.; 4.2). What is withdrawn is the 'evil' which has been promised by God. But this divine retribution in its turn only goes back to the evil which, as human *rā'ā*, is the factor that triggers off events. As Nineveh's aura of evil, it leads human history into paths of error and makes God angry. The doom that has been prophesied will be withdrawn by God if people repent. And for this no atoning substitution is necessary. The Israelite prophet, in the environment in which he was living, may not feel this to be just. But this God attaches no importance to abstract justice. What begins to make itself felt with the prophets of the Babylonian era has here been thought through to the end: human insight and a change of human attitude are now the determining factors. The price is admittedly that the absolutely efficacious power of the *dābār* is no longer assumed. This is the prophecy of conversion, taken to its ultimate conclusion.

8.4 Prophetic theory and political practice

8.4.1 Up to now I have tried to elucidate Israel's prophecy from within, and to trace from the texts the thinking of its great representatives. At the end of our account, it may be useful to look briefly at prophecy from the outside, in its political context. What we can extract from the prophetic books are ideas and pronouncements which give metahistorical significance to the present at any given time. They do this by prophesying a corresponding future which God is going to bring about, with the purpose of rectifying society, and making history move forward to its logical continuation. This was the theory; and the prophets occasionally say explicitly that where the future is concerned, it is a theory that requires faith. Did it have any effects beyond the realm of thought and the religious emotions?

During the period of Israel's monarchy, the pre-literary nabis had directly designated individuals as divinely chosen or divinely rejected. By doing so they allowed the history of the Northern Kingdom to become a succession of 'divinely willed revolutions' (Vol. I, section 3.6). The critical prophets did not aim at individual political actions of this kind. And yet we are bound to ask whether they did not nevertheless have an eminently political effect. Did not the prophecies of doom uttered by men like Amos, Hosea and Isaiah contribute to the downfall of the Israelite states, north and south alike, by undermining the moral power of resistance of at least a considerable section of the people? In the case of Jeremiah it was obvious. We can be sure that his call to the defenders of Jerusalem's walls to desert impelled some Judaeans to abscond to the Babylonian camp. At the same time, the downfall of Israel and Judah would in all probability have come about even without the critical prophets. So it is not a case of self-fulfilling prophecy.

8.4.2 Another picture emerges after the great catastrophe which overtook both people and state in 587/6. Israel's national religion was bound through the traditions of salvation history to the history of the people itself. Her cultic religion was centred on the temple on Zion (cf. Deuteronomy). In these circumstances it seems nothing short of a miracle that the religion should have survived the exile at all. Surely the victory of the Babylonians and the cessation of every sacrifice to Yahweh must have seemed a striking refutation of Israelite monolatry? In the centuries of foreign rule that followed, a good proportion of Israel's neighbours lost not only their national religion but their ethnic identity as well (e.g., the Philistines and the Moabites). The fact that Israel did not undergo the same fate was due not least to the literary prophets. They announced the downfall of their nation and, paradoxically, thereby made its continued existence possible, beyond the catastrophe. Before 587/6, the prophets who predicted doom were only a minority among the numerous nabis in the country. Moreover they seldom found a willing ear with the king or among the people. After the catastrophe they became key witnesses to the fact that the downfall had been the nation's own fault. Far from proving Yahweh's impotence, Israel's fall was evidence of his unbroken will to *mišpāṭ*. (Proof of this appeal to prophecy as the only way of explaining the course of events is furnished by the Deuteronomic History – Joshua to II Kings – which was composed during this period. There attention is continually drawn to Yahweh's servants, the prophets, whose predictions are shamefully ignored and therefore have to find their fulfilment in disaster.) But the people of the exilic period also found prophecies of salvation in these writings – predictions about an Israel which would be renewed in the future. If the prophecy of the divine visitation for evil has been fulfilled, surely the prediction of the eschatological visitation for good must come true as well? During the exile, prophecy certains did not evoke any specific political actions – at least we have no evidence of any. But, in the people's hopeless situation, it did awaken the faith which, in the long run, was the only thing that secured the survival of Israel as a people, and the continuity of her religion.

So when, as a result of Cyrus's edict, a group of exiles returned home towards the end of the century, the sounds of Ezekiel or Deutero-Isaiah were surely echoing in their ears. But it is with Haggai and Zechariah especially that prophecy demonstrably becomes a power that moulds history. For these two prophets provided the spiritual and moral equipment for the tremendous task of rebuilding the temple. Their success was marked by the consecration of the temple in 515 BC; and it represents the zenith of prophetic activity as a whole, if this is viewed from the angle of political history. From that time on, the temple provided a bond of unity which held together Israelites both in the homeland and in the Dispersion. Historically speaking, what this meant for succeeding centuries, down to the turn of the era, can hardly be over-estimated.

8.4.3. Prophecy probably put an even more enduring stamp on political measures at the very point where hardly any scholars assume its influence: in Ezra's reform. Ezra was a priest living in exile. In the seventh year of the reign of Artaxerxes I (458 BC), he organized a party of Israelites who wanted to return home. Previously he had succeeded in acquiring a royal decree which had entrusted him with a reorganization of the cult in Jerusalem, 'in accordance with the *tōrā* of God which you have in your hand'. This law, which had been written down in Babylonian exile and which Ezra took with him to Palestine, was probably the Priestly Writing, one of the main sources of the later Pentateuch (the five books of Moses). Ezra introduced the constitution which gave the Israelite national group the organized form of a cultic community centred on the temple in Jerusalem. It was a structure that endured until the fall of the second temple in AD 70.

Anti-eschatological, theocratic leanings are generally ascribed to Ezra. But the texts show nothing of this. It is true that in his memoir (Ezra 7–10; Neh. 8f.) Ezra does not draw explicit attention to prophetic utterances; and he has no reason for making eschatology a particular theme in what he says. But many striking measures which he implemented can be explained as a cast back to prophetic expectations. For example, he arranged the march from Babylon to Jerusalem as a cultic procession, beginning on New Year's Day (in a sabbatical year, i.e., a year of release, Isa. 6.12), organizing it as a second exodus (cf. 5.5.1 above); he even grouped the participants according to the model of the Mosaic period. Haste is avoided in this exodus, in accordance with Isaiah 52.11f. But all the more emphasis is laid on the purity of those who carry the vessels sacred to Yahweh. It is true that Ezra initially adhered to the laws of the Priestly Writing. But for him their fulfilment was evidently a partial step towards eschatological salvation. He saw the Torah as a means of acquiring the holiness without which Yahweh's eschatological glory could not break in (cf. Malachi). His attempt to set up a twelve-tribe amphictyony in Israel (though with other names, since some of the original tribes had meanwhile disappeared) followed the organization recorded in the Priestly Writing (Num. 1–10); but it was also in accordance with prophetic voices (Isa. 49.6; Ezek. 37. 15ff.).

Ezra's relationship to prophecy has hardly ever been investigated up to now.[36] The priest shows himself to be an extremely far-sighted thinker, who understands how to pick out the features of the prophetic hope which could be realized in practical political terms. He casts aside all exaggerated, utopian ideas. But his fellow-countrymen would hardly have followed him had he not been able to find support for his work in the expectation that was so widespread at the time.

8.5 The decline

Not only did the composition of prophetic books cease after the early Persian period; prophecy in general evidently came to an end in Israel. After Ezra, we hear hardly anything more about a nabi. Ezra's younger contemporary, Nehemiah, does mention people of the kind, but they play a dubious role and are open to the bribes of the political parties. How could prophecy disappear so rapidly from the historical stage so soon after it had reached its crowning point with the successful building of the temple? Part of the reason will be that, during the

Persian period, Israel was not able to engage in political activity, and therefore postponed all eschatology to the far-off future. Itinerant nabis did exist. But some verses in Trito-Zechariah (13.2–6) make it clear that they were viewed with contempt by the general public. The passage prophesies that in the immediate future Yahweh will not only eradicate idols from the country: 'Also I will remove from the land the prophets and the spirit of impurity.' So the prophets' words and impurity are closely connected. If anyone continued to insist that he was a nabi, his own parents would kill him the very same day: 'for you speak deception (*šeqēr*) in the name of Yahweh.' As soon as the eschatological turn of events comes about, no one will don the haircloth cloak any more (this being the characteristic of the nabi orders at the time). Whoever has tried to be a prophet up to then will deny it, and pretend that he has been a farmer. But if he is asked about the tattooing on his hands (which he had evidently cut into them when he was in ecstasy, as a proof of his prophetic calling), he will talk himself out of the affair, saying that he got the injuries in a brothel. So having dealings with a prostitute will then count as less shameful than being one of the nabis.

Later, in the second century BC, it is explicitly recorded that there are no prophets any more. They need only be looked for again when the eschatological future dawns (I Macc. 4.46; 9.27. Cf. II Bar. 85.3).

In spite of this, the prophetic books continued to be passed on, read and used, even in the late Persian and early Hellenistic periods – centuries of which we know very little. So at that time it was not so much the living prophets as the dead ones who exerted an influence. In the course of continual copying, the prophetic books (like all Old Testament writings) were given interpretative glosses, emendations and additions. But the editorial history of the prophetic books has hardly undergone any investigation up to now.

At the end of the third century BC, with the apocalypses (I Enoch; Daniel), a movement began to make itself felt which aimed to give new life to prophecy. How far it succeeded is still a matter of dispute. There is no doubt that some apocalyptic themes do point back to the prophecy of the Persian era (e.g., God's final struggle with the last world empire). But when, or to what extent, apocalyptic ideas began to crop up in the prophetic writings cannot yet be definitively said. Interpreters are often inclined to apply the description 'apocalyptic' much too readily. For example, Isa. 24 to 27 goes under the name of the Isaiah Apocalypse in scholarly literature. These chapters are undoubtedly a later interpolation, describing the downfall of an imperial capital. But only parts of them can be called apocalyptic – the poem about the punishment of the heavenly host, for instance, the banquet for the nations, and the annihilation of death (24.21–23; 25.6–8). Apocalyptic is certainly not a description that can be applied to the chapters as a whole. Until scholarly research can arrive at clarity about what can be termed apocalyptic and what cannot, it will be impossible to say anything definite about the extent to which apocalyptic is anticipated in the prophetic books.

9. Retrospect and Prospect

9.1 The meaning of literary criticism

The longer I am engaged in the interpretation of the prophetic books of the Old Testament, the more sceptical I become about literary criticism in its prevailing form. With insouciant confidence, it sifts out a profusion of non-genuine material from these writings, on the grounds of stylistic 'doublets', or what it takes to be factual contradictions. At the moment, this occupation is absorbing the energies of Old Testament scholars to such an extent that publications dealing with points of literary criticism must outnumber those investigating a prophet's ideas by about ten to one.

Now, the necessity of literary criticism and analysis is unquestionable. For we have not received the prophetic books directly from the hand of their original authors. What we possess is the final stage of a tradition, lasting until the fourth or third century BC, According to this tradition, it was a sacred duty to link the transmission of the prophets' words with explanations and topical allusions designed to give them contemporary relevance. But literary criticism can only lead to significant results when it takes its bearings from linguistic facts (e.g., Deuteronomic turns of speech), from the form criticism of ancient oriental writings, and from the semantics of biblical Hebrew. But this approach is largely ignored. German scholars especially often dissect the Hebrew text as if they were teachers correcting a school essay, underlining in red every superfluous repetition, every unrelated leap from one idea to another, and every unattributed borrowing from an outside source. It seems to me that to apply the criteria of modern taste to texts of the first century BC is not a very promising approach. Moreover it is incompatible with historical criticism. I have therefore described passages as 'later interpolations' far less often than other books and articles on the subject. However, differences of literary judgment about the texts for the most part affect the account of individual prophets. They hardly influence the characterization of prophecy in general, and it is to this to which I should now like to turn.

9.2 The new interpretation of reality

Anyone who looks at the life and activity of the critical prophets is
bound to admire their courage and their steadfastness. From Amos
onwards, they were prepared to risk their personal well-being, their
family happiness, even their lives, for the divine cause which they
recognized as true. But God's cause is also (even if not unreservedly)
the cause of suffering human beings, the poor. The prophets may rebel
inwardly against the burden laid on them by the divine voice (see
Jeremiah's Confessions); but outwardly they show nothing of this.
They go on proclaiming what no one wants to hear, and yet *has* to
hear. In their readiness to blaze the trail for a truth important for
human existence, without themselves falling victim to a merciless
fanaticism, these men have remained exemplary for all time.

But a prophet wants to be taken seriously for the sake of his message,
not because of his behaviour as a human being. What was new about
prophecy? What was of permanent importance for an understanding
of human existence in this world and before the one God? Let me try
to sum up the prophetic achievement under a few headings.

9.2.1 The pre-eminence of moral responsibility. Anyone who opens a
prophetic book stumbles on passionate social criticism on almost
every page. Again and again the prophet's finger points to the
incomprehensible failure of human beings and its destructive effect –
on other people first of all, and then for the active subjects as well.
Whether foreign policy or home affairs, whether religion or the
administration of justice – everywhere the prophets are appalled by
the extent of their people's sin. And yet these people continue to boast
that they enjoy a particular relationship to God!

If we want to understand what is under discussion here, we have
to divest the concept of sin of the pseudo-Christian notion that it has
to do with what is, or is not, personally edifying. Sin has this
connotation in our everyday language. But the prophets do not start
from authoritarian, previously given divine commandments, which
ought to be obeyed blindly and yet are not being obeyed at all. What
they attack as wickedness is lack of faithfulness to the community, a
failure of loyalty and solidarity in inter-personal relations within the
social institutions that sustain men and women. It is true that, towards
the end of the prophetic eras, the idea of listening to Yahweh's voice
(Jeremiah C), or edicts and commandments as the criteria for good
or evil behaviour (Ezekiel), do emerge. But even then these forces are
only intended to support and elucidate what – as the healthful
ordering of society – remains the highest goal by which action can be
determined.

Since they assume that human life can only be successful within a harmonious society, the critical prophets are scandalized by the prevalent exploitation, oppression, injustice and – the other side of the coin – the ostentation and arrogance of the mighty, and their attempts at ingratiating themselves with foreign powers. The social criticism is never confined to evidence of a derangement in inter-personal relations. It looks beyond society and sees the failure as springing from a deranged relationship to God. That is why the reproaches culminate in expressions like sin, religious rebellion, and polluting guilt. The Hebrew was convinced that there was a connection between act and personal destiny. The speaker shares this view with his listeners. So evil conditions must be followed by the downfall of the guilty and those round them. For the aura of an act that is contrary to the interests of the community does not cling to the perpetrator alone; nor is it on him only that it has an invisible effect. It enfolds all the people with whom he has to do. A degree of social criticism had been an inherent component of north-west Semitic divination from time immemorial (cf. Vol. I, section 2.3). The critical prophets now elevated this into a criticism that was fundamental. They claimed that the system in force in Israel was so burdened by sin and so corrupt that unconditional downfall was completely inevitable. And in what they said the speakers did not set themselves aside from the general fate.

When the collapse came, it confirmed for most Israelites not merely the correctness of the prophets' predictions of doom, but also the prophetic pointer to the sinfulness and faultiness of the Israelite people. It was only after this that the prophetic insights really began to penetrate the minds of the people. On the other hand, from the hour of downfall, the prophets for their part laid aside condemnation. Overnight, as it were, they began to implant hope in the midst of what had hitherto been a picture painted in unrelievedly sombre colours. Now they turned into preachers of repentance. They became pastors, talking about conversion as an encouraging and hopeful possibility.

How, earlier, did they arrive at such a pessimistic judgment about human behaviour and social conditions? Elsewhere, too, the ancient East was very well aware of human failings – the Babylonians and Hittites more so, perhaps, than the Egyptians and Canaanites. In the advanced civilizations, offences against the social order were held to be blemishes which touched the precincts of the holy as well, adversely affecting the relation to certain gods. To this extent religion and morals belonged together. But for these people the social and ethical sphere was only one segment within a wide field of impurity, 'anathema' and curse. An evil fate could spring from any of these things. In many cases cultic violations or ritual misdemeanours which were committed unknowingly were considered more serious than theft, profiteering or exploitation. The same still applied in pre-prophetic Israel. We have only to think of the reasons given for the downfall for the first of the kings, Saul (I Sam. 13–15; 28); or we may compare the pre-prophetic ritual decalogue with its post-prophetic ethical equivalent (Ex. 34.10ff.).

From Amos onwards, it is solely in the ethical realm, hardly in the ritual one any more, that the critical prophets seek for the offences that influence destiny. This transformed the understanding of society, since for the first time the community of human beings now became a separate and independent field of action. But it did more even than that. The understanding of man changed too; for now conscious, responsible actions were declared to be the heart of every cohesion linking act and destiny. The sphere of contagious magic, as the source of a taint and the germ of future evil, receded completely into the background. It is really now, for the first time, that human responsibility comes to mean responsibility for society, especially for its weaker members. And the will of God, which stands behind the national and religious community, is experienced as a moral will.

A pre-eminent example of this is the change in the concept of the *tōrā*. Originally the word meant a divine precept, uttered through a priest, which touched on behaviour affecting the borderline between sacred and profane, pure and impure. (It is still used in this sense in Haggai 2.10ff.) From Deuteronomy onwards, the word becomes the quintessence of all divine precepts and commandments affecting the order of human society. Later it becomes the expression for the law of Yahweh *per se*. It is in this sector that from now on the fate of men and women is decided. Earlier, too, Egyptian sages could certainly express the conviction that upright behaviour was more pleasing to the god than the sacrifice of an ox.[37] But in literary prophecy casual utterances of this kind became a fundamental judgment. Hosea already saw the knowledge of God as synonymous with morally responsible dealings with other people. Ezekiel still believed that the final goal of history – to know 'that I (am) Yahweh' – included faithfulness to the community; and that this would become a matter of course in the newly constituted human society.

Moral behaviour that was an expression of faithfulness to the community also counted as reasonable. The key word 'know' or, to be more exact, the statement that the Israelites do *not* know, runs like a scarlet thread through prophetic criticism, from Amos (3.10) to Ezekiel and beyond. Unreasonableness, the prophets maintained, had become the mark of Israelite conduct, from the king down to 'the man in the street'. In Israel, at least, everyone was in a position to know what was in accord with the community and what healthful behaviour meant. But even the animals living in the country were wiser than the people (Isa. 1.2f.). By continually acting contrary to their better judgment, people had lost their ability 'to know'. Their insight had become clouded, so that their reason-heart could no longer be expected to guide their conduct (Isa. 6.9f.; Jer. 17.1f.). At this point prophetic anthropology is fundamentally different from that underlying Greek philosophy, where – from Socrates onwards – people were convinced that anyone who had once perceived the Good would inevitably do it. But there is also a gulf between the prophetic view and a commonly accepted form of Christian theology, a 'vulgar error' which, ever since the Middle Ages, has assumed that there is a fundamental difference between faith and knowledge. The God of the prophets demands nothing of men and women except what is reasonable. But human beings fail, and fall prey to irrational self-isolation.

The moral and reasonable God whom the prophets experience and proclaim is still a God who has to be worshipped in the cult. But it is Israel, rather than Yahweh, who is dependent on religious ceremonies; because it is these which communicate the capacity for behaviour that reflects faithfulness to the community. For when Yahweh encounters human beings at the temple, he at once descends on them with his *ṣedeq*. Old Testament scholars used once to attribute to Amos or Jeremiah a fundamental rejection of the cult. But this is increasingly coming to be seen as a Protestant prejudice. The same Isaiah who castigates the festal ceremonies of his contemporaries as useless, if not actually disastrous in their effect (Isa. 1.10ff.), still clings to Yahweh as the Holy One of Israel; and the Hebrew expression for holy is related to multivolipresence, especially in the cult (cf. Vol. I. section 4.9.1). It is true that, in the closing phase of prophecy, animal sacrifices are denounced as superficial and pernicious (Isa. 66.3). But even then we must remember that at no time did cultic ceremonies in Israel consist entirely of sacrifical offerings. The person who rejects sacrifice does not necessarily condemn the cult.

Why, in the middle of the eighth century, did the prophets discover the conscience, so to speak? Why did they now make the moral element of central significance in the fate of individuals and society? For this we still have no sufficient explanation. The prophets themselves are by no means aware of the novelty of their position. In their polemic they fail to see that it is their opponents who can generally more justly claim the support of Israel's religious traditions. Of course the moral disruption caused by a hundred years of Aramaean wars contributed

something towards a new orientation in the Northern kingdom. It is
also probable that the new anthropological and theological outlook
was pioneered by a succession of seers and nabis, even though we are
no longer able to reconstruct the chain of transmission. For we already
find social involvement in Elijah and Elisha, a hundred years earlier.
Perhaps, too, these earlier nabis offered a training in visions and
experiences of Yahweh in which the schooling of the conscience was
a prominent element. But the exact precursory conditions are still
obscure. The same has to be said about the other components of
prophetic theory, to which we shall now turn our attention.

9.2.2 On the road to monotheism. (a) The empirical sequel of all talk about God.
The prophets feel that they are claimed by their God, down to the
ultimate fibres of their existence. But their own emotional involvement
with God is not the only source of their proclamation. Two parallel
fields of experience provide the foundation for their preaching: their
secret (extra-sensory) experience of visions and spoken messages on
the one hand; and, on the other, the general experience of the Israelites
in their own history. There is no need to emphasize the extent to which
the prophets are influenced by secret experiences, in which they
become aware of God's own voice. They also simultaneously and
attentively register conditions in their environment; that, too, goes
without saying, and we find the evidence for it in every 'indication of
situation'. The interesting thing is that the legitimation of the secret
experience should occasionally be tested against the general experience of the people (Jer. 28.7–9).

The empirical basis of their argumentation prevents me from
ascribing a 'theology' to the prophets (though this is often done). For
theology's method is primarily deductive. It bases its conclusions on
dogmatic or methodological axioms. The prophets, on the other hand,
think inductively. Yahweh's real nature is not established in ultimate
terms. Theory about what he is, is continually corrected by experience.
The individual prophets stood in the lines of different traditions, and
needed these in order to be able to express in meaningful terms what
at the moment of perception appeared chaotic. But these roots in
tradition certainly did not mean that for the prophets the knowledge
of Yahweh was something that was concluded and complete. For
example, under the impression of his third vision (Amos 7.7–9), Amos
modifies the commonly accepted understanding of a God who is
always prepared to forgive – a view which he had still shared in his
two earlier visions. Corrections of this kind become even more evident
if we compare different prophetic eras. Take, for example, the concept
of Yahweh's efficacious word, which gives a new direction to historical

events: here Amos and Isaiah share the traditional conviction that a *dābār*, once proclaimed, cannot be rescinded because of human counter-measures, not even through repentance and prayer. But Jeremiah realizes that for him repentance was possible; while Deutero-Isaiah assumes that his generation was ready to repent; and from this time on, human repentance gradually becomes a factor which moves Yahweh to an unconditional withdrawal of his *dābār*. This is the explicit teaching of the little Book of Jonah.

Something similar can also be seen in respect of the conviction about a collective correlation between action and destiny, and about the divine visitation – convictions which were of such essential importance. In the Assyrian period this complex of ideas still provides the undisputed foundation for the transition from the indication of situation to the prediction, in every prophecy of doom. But in Jeremiah, and still more in Ezekiel, Yahweh's direct relationship to the individual Israelite is felt so strongly that the collective component is already attacked as failure to understand God's order and justice (Ezek. 18). So there is no dogma which teaches the prophets what God is. The traditional picture of Yahweh certainly provides the horizon of understanding, but it is modified afresh by every historical experience of far-reaching importance.

(b) The distance between man and God, in the present and in principle. The reader of the Bible does not feel the God of the prophets to be nearly as personal and familiar as the God presented by the early stories in the historical books – in the story of Abraham, for example. In the period before the literary prophets, Yahweh's interests and Israel's amounted to the same thing, and God above all embodies Israel's national spirit (though he was characterized by other relationships as well). But for critical prophecy there is a gulf between God and Israel. It emerges from the now untenable internal and external political situation that Yahweh has moved far away. Amos (5.14) already mocks his listeners' words, 'Yahweh is with us', seeing this as a dangerous illusion. Because of the number of atrocious deeds which Israel has committed, Yahweh has departed from people and land, and has even withdrawn his glory from the holy place on Zion (Ezek. 8–11). God knows no fellowship with sinners. Israel's forbears had maintained that Yahweh was gracious and merciful and ready to take away human sin (Ex. 34.6f.). But the prophets arrive at a different insight: they believe that the positive foundation of all reality has become tired of taking on himself the incessant guilt of this group of men and women (Isa. 1.14; 43.22–24). The God of the prophets can assume almost merciless features. He has become a stranger to the present generation. This estrangement is initially temporary, even if

it lasts for decades. When the eschatological revolution comes, the estrangement will be ended once more, and man and God will come close to one another again. But this is by no means the beginning of the intimate relationship which earlier generations expected.

The experience that the fundamental power held himself aloof from the contemporary sinner, led to another awareness which increased as time went on: the sense that there was a fundamental distance between the deity and human beings. 'Am I (only) a God at hand and not (rather) a God afar off?' (Jer. 23.23). The more moral conduct becomes the determining standard, the more the qualitative difference between God and every human being – even the Israelite – makes itself felt (Isa. 31.3). The secret experiences of the prophets tells the same story. Nothing more is heard of the intoxicating ecstasy of earlier nabis, or of an 'infusion of the spirit' through music or dance. In Jeremiah's Confessions particularly the difference emerges in all its harshness.

The growing awareness of the cleft between this God and this people is only partially counterbalanced by the fact that other nations now fall under Yahweh's historical guidance; so that in the oracles about the nations Yahweh's impending visitation is extended to all dwellers upon earth. For the divine relation to the nations is only a personal one to a limited degree (Isa. 56.7 is an exception). Nevertheless, from creation onwards the other nations are included in the divine plan and providence, even down to details such as the seventy years of the neo-Babylonian empire (Jer. 25). So Yahweh is no longer thought of (as he was in the book of Judges) as one actor among others on the battlefield of history, even if a particularly mighty one. He is now seen as the primal ground of all positive reality and all 'progressive' history. He does not only allow spheres of human action all over the world to mature into their corresponding destinies. He is also efficacious in natural forces, such as the waters of the Euphrates (Isa. 8.7). In this way the prophets take up Israel's monolatry as it had been passed down to them, and develop it into monotheism. In Isaiah this becomes a definite and emphasized theme (e.g., Isa. 45.7). That is not to deny that beneath (or above) the Babylonians, for example, powers such as Bel and Nebo do 'exist'. But they are nothing more than the embodiment of their nations, and just as helpless (Isa. 46.1).

The nineteenth century interpreted this change of attitude to mean that the prophets spiritualized the concept of God and discovered his transcendence. What a misunderstanding! Even though the prophets bitterly oppose the identification of Israel and Yahweh, the God whom they experience is neither located beyond the world (except possibly in Zechariah's Night Visions?); nor is matter ever divided from spirit.

Deutero-Isaiah is still convinced that Yahweh is actually present in space, even if he is not formally palpable; he accompanies Israel through the wilderness and goes before the people to Jerusalem. In addition, the warp and weft of divine active powers means that all the prophets, even if in different degrees, assume that it is impossible to conceive of Yahweh as existing in transcendent self-sufficiency.

This lack of interest in transcendence also explains why the prophets never apostrophize their God as judge. For a judge stands outside the entanglements which he has to appraise; whereas Yahweh is involved everywhere. It is certainly usual for scholars to talk about critical prophecy as a prophecy of judgment, ascribing to it words of judgment, a message of judgment, a proclamation of judgment, an announcement of judgment, and so forth. Modern translations pander to the same view, pinning down a whole series of Hebrew expressions (*rīb, dīn, mišpāṭ*) to the rendering 'judge' or 'judgment'. Now, it is certainly possible, by the method of transferred speech, to present the divine visitation predicted by the prophets in our terms, so that for these men world history was clearly becoming world judgment. But one must remain aware that this is a metaphorical use of language. For it must always be remembered that, apart from some accusations which Yahweh brings before a cosmic forum – as prosecuting counsel, not as judge (for example, Micah 6.1–8; Isa. 1.2f.; Jer. 2.12ff.) – every forensic feature is lacking, and a judge's sentence is never spoken. The usual self-assured transference to Old Testament writings of terms belonging to a Western theology which has adopted the legal concepts of its own civilization, is justified neither by form criticism nor by semantics.

But if 'judgment' does not provide the guideline for prophetic thinking, then the only possibility open to us is to assume that here *history* is the field which keeps the prophets in a state of suspense from the first word to the last.

Every prophecy is an attempt to hold together in a logical cohesion present conditions and future events. This necessarily implies a theory of history, even if history does not mean here what it means for modern historical studies. Above all, there is no question of an antithesis between history and nature. Some of what I want to say here about what is called (supra-) history will become clearer later, when we come to discuss eschatology (cf. also Vol. I, section 7.8).

9.2.3 Monanthropology between particularism and universalism. Their sensitivity in recording every damage inflicted in relations between human beings, and their discernment of sin everywhere, and in all walks of life, means that for the prophets differences of class and nation take on merely relative importance. Prince or peasant, man or woman, they all receive the mark 'unsatisfactory'. This does not apply merely to the prophet's own countrymen. Amos establishes that Damascus and the other neighbouring peoples are rebelling against the divine Lord of history in the same way as his own nation. Isaiah discovers the arrogance of the mighty just as much in Judah as in the Assyrian king. As the distance between God and man increases, because the holy God does not walk together with sinners, so, in the same measure, men and women draw closer together becoming a community with a common liability. They are all going to be overwhelmed and crushed by the Day of Yahweh.

But human beings do not belong together merely in the negative sense. The more God is understood as the creator of mankind, the more closely political rule throughout the whole inhabited earth is intertwined. A great king like Nebuchadnezzar (see Jeremiah) or a messiah like Cyrus (see Deutero-Isaiah) is required if *šālōm* is to be ensured among all the nations. Yahweh sees to it that these men are to hand at the proper time for human beings in general. The common fate of all human beings remains, even in the future era of salvation beyond the catastrophe. The knowledge of Yahweh becomes the goal for all nations (Ezekiel); all the ends of the earth will then see the salvation brought about by Yahweh (Deutero-Isaiah, cf. Isa. 2.2–4). So the national particularism of the Yahweh religion in its traditional form is now restricted, as is its commitment to the traditional order of classes and 'estates'.

But this does not imply any kind of cosmopolitan or religious universalism, which tears down the barriers between Israel, as Yahweh's own people, and the other nations, who do not know Yahweh. In order to explain both the unity of the nations and the difference between them, the prophets develop a monanthropology – a theory of man as the earthly author of history and nature, with concentric circles, each of which takes in a different manifestation of humanity, according to geography, race and language. Mankind has its cultic centre in the king or high priest on Zion, Yahweh's sacred precinct. Round this, Israel/Judah forms an inner circle, because it lives in God's own land, speaks Yahweh's language, Hebrew, and is bound to him in the covenant, or has been 'chosen', to take the word used from Deuteronomy and Deutero-Isaiah onwards. In these writings, 'to be chosen' does not imply exclusiveness. The phrase is meant to be understood in a functional sense: Israel has been set aside from the nations so that it may exercise a representative and priestly function on behalf of all human existence. It is quite understandable that this people should at that time have seen itself as the hub of the civilized world, in view of its historical experience, as well as its geopolitical situation on the neck of land joining Asia and Africa. And it was a standpoint borne out by the special character of Israel's religion and cult.

9.2.4 The eschatological community with God and the community of the nation. It is with the prophetic books that an eschatology emerges for the first time in the history of religion. It is an eschatology within history, not an eschatology at history's end. The new era of salvation that has been proclaimed is expected to bring with it a better history for all mankind. A new salvation history will begin and in this sense the primordial era will return in the form of the End-time; but the new age will go far beyond anything that has existed hitherto. It will not merely evoke marvellous changes in nature. It will also fundamentally transform the structures of man. A history of disaster of the kind Israel is now experiencing and suffering will henceforth be impossible. Features of this kind make it permissible to talk about 'eschatology'. Numerous references to earlier prophecies of salvation show that this eschatology does not assume that human history will break off; but it does expect an essentially new direction, which will be brought about by Yahweh's creative intervention. The prophetic passion lives from the expectation of what is going to happen at this new beginning, and afterwards. All previous revelation will become unimportant in the face of such exciting, revolutionary events (Jer. 23.7f.; Isa. 43.18f.). Prophecies of this kind give religious thinking a futuristic direction for the first time.

History is hastening towards a catastrophe of hitherto unknown dimensions, and human spheres of misdeeds and consequent disaster mean that this trend is simply unavoidable. People are the subjects responsible for this phase of history. It is different with the succeeding turn of events. Whatever the position of a remnant of Israel may be, it certainly does not offer a sufficient reason why salvation history should have a new beginning. The expected turn to salvation can only be deduced from the monotheistic pole of being and reality, not from the monanthropological counter-pole. But in the opinion of the prophets there are, happily, signs that this new beginning is going to come. For Yahweh has made himself known as a kind of father, whose first-born son is Israel (Hos. 11.1–9); and in the long run Yahweh will not let there be any lack of family solidarity (this being the first implication of *ṣᵉdāqā* among human beings).

We find another complex of ideas in Isaiah. The Holy One of Israel in whom the prophet hopes dwells on Zion. He can certainly dispense with human offerings and sacrifices, but he will not basically renounce his ties with a special human group. Deutero-Isaiah's reasoning is different again. In what he says, God emerges as the one who is in duty bound to redeem his kindred, Israel, quite unconditionally. Ties of this kind never lose their binding force. So past history provides a wealth of intimations that, in spite of his impending day of doom, Yahweh will remain faithful to the constructively developing history which he set in motion in primordial times. This God is essentially interested in allying himself with human beings, in being known by human beings, in acting through human beings and in manifesting himself in them as the power that brings blessing. The prophets can imagine a godless person more easily than a God who is without human beings. That is why they wait for the ending of the estrangement between God and Israel, or mankind. The number of sins on earth and the weight of human guilt have increased so appallingly that they have to be eliminated through a painful operation; for even a God cannot simply ignore them and get on with the agenda. But in the long run this process does not offer any hindrance to the purposeful, positively directed creative will, which reigns supreme behind the incessant change of all existing things. A steadfast community between this God and these people remains the goal of the divine 'way'. Seen from this angle, the hope for a new covenant, a new constitution for Israel, does in fact reflect Yahweh's final purpose. We find this hope in Hosea, afterwards in Jeremiah, and then down to Deutero-Isaiah and Malachi (whether the relevant passages are attributed to the prophets themselves or to later interpretative strata). It was a hope which, like nothing else, provided the secret focus for prophetic eschatology.

The separation of people from their God which the prophets have to deplore at present certainly rests on an ontological difference, as was shown above. But at the moment the cleft goes infinitely deeper than would be required by the difference in nature between God and man. God will mitigate this excessive distance. Yet in spite of their rhapsodic enthusiasm for the impending approach of God and the blessings of his salvation, the prophets still do not revert to the picture of God held in earlier centuries, when so to speak Yahweh embodied Israel's national spirit. It is true that Yahweh's glory will return to the temple in Jerusalem and to his people, and from that focus will dispense inconceivable blessing to the whole earth as well. But the separation of powers between king and priest will remain, and neither of them is granted the intimate relationship to God which the pre-exilic kings claimed for themselves (compare Ezekiel 43–46 e.g. with Ps. 45.7).

When the estrangement between God and human beings ends, the alienation between human beings will end as well. The visionary colours deepen as the prophets paint in utopian terms the salvation that wells up from common faithfulness to the community of all. The divine *ṣedeq* that will then rain down will make people everywhere act spontaneously in *ṣᵉdāqā* (Isa. 45.8). The messiah belongs within the same context. He is hardly ever described in warlike terms, let alone as dictator. His chief task is a moral and religious one – indeed his blessing will extend to nature itself. All this belongs to his *ṣᵉdāqā* (Isa. 9.7; 11.1–9). Administrative and political functions recede into the background.

The eschatological transformation does not merely mean something for the men and women who will then become 'a people' – i.e., a community without estrangement and with a common purpose. It also has a meaning for Yahweh himself, since he will then finally become 'God for them', as the frequently used covenant formula stresses (Jer. 7.3; 31.33; Ezek. 11.20; 37.23, 27, and frequently elsewhere; cf. Hos. 1.9). Strange and even displeasing though it may seem to the modern reader, the prophets can evidently conceive of God as 'becoming'. He is not thought of as unchangeable. (Apocalyptic was later to restrict this 'becoming' to the kingdom of God.) So it is not only the expectation of salvation which is directed towards the future consummation. The whole understanding of God tends in the same direction. Here, for the first time, we see the beginnings of an ethical and futuristic monotheism.

9.3 The prophetic influence

9.3.1 Prophecy and the major world religions.
Christianity, Judaism and Islam – the three monotheistic religions of the world which are within the biblical orbit – all grew up on the foundation of Israel's prophecy. (Mohammed called himself a prophet, thereby following Old Testament precedent, and not Son of God or saviour, on the analogy of the New.) It is far from my intention to call in question the differences between these three religions. Each of them contains elements springing from sources other than Israelite prophecy. Each of them lays stress on different things. For Moslems, religious thinking is dominated by the acknowledgment of the uniqueness of God. Jews stress the importance of conduct that is in strict accordance with the will of God; whereas Christian doctrine puts more emphasis on human sinfulness and the need for redemption. But in each case many threads can unmistakably be traced back to what was perceived and formulated from Amos down to the little Book of Jonah:

(a) The conviction that there is only one God and that, because of his unique sovereignty, all idolatry must be decisively rejected;

(b) God's revelation is made on the level of speech, in the word of promise and of the law;

(c) For practical living, moral conduct is of pre-eminent importance. Zeal for righteousness among human beings is the proof of true piety. Its value is far higher than the fulfilment of every religious observance. This conviction is bound up with the insight that people generally fail to live up to the divine purposes, and fall into sin;

(d) There is an eschatological unrest which does not remain content with the present suffering on earth. It looks for the salvation which God is going to bring about in the Last Days.

(e) If all these suggestions and insights are related to one another, they trace the metahistorical contours of the providence which guides the history of human beings and nature.

Western and Eastern cultures have internalized the first three themes to such an extent that they have become no more than platitudes. We can still discuss among ourselves whether there is a God or not; but a plurality of gods has become inconceivable. And whatever we mean by the word 'God', it belongs mainly in the context of word and spirit. We can argue the question whether the Christian (or Jewish or Moslem) religion has furthered humanity or not; but no one today would fall victim to the notion that there could be such a thing as religion without a moral imperative, or an active relationship to God without a corresponding relationship to other people.

However, when we come to the last two points, matters become more complicated. Ever since its beginnings – ever since the catastrophe that followed the revolts against Rome in AD 70 and 135 – Judaism has repressed eschatology and metahistory. Ever since the beginning of modern times these two themes have also receded into the background in Christian thought – or they have been secularized into ideas of human advancement. But we may well ask ourselves today whether the Christian faith can afford to do without eschatology and metahistory. Once the theologians eliminate them from the biblical heritage, is the Almighty Creator we find in the Bible not trivialized into a highly personal 'godlet', whose only importance is for the religion of the heart, the private piety of every individual? Theology is at all times tested against the standard set up by Israel's critical prophecy. Does it meet these standards at the present day?

9.3.2 The limitations of prophetic thinking. Its development in apocalyptic.
When, at the end of antiquity, the three religions took over the prophetic heritage, they already found it modified through interpretation, its original light refracted through the filter of apocalyptic. This is quite understandable. Anyone who writes about what the prophets

achieved for the understanding of God and man, has also to point to the limitations of their thinking.

(i) Under the spell of the collectivist anthropology of ancient oriental civilizations, the individual is not really taken into account. Even when an attempt is made – for example, when the correlation between act and destiny is limited to a single life (Ezek. 18) – the solution is not convincing. It appears artificial, and runs counter to all experience. But succeeding centuries have been able to conceive of the religious conscience only as the conscience of any given individual. Are they not completely right?

(ii) In spite of their stress on the invisible background of all reality, the prophets take over from pre-prophetic religion the this-worldliness of all life, and the earthly character of the benefits of salvation. To this they cling tenaciously. But is such a viewpoint capable of eliciting and formulating a final, convincing meaning for human existence? Does this view not ascribe undue religious weight to political history?

(iii) The monanthropology which is characteristic of the prophets puts down all the sufferings of the world exclusively to the human reason-heart, with its paradoxical, unreasonable behaviour. But can *evil* – by which I mean not merely moral evil, but 'natural' evil too – be laid to the charge of human responsibility alone? Can the theodicy problem be settled as easily as this?

Two hundred years after the end of prophecy, apocalyptic began with these very problems. It chose different approaches from prophecy. Unfortunately apocalyptic is a field which has still hardly been investigated. But a certain amount is clear. Where the points we have just mentioned are concerned, apolcalyptic solutions are in the direction of the resurrection of the dead and eternal life, and towards a satanic world as the origin of evil. These solutions have their own inherent difficulties. But they imply questions to prophecy which in themselves seem justified. These questions were taken up by the three religions we have mentioned, each in its own way. If we are honest, are they not the very questions that still exercise our minds today?

BIBLIOGRAPHY

For literature on prophecy generally see Vol. 1. This bibliography is a select list of literature on individual prophetic books which makes it possible for the reader to become acquainted with current problems.

1. Deuteronomy

Commentary: G. von Rad, *Deuteronomy*, ET Old Testament Library 1966.
S. Loersch, *Das Deuteronomium und seine Deutungen*, Stuttgart, 1967, gives a survey of exegesis. The investigation by M. Weinfeld, *Deuteronomy and the Deuteronomic School*, Oxford 1972, seeks to derive the book from a school of court scribes in Jerusalem. Cf. also E. W. Nicholson, *Deuteronomy and Tradition*, Oxford and Philadelphia 1967.

2. Jeremiah

Commentaries: W. Rudolph, *Jeremiah*, Handbuch zum AT 12, Tübingen, ³1968: J. Bright, Anchor Bible XXI, 1965.
J. B. Berridge, *Prophet, People and the World of Yahweh*, Zurich 1970. Cf. also R. P. Carroll, *From Chaos to Covenant*, London and New York 1981. W. L. Holladay has written a number of valuable articles, cf. his survey in *Interpreter's Dictionary of the Bible*, 470–2, and his popular account, *Jeremiah: Spokesman out of Time*, 1974. E. W. Nicholson, *Preaching to the Exiles*, Oxford and New York 1970, attempts to demonstrate a redaction in the Deuteronomic style. A. Neher, *Jérémie*, Paris 1960, works out impressively the connection between the man and his prophecy.

3. Habakkuk

Commentary: W. Rudolph, *Micha – Nahum – Habakkuk – Zephania*, Kommentar zum Alten Testament XIII, 3, Gütersloh 1975.

4. Obadiah

Commentaries: W. Rudolph, *Joel – Amos – Obadja – Jona*, Kommentar zum Alten Testament XIII, 3, Gütersloh 1971; H. W. Wolff, *Obadiah – Jonah*, Hermeneia, ET Philadelphia, in preparation.

5. Ezekiel

Commentaries: J. W. Wevers, *Ezekiel*, The Century Bible 1969; W. Zimmerli, *Ezekiel*, Hermeneia, two vols, ET Philadelphia 1979, 1983.

6. Deutero- and Trito-Isaiah

Commentaries: J. L. McKenzie, Anchor Bible 20, 1968; C. Westermann, *Isaiah 40-66*, Old Testament Library, 1969. *Interpreter's Dictionary to the Bible*, Supplement, 459f., gives a survey of research. A. Schoors, *I am God Your Saviour*, Vetus Testamentum Supplement XXIV, Leiden 1973, gives a form-critical treatment. C. Stuhlmueller, *Creative Redemption in Deutero-Isaiah*, 1970, is illuminating on the theology. C. R. North, *The Suffering Servant in Deutero-Isaiah*, ²1956, and H. H. Rowley, *The Servant of the Lord*, ²1965, give a good survey of the Servant of Yahweh liturgies.

7. Haggai and Zechariah

Commentaries: W. Rudolph, *Haggai - Sacharja 1-8, Sacharja 9-14 - Malachi*, Kommentar zum Alten Testament XIII 4, Gütersloh 1976. Redaction-critical questions are investigated by P. R. Ackroyd, 'Studies in the Book of Haggai', *Journal of Jewish Studies* 2, 1951, 163-76; id, 'The Book of Haggai and Zechariah I-XIII', ibid., 3, 1952, 151-6, and W. A. M. Beuken, *Haggai-Sacharja 1-8*, 1967. K. Seybold, *Bilder zum Tempelbau*, Stuttgart 1974, investigates the structure and themes of the Night Visions. P. D. Hanson, *The Dawn of Apocalyptic*, Philadelphia 1975, indicates the traces of the beginnings of apocalyptic from Trito-Isaiah to Zechariah 9-14.

8. Malachi

Commentaries: W. Rudolph and H. W. Wolff, see on 4. above.

9. Jonah

Commentaries: W. Rudolph and H. W. Wolff, see on 4. above.

For the theme of the taking back of words of Yahweh after human repentance cf. R. E. Clements, 'The Purpose of the Book of Jonah', *Vetus Testamentum Supplement* 18, 1975, 16ff.

NOTES

1. J. Wellhausen, *Prolegomena to the History of Ancient Israel*, ET Edinburgh 1885, reissued Cleveland 1957, p. 399.
2. Ibid., p. 402.
3. Cf. for example the Code of Hammurabi §199, in H. Gressmann (ed.), *Altorientalische Texte zum Alten Testament*, Tübingen ²1906 (=*AOT*), p. 401, with Ex. 21.26f.
4. A. Alt, 'The Origins of Israelite Law', in *Essays in Old Testament History and Religion*, ET Oxford 1966, pp. 79–132.
5. M. Noth, *The Laws in the Pentateuch*, ET Edinburgh 1967.
6. Cf. H. Gunkel, *Schöpfung und Chaos*, Göttingen 1895.
7. Cimmerians and Medes.
8. J. B. Pritchard, *Ancient Near Eastern Tests relating to the Old Testament*, Princeton NJ ³1969 (=*ANET*), p. 534.
9. Cf. G. von Rad, *The Problem of the Hexateuch and Other Essays*, ET Edinburgh 1966, pp. 1–78.
10. P. Volz, *Jeremiah*, Tübingen ²1928.
11. Cf. K. Koch, *The Growth of the Biblical Tradition*, ET London 1969, pp. 171ff.
12. Cf. M. Weinfeld, *Ugarit-Forschungen* 4, 1972, pp. 133 ff.
13. In O. Eissfeldt, 'Baʿalšamem und Jahwe', *Kleine Schriften* II, Tübingen 1963, pp. 171ff.
14. F. Cumont, *Astrology and Religion among the Greeks and Romans*, 1912, reissued New York 1960, pp. xvf.
15. Andre Neher, *Jérémie*, Paris 1960.
16. W. Rudolph, *Jeremiah*, Handbuch zum Alten Testament 12, Tübingen ³1968, p. 175.
17. G. von Rad, *Old Testament Theology* II, ET Edinburgh 1965, p. 212.
18. *mellammu, pulhu*, cf. J. B. Pritchard, *The Ancient Near East in Pictures relating to the Old Testament*, Princeton ²1969 (=*ANEP*), p. 536.
19. *ANEP*, p. 529.
20. For further comparative material see O. Keel, *Jahwe-Visionen und Siegelkunst*, Stuttgart 1977.
21. In *Festschrift für Karl Schneider*, 1947.
22. In Y. Spiegel (ed.), *Psychoanalytische Interpretationen*, Munich 1972, pp. 232ff.
23. Cf. K. Koch, 'Tempeleinlassliturgien und Dekaloge', *Studien zur Theologie der alttestamentlichen Überlieferungen*, ed. R. Rendtorff and K. Koch, Neukirchen 1961, pp. 45 ff.

24. K. Budde, *Die Religion des Volkes Israel*, Giessen 1900, p. 195.

25. R. Bultmann, in G. Kittel (ed.), *Theological Dictionary of the New Testament* I, pp. 696 ff.

26. Cf. K. Koch, op. cit. (n. 23).

27. B. Duhm, *Israels Propheten*, Tübingen 1916, p. 236.

28. But cf. H. D. Preuss (ed.), *Eschatologie im Alten Testament*, Darmstadt 1978.

29. *AOT*, pp. 368 ff.; *ANET*, pp. 315 ff.

30. Translation from *ANET* (n. 28 above), modified along the lines of *AOT*.

31. Cf. *ANEP*, 249 f.

32. J. Hempel, *Apoxysmata*, Berlin 1961, pp. 174–97.

33. O. Eissfeldt, *The Old Testament: An Introduction*, ET Oxford 1965, p. 443.

34. P. R. Ackroyd, *Exile and Restoration*, London 1968, pp. 244 f.

35. Fingert, *Psychological Review*, 1954, pp. 55 ff.

36. Cf. K. Koch, 'Ezra and the Origins of Judaism', *Journal of Semitic Studies*, 1974, pp. 173 ff.

37. *AOT*, p. 35; W. Beyerlin (ed.), *Near Eastern Religious Texts relating to the Old Testament*, ET 1978, p. 46.

INDEX OF BIBLICAL REFERENCES